T0300436

MARKET-DRIVEN THINKING

THINKING

Achieving Contextual Intelligence

MARKET-DRIVEN THINKING

Achieving Contextual Intelligence

Arch G. Woodside

Professor of Marketing
Boston College
Boston, Massachusetts

Routledge
Taylor & Francis Group

LONDON AND NEW YORK

First published 2005 by Elsevier Butterworth–Heinemann

Published 2014 by Routledge
2 Park Square, Milton Park, Abingdon, Oxon OX14 4RN
711 Third Avenue, New York, NY 10017

Routledge is an imprint of the Taylor & Francis Group, an informa business

Library of Congress Cataloging-in-Publication Data

Woodside, Arch G.
    Market-driven thinking : achieving contextual intelligence / Arch G. Woodside.
      p. cm.
    Includes bibliographical references and index.
    ISBN 0-7506-7901-8 (alk. paper)
    1. Marketing–Decision making. 2. Marketing–Psychological aspects. 3. Consumer behavior–
Psychological aspects. I. Title.

    HF5415.135.W66 2005
    658.8′342–dc22

                                                                                    2004028555

British Library Cataloguing-in-Publication Data
A catalogue record for this book is available from the British Library.

ISBN: 978- 0-7506-7901-5 (hbk)

To my daughters,
Christine Ann, Judith Beth, and
Martha Jane Woodside

CONTENTS

I A PRIMER IN LEARNING MARKET-DRIVEN THINKING

V LEARNING HOW INITIAL BEHAVIOR AFFECTS FUTURE BEHAVIOR

PREFACE

Meta-thinking, or thinking and research on thinking, includes three principal areas of inquiry:

- Descriptive research on how thinking and action occur and relate to each other.
- Prescriptive research on what steps and tools can be applied effectively to increase the quality of thinking.
- Normative research on how thinking should occur according to game theory and rational models of behavior.

Humans are the only organisms who raise and attempt to answer the three principal questions that relate to these three areas:

- How do we actually go about thinking?
- How can we get better at thinking?
- What's the best way to think given a particular context?

This book focuses on examining the first question within the context of business-to-business (B2B) and business-to-consumer (B2C) marketplaces in developed nations. The nitty-gritty focus of the book is on how to go about learning what executives and customers think before, during, and after doing things. But before considering this issue, let us briefly consider some useful sources for learning about all three of the main issues on thinking.

The *Journal of Contemporary Ethnography* is one of several very useful sources for descriptive research on the study of real-life thinking and action. The *JCE* provides "thick descriptions" of thinking and actions as they occur in real-life situations. The *JCE* aims to provide deep understanding and description of the dynamics of thinking and acting. While many other journals have some reports on thinking and actions in real-life contexts, the *JCE* is unique in its consistent focus on this area of study. The *JCE* publishes articles that provide contextual intelligence: wisdom about the thinking, actions, and outcomes occurring in specific situations. The behavioral science literature supports the views that most thinking occurs unconsciously and situational forces strongly influence thinking; these two conclusions imply that you have to get out there—learn about thinking in real-life contexts—and not rely on written surveys and focus-group reports.

The best readings on prescriptive research include the following books:

- *Winning Decisions: Getting It Right the First Time* by J. Edward Russo and Paul J. H. Schoemaker (2002); an easy-to-read primer on how to improve thinking, judgments, and decisions, with lots of references to important studies on prescriptive thinking topics.
- *Sensemaking in Organizations* by Karl E. Weick (1995); the seminal work on prescriptive thinking. Here's an appetizer:

People discover what they think by looking at what they say, how they feel, and where they walk. The talk makes sense of walking, which means those best able to walk the talk are the ones who actually talk the walking they find themselves doing most often, with more intensity, and with most satisfaction. How can I know what I value until I see where I walk? (Weick, 1995, p. 182–3)

- *Adaptive Thinking: Rationality in the Real World* by Gerd Gigerenzer (2000); an advanced treatise on prescriptive research tools and findings on how to improve the quality of thinking and deciding.

Games and Economic Behavior (a journal) is a major source of normative research contributions into how thinking and deciding should occur according to various economic game theories. While useful for deepening insight into how thinking may be improved within specific economic contexts, decision outcomes from normative research have been shown to be less accurate in predicting real-life decisions than role-playing studies (see Green, 2002).

AIMS OF THIS BOOK

This book focuses on descriptive research on thinking for achieving contextual intelligence. It examines the actual thinking and actions by executives and customers that relate to making marketplace decisions. The book aims to achieve three objectives:

- Increase your knowledge of the unconscious and conscious thinking processes of participants' marketplace contexts.
- Provide research tools useful for revealing the unconscious and conscious thinking processes of executives and customers.
- Provide in-depth examples of these research tools in both B2B and B2C contexts.

When Your Unconscious and Conscious Thinking Conflict

The thought, "A Jewish couple buys [or wants to buy] a German car" reflects the paradox or imbalance that sometimes confronts decision-makers when they are making choices. Such imbalances reflect conflicts between unconscious and conscious thinking. Chapter 4 takes up the conflict and resolution of the Jewish couple buying the German car.

A key research finding important for executives desiring to increase mindful thinking is that most thinking occurs unconsciously (see Wilson, 2002; Zaltman, 2003). Most thoughts and actions occur automatically, without conscious effort. Automatic (unconscious-based) thinking builds from cultural and early-experience imprinting.

Overconfidence

A second important research finding: overconfidence is the biggest cause of poor decisions and actions. Overconfidence[2] (overconfidence squared) is the problem of believing that you do not suffer from the overconfidence bias. Independent testing confirms that we all suffer from overconfidence in believing that our (unconscious-based) thoughts are correct.

What to do? What steps are useful to apply to overcome overconfidence and overconfidence[2]? The literature that answers this question and similar questions is substantial and very helpful. If considering such questions represents new thinking for you, reading Gilovich (1993) is an excellent place to start to learn about such problems. Even the title of Gilovich's book is impressive: *How We Know What Isn't So*. The book by Russo and Schoemaker (2002) also offers impressive training in making critical judgments. For an advanced treatise that includes helpful computer software programs, *Making Hard Decisions* by Clemen and Reilly (2001) is recommended.

Learning About How Executives and Customers Think

This book's principal aim is to provide a useful mental model and tools for learning about how executives and customers think within marketplace contexts. When the need to learn about how executives and customers think is recognized, a solution is usually implemented automatically, with no thought given to the relative worth of alternative methods. Thus, the "dominant logic" (most-often-implemented methods) to learn about thinking are written surveys and focus-group interviews—two research methods that almost always fail to provide valid and useful answers on how and why executives and customers think the way they do in specific contexts. If written surveys and focus groups are so bad, why are they the dominant logic for learning about executive and customer thinking? Because they give the appearance of making sense. For example, if we need to know what tourists think about the Summer Olympics that were held in Greece, let's ask them. The problem with framing such a question is that the question often assumes that tourists are aware of the Summer Olympics and that they sometimes think about Greece. For a sizeable share of tourists, these assumptions are likely to be inaccurate.

All of us tend to be overconfident in thinking we can frame meaningful and unbiased questions. However, a substantial literature supports the conclusion that most written surveys and focus-group studies are highly biased in ways unrecognized by the researcher (see Woodside and Dubelaar, 1993 for a review and an empirical study on this point). Even highly trained researchers often design highly biased—badly framed—questions (see Feldman and Lynch, 1988 for details).

If written surveys and focus-group research are poor choices for learning how executives and customers think, what methods are useful? This book recommends and demonstrates several approaches, including being there—that is, "direct research" (see Mintzberg, 1979) of observing and asking open-ended questions during the occurrences of real-life situations, as well as several other methods (e.g., applying "the long interview," the forced metaphor elicitation technique (FMET) to uncover unconscious thinking, observing behavior over several time periods, or asking what attributes and benefits evoke what brands rather than mentioning brand names first to respondents to learn their beliefs and feelings about each brand).

In real life, almost all customers may associate little or nothing with your brand but will offer opinions about your brand if you frame questions that begin by mentioning your brand name. "Canada" as a tourism brand is an example of this phenomenon; most Americans know the brand name, but the principal finding from in-depth interviews in customer research sponsored by the Canadian government is that most Americans do not think about Canada unconsciously or consciously as a vacation destination (Taylor,

1988). Canada is most often in Americans' inert mind set, not consideration set, as a destination option.

You might ask about how to generalize findings from a small number of cases to a large population if written surveys (e.g., completed by 1,000 respondents) are replaced with long interviews (e.g., face-to-face on-site interviews with 30 customers). Answer: You both generalize and go deep by identifying highly representative customers that fit very specific profiles before conducting five or so long interviews that fall within each profile, treating each interview as one complete experiment that is replicated five times, and supporting the surface conscious answers with direct observation and unconscious automatic retrieving questions. Also, the 30 completed long interviews usually represent a 70 percent useable completion rate among the 35 to 40 initial contacts, versus the useable completion rate of 10 to 15 percent that usually occurs for the 1,000 written surveys. Ask yourself which study you would want to read and use:

- The study achieving a response rate of 30 of 40 completed interviews, each interview lasting two to three hours, without the informant learning the sponsor's identity.
- The study using closed-end, fixed-point questions (e.g., seven-point "strongly disagree" to "strongly agree" items) along with requiring written open-end comments by respondents that achieved 1,000 completed interviews from a mailing of 10,000.

This book includes five parts, with two to three chapters in each part. While later parts and chapters build on the earlier discussions, the book presents each part and chapter as a stand-alone unit. Thus, a few of the figures appear in more than one chapter for ease of discussion. Now we turn to a brief introduction to each part and chapter.

Part I: A Primer in Market-Driven Thinking

Part 1 describes how thinking by executives and customers is a combination of unconscious and conscious processing of internal (memory-based) and external cues, stories, and information. Chapter 1 presents some similarities and departures in the thinking done by executives and customers. Chapter 1 observes that automatic (unconscious-based) mental processes (see Bargh, Chen, and Burrows, 1996) rather than strategic thinking tends to occur in all phases of thinking by both executives and consumers; neither executives nor consumers frequently explicitly consider alternative ways of framing and solving problems.

Chapter 2 presents details on how to go about doing case study research and develops the argument that dynamic thinking and actions through multiple time periods need to be included for learning market-driven thinking.

Chapter 2 provides several nitty-gritty illustrations and key sources for you to track down for further reading.

Chapter 3 provides an in-depth case study on the contingent nature of market-driven thinking. The chapter takes an admiring look at how Sam Walton went about learning about market-driven thinking to help craft strategic action for his company (Wal-Mart).

Part 2: Tools for Illuminating the Unconscious and Conscious Mind

Part 2 provides both theoretical and empirical tools for collecting data on the unconscious and conscious thinking processes of executives and customers. Part 2 advocates the view that answering questions requires introspection on whether the interviewer is the same person asking the question. Thus, examining "subjective personal introspection" is worth our attention. And we need to apply additional learning tools to enable the introspector to reach into her unconscious, retrieve, interpret, and report what she finds.

Chapter 4 demonstrates how mental anguish and lesser conflicts arise between unconscious and conscious thinking and how individuals go about resolving such conflicts. Heider's (1958) balance theory helps increase our understanding of such processes.

Chapter 5 presents means–end chains in thinking research as a way to uncover core values that relate indirectly via behaviors/consequences/benefits/attributes to brands of products and services. The chapter provides ways to increase the value of means–end research and illustrates these improved methods empirically.

Chapter 6 develops a thinking model of how introspection occurs when someone is asked a question. The chapter presents and illustrates the use of new tools to advance from subjective to confirmatory personal introspection.

Part 3: Customer Associate-to-Vendor (Store) Retrieval Research

Field studies on market-driven thinking can go beyond narrative (qualitative) reporting of executive and customer thinking in several different ways. Part 3 applies empirical positivistic tools (i.e., statistical hypothesis testing) in research on customers' automatic associate-to-brand (store) retrievals.

Chapter 7 illustrates how to build multiple regression models based on customers' automatic retrievals of brand names when asked what brand first comes to mind for a given benefit or attribute. Thus, the chapter applies a useful rule of thumb in learning market-driven thinking: ask *not* what your brand evokes; ask what evokes your brand.

Chapter 8 compares an industrial distributor's mental model of customer thinking with customers' own mental models. The differences are striking. This chapter offers a template on how to go about collecting thinking data for such studies.

Part 4: Case-Based Research for Learning Gestalt Thinking–Doing Processes

Zaltman (2003, p. 237) points out, "Managers must also understand their own unconscious thoughts about consumers and marketing—and think in entirely new, interdisciplinary ways." Part 4 focuses on how to apply the long interview method to uncover the thinking processes of managers and compare such mental models with customers' own thinking.

The long interview method starts with careful selection of five or six households or business firms for each of several categories of customers or executives. The long interview is best conducted on site—in the locations where the action occurs. For example, if you were studying the thinking and actions of gardeners, you would conduct the long interviews in the homes and gardens of gardeners. Lots of open-ended questions and props (e.g., seed packets and catalogs) are shown, and think-aloud responses are collected from informants.

Chapter 9 describes long interviews with two executives about the thinking and actions of customers. Then the "mental models" of these two executives are compared with the thinking and actions reported by customers in a second set of long interviews. The approach allows for "building in degrees of freedom" in case study research for testing opposing mental models of reality.

Chapter 10 applies the long interview among customers who are confirmed recent buyers of the product category. This chapter illustrates how to conduct brand-user interviews to learn the thinking and actions by customers occurring before and during brand use. The specific application in Chapter 10 was helpful in deciding whether or not the brand was strong enough (in the minds of customers) to stand alone from the parent brand in communicating to customers—it wasn't.

Part 5: Learning How Initial Behavior Affects Future Behavior

Because most thinking occurs unconsciously, inferring thinking processes from observing behavior rather than asking questions is useful. For example, female Wolf spiders are much more likely to mate, rather than eat, black-foreleg versus brown-foreleg male spiders when the females have had pre-adult exposure to black-foreleg adult male spiders; and female Wolf spiders are much more likely to eat, rather than mate with, brown-foreleg spiders when the females have had pre-adult exposure to black-foreleg adult male spiders. The reverse pattern occurs when female Wolf spiders experience pre-adult exposure to brown-foreleg adult males. See Chapter 11 and Hebets (2003) for details.

Chapter 11 provides evidence that imprinting in the form of first-brand purchase–use experience by customers has a bigger impact on long-term brand choice than do short-term marketing influences (e.g., coupons and limited-time-period price reductions). Believing that a brand wins in two ways, many advertisers seek young audiences when placing ads. The two ways are achieving an imprinting experience for the brand and successfully promoting variety-seeking behavior—(1) promoting the first-brand purchase–use experience by the customer and (2) the young customer being willing to seek variety by trying different brands. Chapters 11 and 12 provide evidence that confirms both views. Such studies lend credence to the practice of paying higher ad rates to advertise on David Letterman than on Jay Leno—Leno offers the bigger audience, but Letterman offers the younger audience.

An Invitation

Meta-thinking, that is, thinking about thinking, deserves our attention. Meta-thinking is the best antidote for confirmation bias—the hardwired bias to favor evidence that supports our current beliefs and to dismiss evidence that challenges them. Confirmation bias and overconfidence are twin forces leading to inaccurate mental models—bad thinking. Bad thinking produces bad decisions and disastrous outcomes, and good thinking leads to better decisions and desirable outcomes; for proof of this conclusion, please see Armstrong (1986), Baron's (2000) Chapter 9, and Herek, Janis, and Huth (1987).

Confirmation and overconfidence biases are at work when we think we know how to think without reading the literature on meta-thinking. You are invited to join me in annually completing self-assigned readings and applying the principles learned from the meta-thinking literature.

Improving market-driven thinking begins by explicitly recognizing that you know less than you think you know about how executives and customers actually think—going beyond your own thinking is a necessary step. Think about Sam Walton getting up each morning at 3 a.m. to go to talk with Wal-Mart truck drivers to learn what was really happening—he did this more than once each week, 50 weeks each year.

Confirmation bias and overconfidence bias are at work when we think we can design a questionnaire to ask executives and customers what they are thinking and doing without reading about how to frame questions and how to collect doing (i.e., behavior) data. This book invites you to apply alternative methods to learn how executives and customers think; it suggests *not* applying the dominating logic of written surveys sent by mail or by Internet, and it suggests reading the literature on meta-thinking.

ACKNOWLEDGMENTS

Some contents in a few of the chapters in this book include updated discussions of studies reported elsewhere. I am very grateful and would like to acknowledge the contributions of my colleagues to the ideas and field research work resulting in these earlier publications, as well as permission from the publishers to publish excerpts from these studies. Chapter 1 is adapted, in part, from Elizabeth J. Wilson and Arch G. Woodside (2001), "Executive and Consumer Decision-Making: Increasing Useful Sensemaking by Identifying Similarities and Departures," *Journal of Business & Industrial Marketing*, 16(5), 401–414. Chapter 2 is adapted, in part, from Arch G. Woodside and Elizabeth J. Wilson (2003), "Case Study Research for Theory-Building," *Journal of Business & Industrial Marketing*, 18(6/7), 493–508. Chapter 3 is adapted, in part, from Arch G. Woodside (2003), "Middle-Range Theory Construction of the Dynamics of Organizational Marketing-Buying Behavior," *Journal of Business & Industrial Marketing*, 18(4/5), 309–335. Chapter 4 is adapted, in part, from Arch G. Woodside and Jean-Charles Chebat (2001), "Updating Heider's Balance Theory in Consumer Behavior," *Psychology & Marketing*, 18(5), 475–496. Chapter 5 is adapted, in part, from Arch G. Woodside (2004), "Advancing Means–End Chains by Incorporating Heider's Balance Theory and Fournier's Consumer-Brand Relationship Typology," *Psychology & Marketing*, 21(4), 279–294. Chapter 6 is adapted, in part, from Arch G. Woodside (2005), "Advancing from Subjective to Confirmatory Personal Introspection," *Psychology & Marketing*, 22(10). Chapter 7 is adapted, in part, from Arch G. Woodside and Eva M. Thelen (1996), "Accessing Memory and Customer Choice: Benefit-to-Store (Brand) Retrieval Models that Predict Purchase," *Journal of the European Society for Opinion and Marketing Research*, 24(4), 260–267. Chapter 8 is adapted, in part, from Arch G. Woodside (1987), "Customer Awareness and Choice of Industrial Distributors," *Industrial Marketing & Purchasing*, 2(2), 47–68. Chapter 9 was co-authored by Elizabeth J. Wilson (Suffolk University, Boston) and Arch G. Woodside. Chapter 10 is adapted, in part, from Arch G. Woodside, Roberta MacDonald, and Marion Burford (2004), "Grounded Theory of Leisure Travel," *Journal of Travel and Tourism Marketing*, 14(1), 7–39. Chapter 11 was co-authored by Mark Uncles and Arch G. Woodside.

PART I

A PRIMER IN LEARNING MARKET-DRIVEN THINKING

I

THINKING, DECIDING, AND ACTING BY EXECUTIVES AND CUSTOMERS

Synopsis

Both marketing executives and consumers engage in a combination of automatic and strategic (i.e., controlled) thinking and doing processes when they become aware of problems and opportunities. Similarities and departures in these processes among executives and consumers occur through all stages of their decisions. This chapter includes a paradigm describing similarities (S_i) and departures (D_i) in the stream of thinking and behaviors of executives and consumers. For example, both executives and consumers apply simplifying categorizing rules for defining decision contexts; for repetitive decision-making contexts, categorization rules are more often formalized in writing by executives but not by consumers. The literature on the quality of decision processes offers several easy-to-apply, but often unknown, rules helpful for both executives and consumers for improving the quality of their decisions. These rules are examined briefly within the framework of similarities and departures. Formal study by business-to-business (B2B) and business-to-consumer (B2C) marketers of such similarities and departures of consumer/business buying decisions may be helpful for recognizing nuances critical in selling–buying processes for achieving desired outcomes—such as getting a sale or building a marketing relationship.

INTRODUCTION: ACHIEVING A DEEP UNDERSTANDING OF WHAT'S HAPPENING

Examining similarities and departures in the thinking processes among executives and consumers helps to achieve more useful "sensemaking" (Weick, 1995) of real-life decision-making. For example, research on executive and consumer decision processes includes modeling the *implicit* thinking and deciding processes by decision-makers. What we've learned from such research: even when B2B marketers and consumers report following explicit rules for searching and making choices, thick descriptions of what happens in real life do not support their reports (see Woodside, 1992). Automatic thinking, rather than explicit (or "strategic") thinking (see Bargh, 1994), appears throughout most phases of decision-making, and often the decision-makers are unaware of how such unintended thoughts are influencing their choices.

Why is the direct research logic particularly valuable for studying executive and consumer decision processes? Part of the answer lies in the work by Gilovich (1991). He identifies overconfidence in our individual perceptions of reality as likely to be the single greatest shortcoming to improved knowing. The human tendency is very strong to believe we know even though what we know "isn't so" (Gilovich, 1991). Thus, answers to closed-ended questions by executives or consumers in a mail survey fail to account for what is reported by these decision-makers that just isn't so, as well as what they fail to report that is so. Because direct research often combines the collection of supporting documents, confirmation of thoughts from multiple interviewing of multiple respondents, and direct observation of some interactions of people participating in the processes, direct research studies increase the quality of data reported compared to one-shot survey-based studies.

It is useful to consider whether executives and consumers exhibit similarities or differences in their decision-making. Critical nuances in conversations, thought processes, and behaviors associated with individual business and consumer case studies support the view that every decision process is unique (see Woodside, 1996). Yet a compelling need to categorize and simplify exists in both theory and management practice that results in grouping cases into a manageable number of processes. Effective thinking requires building and comparing typologies and categories. For example, associating unique decision processes with executive versus consumer problem-solving implies two process categories that differ significantly.

This compelling need is to achieve a deep understanding of what is happening, what outcomes are likely to occur or not occur, and the reasoning (i.e., the implicit "mental models" being implemented by the decision-makers; see Senge, 1990) supporting the observed decision processes. This chapter does not offer an in-depth review of this literature, but it does describe specific similarities and departures between executive and consumer decision processes. Crafting such propositions provides useful ground for context-based models that describe the contingencies resulting in observed similarities and departures. By the end of the discussion, the thesis presented here reaches two central conclusions:

- it is useful to describe and test noteworthy similarities in executive and consumer decision processes, to achieve greater sensemaking of both processes;
- for every similarity proposition, stating a relevant departure proposition may be supportable empirically.

Consequently, the study of similarities and departures in such decision processes presents multiple meanings and cues. The answer most useful in the principle issue is that both similarities and departures should be expected in studies of thoughts, decisions, and behaviors among executives and consumers.

Using "direct research" (Mintzberg, 1979) to examine similarities and differences in the decision processes of executives and consumers helps fulfill a compelling need for deep understanding. Direct research compels explicit model building when studying the nuances behind the similarities and differences—and how both the executive and the consumer might improve their thinking processes. Direct research includes face-to-face interviews with decision-makers—usually multiple interviews of the same persons in two or more sessions and/or interviews with additional persons mentioned during initial interviews. Direct research of decision-making attempts to capture deep knowledge of the streams of thinking and actions of "emergent strategies" (Mintzberg, 1979). Such emergent strategies include the nuances arising from transforming planning with implementing decisions/actions, including adjustments in thinking, searching for information, modifications to decision rules, last-minute third-party influences, and unexpected contextual influences. Mintzberg (1979) provides seven basic themes for direct research:

- The research is as purely descriptive as the researcher is able to make it.
- The research relies on simple—in a sense, inelegant—methodologies.
- The research is as purely inductive as possible.
- The research is systematic in nature—specific kinds of data are collected systematically.
- The research, in its intensive nature, ensures that systematic data are supported by anecdotal data because theory building seems to require description, the richness that comes from anecdote.
- The research seeks to synthesize, to integrate diverse elements into configurations of ideal or pure types.

Because direct research runs counter to the dominant logic of empirical positivism (i.e., surveys or experiments that test deductively developed hypotheses), it may be surprising to learn that a substantial body of literature is available in organizational marketing and consumer research that uses direct research methods. Direct research examples in organizational marketing include the following studies:

- Based on data from direct research, Morgenroth (1964) and Howard and Morgenroth (1968) developed binary flow diagrams and a computer program that accurately predicts distribution-pricing decisions by Gulf Oil executives.

- Howard *et al.* (1975) reviewed a series of organizational marketing studies employing direct research—which they label "decision systems analysis" (DSA).
- Montgomery (1975) showed the stream of thoughts (including heuristics and decisions) within one supermarket's executive buying committee through their deliberations on whether to buy new grocery products.
- Woodside (1992) included in-depth reports of ten field direct-research studies conducted in Europe and North America by a team of academic researchers.
- Woodside and Wilson (2000) showed what-if decision trees based on "thick descriptions" of marketers' and buyers' decision processes involved in the same B2B relationships.

Direct research examples in consumer research include the following studies:

- Cox (1967) conducted face-to-face interviews with two housewives separately each week for twenty weeks to gain deep understanding of their automatic and implicit thoughts related to grocery purchases.
- Bettman's (1970) doctoral dissertation employed direct research to learn the heuristics implemented by two housewives when deciding what to place in their supermarket shopping carts.
- Woodside and Fleck (1979) twice interviewed two beer drinkers separately in their homes—each of the four interviews lasted three hours—to learn their thoughts, feelings, and actions regarding beer as a beverage category, brand preferences, product/brand purchase decisions, and beer consumption decisions.
- Payne *et al.* (1993) compared and contrasted findings from consumer field and laboratory studies employing direct research methods.
- Fournier (1998) employed direct research to learn how brands relate to how consumers come to understand themselves.

Direct research often includes two or more face-to-face interviews with the same respondents spaced over weeks or months. The use of such a method allows respondents to reflect on their answers given in earlier interviews. Because reflection clarifies and deepens understanding (see Weick, 1995), respondents often provide deeper insights into the reasons for their decisions and actions than expressed earlier. Multiple interviews with the same respondents permit these respondents to learn what they really believe and feel related to the topics covered in the study. Weick (1979, p. 5) captures this point well when discussing the criticality of retrospection: "How can I know what I think until I see what I say?"

The Fallacy of Centrality

Closely related to the principle of overconfidence is the "fallacy of centrality" (i.e., experts underestimating the likelihood of an event because they would surely know about the phenomenon if it actually were taking place; see Westrum, 1982, and Weick, 1995). "This fallacy is all the more damaging in that it not only discourages curiosity on the part of the person making it but also frequently creates in him/her an antagonistic stance toward the events in question" (Westrum, 1982, p. 393).

Consequently, thinking we know the answer to the issue of whether executives and consumers match or differ in their decision processes is likely to be a false premise. To overcome the overconfidence bias and the fallacy of centrality, data and information from field studies are needed on the decision processes enacted by executives and consumers. Fortunately, field studies are available in the literature for both consumer and executive decision processes (e.g., Payne *et al.*, 1993; Woodside, 1992).

These field studies provide findings and conclusions about how decisions are framed and made by consumers and executives. Consequently, rudimentary comparisons of similarities and differences in the decisions implemented by consumers and executives can be compared. Such comparisons are rudimentary because the studies reported were not done with such comparisons in mind; and usually differing research methods were used for collecting data in the studies. Striking similarities and differences can still be noted in these studies.

Thinking Similarities

Striking similarities include the following core observations. Both executives and consumers apply very limited (low-cognitive-effort) search strategies to frame decision contexts, to find solutions, and to create rules for deciding. Simon's (1957) principle of "satisficing" rather than maximizing applies frequently in decision-making by executives and consumers.

Both executives and consumers frequently create and implement non-compensatory, rather than compensatory, heuristics for both identifying candidate solutions and making final choice decisions. Even when they report use of compensatory rules, careful analysis of the implemented decisions indicates that they didn't use those rules.

Automatic mental processes (see Bargh, 1994), rather than strategic thinking, tend to occur in all phases of decision-making by both executives and consumers. Neither executives nor consumers often explicitly consider alternative ways of framing and solving problems.

For major decisions, looping of thoughts back and forth to memory and thinking about external stimuli occurs frequently during decision-making. For example, consider "new task" problems by executives or "extensive problem-solving" situations by consumers. Such feedback loops are depicted in Figure 1-1 by left-to-right arrows. Mintzberg (1979) in particular emphasizes that feedback loops are often found in the decisions implemented by executives.

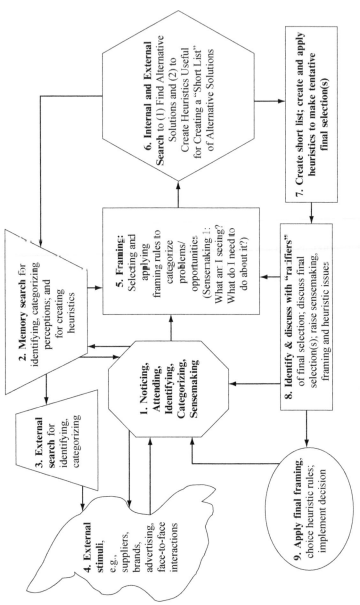

FIGURE 1.1   Decision process by executives and consumers.

Both executives and consumers frequently consult and seek approval from others before making a final decision (see Box 8 in Figure 1-1).

Several differences in decision-making between executives and consumers can be identified in the cited literature. Here are some noteworthy examples:

- Formal, written rules for searching for suppliers and evaluating vendor proposals are created for many categories of decisions within organizations but rarely by consumers.
- Formal performance audits by external audit professionals occur annually for purchasing and in many marketing organizations, but rarely are such audits done for consumer decisions.
- For many categories of decisions, documentation of deliberations and decision outcomes are more extensive in business organizations than in consumer households.

Five formal propositions of similarities and differences are described in separate sections following this introduction; these five propositions are summarized in Figure 1-2. The discussion closes with possibilities of the propositions for improving sensemaking to help plan and implement decisions that achieve desired outcomes.

S$_1$: AUTOMATIC AND CONTROLLED THINKING; D$_1$: META-THINKING

Bargh (1989, 1994) and Bargh *et al.* (1996) empirically support the proposition that most thinking, deciding, and doing processes include combining bits and pieces of automatic and conscious processes. Consequently, all decision-makers can only partly report the motivations and steps taken in their thoughts and actions because they are only partly aware of their own decision processes. "All decision-makers" is a category that would include marketers and buyers in organizations and consumers in households. Such a view has profound implications for theory, research, and marketing practice. Evidence supporting this viewpoint is available in the field of business and industrial marketing (Woodside, 1987; Woodside and McMurrian, 2000) as well as household buying behavior (Cohen, 1966; Thelen and Woodside, 1997).

S$_1$: Thinking, deciding, and actions by marketing and purchasing executives and household consumers often include automatic as well as conscious processing of information.

Meta-thinking is defined as thinking about how thinking occurs, including how thinking should occur. Meta-thinking by decision-makers is a higher

Similarity	Departure	Strategy and Research Implications
S_1: Thinking, deciding, and actions by marketing and purchasing executives and household consumers often include automatic as well as conscious processing of information.	D_1: Research evidence of business and organizational marketers and purchasers engaging in meta-thinking is more substantial compared to household consumers.	Recognizing the multiple categories of thinking will likely improve the quality of decisions made by business and industrial marketers: few may recognize the impact of automatic thoughts.
S_2: Both executives and consumers apply simplifying categorizing rules for defining decision contexts.	D_2: For repetitive decision-making contexts, categorization rules are more often formalized in writing by executives but not by consumers.	How the decision-maker frames the problem/decision has a large impact on his/her willingness to consider new vendors.
S_3: All decision-makers appear to create and use simplifying decision rules when faced with two or more alternatives.	D_3: Formal, written evaluation and choice rules are created and applied more often by professional buyers compared to household consumers.	Beware: Industrial buyers may use formal, written choice rules for comparing outcomes with informal, unwritten choice rules that are, in fact, applied (see Woodside and Wilson, 2000).
S_4: Decisions are often made in groups of two or more persons both in industrial firms and consumer households.	D_4: Formal group procedures are enacted often within industrial firms but not households during meetings to frame problems/opportunities, evaluate alternatives, and in making choices.	Influencing how a problem is framed will likely affect who is influential in the industrial marketing group decision-making (see Wilson, Lilien, and Wilson, 1991).
S_5: Post-experience evaluations and assessments of (dis)satisfaction occur often among both industrial firms and consumer households.	D_5: Performance audits of suppliers, products purchased, and the professional buyers/marketers employed by the organization are done more frequently by industrial firms, but rarely, if at all, by households.	Assessment of best practices for formal performance audits done by business and industrial firms will likely improve marketing strategies; research is needed on B2B performance auditing behavior.

FIGURE 1.2   Exhibit of executive and consumer decision processes: similarities, departures, and strategy implications.

form of conscious thought than conscious thought directly relevant to immediate issues. Here is an example of meta-thinking versus first-level conscious
thinking:

> Meta-thinking: What supplier performance attributes really make a differ-
> ence in my own purchasing performance?

> First-level conscious thinking: Does our major supplier provide on-time
> delivery consistently?

The creation of written checklists, such as safety procedures that must
be followed by a pilot before lift-off, is an example of meta-thinking.
While written procedures on how to think and act with customers and suppliers are often prescribed in industrial marketing and purchasing departments, written guidelines of purchasing procedures are not found in
households.

Written evaluation methods using weighted compensatory models are
required in some industrial purchasing departments (Woodside and
Wilson, 2000) but likely are rarely available in households. In the U.S., the
National Association of Purchasing Managers (NAPM) offers short
courses and educational certification programs to train managers how to
think and act effectively as buyers and purchasing managers; more than
30,000 professional buyers are Certified Purchasing Managers. Similar certification programs for training household consumers do not appear to be
available.

**D₁: Evidence of meta-thinking by business and organizational
marketers and purchasers is more substantial than evidence of such
thinking by household consumers.**

S₂: USE OF SIMPLIFYING CATEGORIZATION RULES;
D₂: FORMALIZING SUCH RULES

Both executives and consumers appear to use a few framing rules when deciding the nature of the problem or opportunity before them. One who learns
these problem/opportunity framing rules can influence the thinking and subsequent actions of both managers and consumers. For example, if a buyer
perceives an upcoming purchase as a standard re-order from current suppliers, a new vendor may need to influence the buyer to reframe the purchase as
a "new task buy" (Howard and Sheth, 1969) before the buyer will consider
the new vendor's product or service. This implication follows from the related
proposition that the amount of effort in searching for alternatives and in
evaluating alternatives is likely to be influenced by how decision-makers
frame problems.

S₂: Both executives and consumers apply simplifying categorizing rules for defining decision contexts.

Three problem dimensions may dominate how decision-makers frame a problem/opportunity (see Wilson, McMurrian, and Woodside, 2000): familiarity, financial commitment, and technical complexity. Assuming two levels are used as a way of simplifying each of these three dimensions, then eight framing categories may be identified (see Figure 1-3). Such problem-framing thoughts are noted in both industrial and consumer research literature (Woodside, 1992; Payne, Bettman, and Johnson, 1993).

D₂: For repetitive decision-making contexts, categorization rules are often formalized in writing by executives but not by consumers.

Several rationales may be suggested for written problem/opportunity framing rules occurring for executives but not for consumers. The formal requirements listed in the occupational specialty often require written order routines that differ by product category (e.g., raw materials versus maintenance, repair, and operating [MRO] items) for purchasers and buyers in firms but not in households. Most household consumers may view the purchase of low-priced consumer goods to be peripheral actions not worth the effort of creating and following written guidelines. Training of new professional buyers is often facilitated by detailed written order routines for all product categories; such written order routines may be prepared only rarely for household consumers because training in buying is more informal and one-on-one, for example, parent–child or sibling–sibling.

S₃: USE OF SIMPLIFYING EVALUATION/CHOICE RULES; D₃: FORMALIZING EVALUATION/CHOICE RULES

S₃: All decision-makers appear to create and use simplifying decision rules when faced with two or more alternatives.

For example, both professional buyers and household consumers create and use simple conjunctive rules to eliminate all but a few possible suppliers or brands when faced with many alternatives (more than seven or so). A conjunctive rule sets minimum levels of performance that must be met or surpassed in the product provided as well as in supplier service performance. Consequently, a "short list" or "consideration set" of three to five alternatives is formed for more in-depth evaluation using some other evaluation and choice rule. A weighted compensatory or lexicographic rule may be applied for evaluating the alternatives in the short list (consideration set). See Payne et al. (1993) for a discussion of these heuristics.

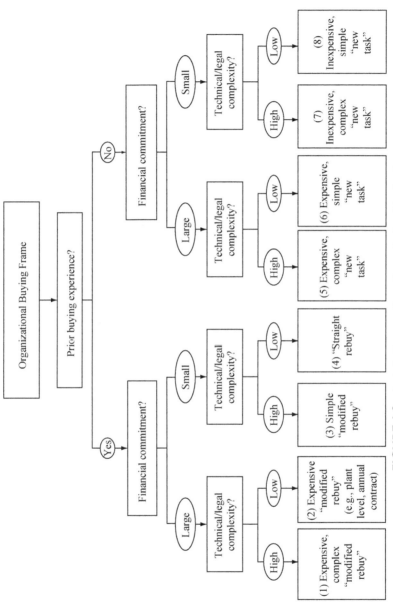

FIGURE 1.3 An inductive paradigm of organizational buying frames.

Thus, a combination of evaluation and choice rules may occur often for both executives and household consumers when faced with many alternatives to evaluate, even though printed forms using weighted compensatory rules for evaluating competing vendors likely are printed only among industrial firms, not households. Consequently, organizational buyers and household consumers depart from each other in the degree of formalization used in creating weighted compensatory heuristics.

D_3: Formal, written choice and evaluation rules are created and applied more often by professional buyers than household consumers.

Organizational marketers should be aware that the final evaluations from customers' written weighted compensatory rules often do not reflect the final choices and purchase agreements (Woodside and Wilson, 2000)—the outcomes of using the weighted compensatory rules may be revised to account for seemingly idiosyncratic preferences in the organization. Woodside and Sherrell (1980) describe such choice behavior examples. Nevertheless, buyers using weighted compensatory rules report that doing the necessary calculations is helpful because the approach forces them to consider more product and service attributes than they would consider without the use of such rules.

S_4: MEETINGS FOR EVALUATING ALTERNATIVE PRODUCTS AND SUPPLIERS; D_4: FORMALIZING RULES OF DISCUSSION AND APPLICATION OF GROUP CHOICE RULES

S_4: Decisions are often made in groups of two or more persons in both industrial organizations and households.

Even when all members of a group name one person as the sole decision-maker, other members of the group as well as group discussion are likely to influence the choices made (Wilson, Lilien, and Wilson, 1991).

D_4: Formal group procedures are enacted often within industrial firms, but not in households, for meetings to frame problems/opportunities, evaluate alternatives, and make choices.

Written procedures of discussion, and minutes of conversations and decision outcomes (including formal purchase agreements), follow from cross-departmental meetings in business organizations more often than from meetings of household members. To achieve effective decisions and savings in bulk purchases, meetings for the purpose of evaluating and selecting suppliers may extend across several manufacturing locations for an industrial firm on an annual basis for several product categories (Woodside and Samuel, 1981). Adult siblings living in separate households rarely hold such meetings. However, Sirsi, Ward, and Reingen (1996) offer an exception to this observation in their direct research report on a consumer cooperative buying organization.

S_5: EVALUATING OUTCOMES OF BUYING TRANSACTIONS AND QUALITY-IN-USE EXPERIENCES; D_5: FORMAL PERFORMANCE AUDITS

S_5: Post-experience evaluations and assessments of (dis)satisfaction occur often among both industrial firms and households.

Some judgments influence intentions toward both suppliers and specific products. Consequently, industrial and consumer marketers often design marketing information systems to measure customer satisfaction with the use of products and services—including service provided by salespeople.

D_5: Performance audits of suppliers, products purchased, and professional buyers/marketers employed by the organization are done frequently by industrial firms but rarely, if ever, by households.

Written guidelines are available on how to evaluate the performance of marketers, the performance of professional buyers, and the strategy of the organization for industrial firms; much of the popular business literature is devoted to reports of such performance audits (see Woodside, 2001). Compared to the ample business-to-business literature, written reports on the effectiveness and efficiency of buying decisions by households are sparse.

IMPLICATIONS FOR BUSINESS AND INDUSTRIAL MARKETING STRATEGY

Of course, the five sets of identified similarities and departures are not intended to be exhaustive. Many additional sets may be described. For example, many key relationships among variables involved in decision processes may go unrecognized by participants when they make decisions (Senge, 1990; Hall, 1984). However, in many industrial contexts, systems analyses (e.g., mathematical models and simulations) have been applied for identifying key leverage points that affect outcomes desired by executives (e.g., Hall, 1984). Such work does not appear to be available in the consumer research literature. Taking the time and making the effort to study feedback loops may be critical for achieving deep sensemaking regarding how our decisions/actions result in desired and undesired outcomes (see Senge, 1990).

Also, many executives in industrial firms and many household consumers resist adoption of products/services built on new technology platforms, even when those platforms have proven to be superior to installed products/services (Ram, 1987; Woodside, 2000b). Although such resistance may lead to decline and death of a business organization (Christensen, 1997), it rarely does so among households.

The main benefit of studying and comparing industrial and consumer research literature may be gaining a deep understanding of the subtleties and unexpected interdependencies in thinking, deciding, talking, and actions of decision-makers. Most likely, sensemaking skills are improved when one learns the similarities and differences in the processes of both categories of decision-making. Thus, the issue of what similarities and differences in decisions and actions occur among business executives and household consumers may be more useful than advocating that the study of decision-making by executives be distinct from the study of decision-making by consumers.

Business and industrial strategists are likely to increase their skill in making effective decisions from studying literature from both industrial marketing and consumer research. Too often the thought expressed is, "My company's situation is unique—it would not be useful to consider the behavior of other firms, let alone household consumers, in similar situations because the situation is really unique to my company." Expression of such a mental model often indicates an inability to create and learn from analogies.

> Better to start by casting a wider net: Let us admit that important similarities in decisions and behaviors do exist between business firms and household consumers, while recognizing that success lies also in studying the nuances occurring in the unique combinations of events in each case study (see Ragin (1987) for a complete development of this point).

2

CASE STUDY RESEARCH METHODS FOR LEARNING HOW EXECUTIVES AND CUSTOMERS THINK, DECIDE, AND ACT

Synopsis

This chapter provides a new definition for case study research (CSR). Achieving a deep understanding of processes and other concept variables, such as participants' self perceptions (an "emic view" of what's happening and "why I did what I did") of their own thinking processes, intentions, and contextual influences, is identified as the principal objective of CSR. Using multiple methods to "triangulate" (i.e., confirm and deepen understanding by using multiple sources all focusing on the same process/event) within the same case is described. This chapter outlines the core criticisms made by case study researchers of large sample surveys. A need exists for a paradigm shift in research on organizational behavior (including modeling the history of new product performance). The chapter outlines the significant weaknesses of CSR as seen by other researchers. The chapter examines Senge's (1990) core propositions related to the "mental models" of decision participants. Details illustrate the use of specific research methods for case studies to achieve different research objectives and the combination of objectives. Finally, the chapter illustrates basic concept variables in case studies and twelve propositions are reviewed briefly. This report reviews classic and recent contributions to the literature of CSR.

INTRODUCTION: ACHIEVING A BROAD PERSPECTIVE WHEN DEFINING CASE STUDY RESEARCH

CSR is an inquiry that focuses on describing, understanding, predicting, and/or controlling the individual (i.e., process, animal, person, household,

organization, group, industry, culture, or nationality). This definition is intentionally broader than the definition that Yin (1994, p. 13) proposes:

> A *case study* is an empirical inquiry that investigates a contemporary phe-
> nomenon within its real life context, especially when the boundaries between
> phenomenon and context are not clearly evident.

For a given study, focusing the research issues, theory, and/or empirical
inquiry on the individual (n = 1) is the central feature of CSR. As Skinner notes
(1966, p. 21), "... instead of studying a thousand rats for one hour each, or a
hundred rats for ten hours each, the investigator is likely to study one rat for a
thousand hours." This view is not intended to imply that CSR is limited to a
sample of n = 1. The reporting of several case studies in one inquiry is possible
when the inquiry is to estimate the size of an effect (i.e., the strength of a relationship between two variables) rather than to generalize to a population. For
example, meta-analyses (e.g., Hunter, Schmidt, and Jackson, 1982) provide
tools for estimating strengths of relationships (i.e., effect sizes). Also, reports of
multiple case studies are available in organization science (e.g., Nutt, 1998)
involving business-to-business contexts. In the marketing literature, Howard
and Morgenroth (1968) illustrate transforming the research context in one supply chain from n = 1 to n > 30 by examining alternative thought/action routes
taken in separate, but seemingly similar, decisions that include five principal
parties: a senior decision-maker, a regional manager, a local distributor, and
two sets of competitors.

A key point to our definition is that CSR is not limited to contemporary
phenomenon or real-life contexts, especially when boundaries between phenomenon and context are not clearly evident. Digging up the bones of U.S.
President Zachary Taylor in 1996 to determine if he was assassinated is an
example of CSR; B.F. Skinner's experiments in controlling the behavior of his
infant daughter are an example of CSR. The defining feature of CSR lies in the
supreme importance placed by the researcher on acquiring data resulting in
describing, understanding, predicting, and/or controlling the individual case.

WHY CASE STUDY RESEARCH IS USEFUL, PARTICULARLY IN INDUSTRIAL MARKETING

A substantial portion of research in industrial marketing focuses on the decisions and the behaviors by individuals and groups within and between organizations (Woodside, 1992; Woodside and Wilson, 2000). The most frequently
used research method in the field involves sending a mail survey of mostly
closed-ended questions covering 10 to 20 research constructs. The request
usually made is that the questionnaire be completed by one person per firm,
without comparison to any other person's answers. The reported response
rates for such studies typically range from eight to thirty percent.

This dominant logic assumes that the responding individual is willing to report her own thinking process, the thinking processes of others involved in the decision process, and the sequence of events that occurred over several days, weeks, months, or years. The dominant research paradigm assumes that the research constructs (e.g., role ambiguity, trust, closeness of supervision) measured on fixed-point scales provide the nuance necessary for capturing the thinking/doing processes under study.

Yet the scientific literature on thinking concludes that about 95 percent of thought is subconscious (Wegner, 2002; Zaltman, 2003) and that people have only limited access to their own thinking processes, not to mention the thinking processes of others. Consequently, research methods attempting to measure ongoing thinking (e.g., van Someren, Baranrd, and Sandberg, 1994) and thinking by the same person using multiple interviews over several weeks (e.g., Cox, 1967; Cyert, Simon, and Trow, 1956; Witte, 1972; Woodside and Wilson, 2000), methods to bring up subconscious thinking (e.g., Schank, 1999; Fauconnier, 1997), and interviewing the multiple participants involved in the thinking/doing under study (e.g., Biemans, 1989) not only are particularly useful steps, they become mandatory if we really want to achieve deep understanding in research on thinking/doing processes in industrial marketing.

"I Hate Lying Like That"

The operational constructs using closed-ended responses developed by researchers fail to uncover the deep nuances and dynamic interactions between thoughts and actions within and between individuals that occur within industrial marketing contexts. The following story illustrates such nuances that CSR can capture in ways unlikely to be captured by closed-ended mail survey responses. The story involves a sales call made by a representative of an industrial distributor of copiers and printing equipment (this sales call was overheard by one of the authors who rode in the same vehicle with the sales rep). During the selling/buying discussion involving the new purchase requirements, the customer mentioned that the copier purchased recently from the sales rep was broken again. Both the sales rep and the customer mentioned that the copier had needed a service technician to repair it almost every week since it was installed six weeks before. The sales rep responded to the customer's concern by saying, "I'm sorry you've experienced so many problems with your new copier. We will get to the bottom of the situation. It's a fine piece of equipment and we will solve the problem so it doesn't keep coming up." After getting back in his car, the sales rep remarked to the researcher, "The copier is a piece of shit; I really hate lying like that [to a customer]. It's really going to hurt my relationship with the guy." The sales rep elaborated that a competing distributor carried a line of copiers that were far superior in performance and reliability compared to his product line.

Three-Person and Five-Way Mental Processing in Industrial Marketing

Most studies in business and industrial marketing usually focus on only one of five mental processes, that is, verbalized thoughts. Figure 2-1 depicts such thoughts as Level 1 thinking. The other four levels shown in Figure 2-1 include the following mental processes.

Level 2 mental processing includes conscious editing of thoughts surfacing from unconscious processing, spreading, and combining of thoughts held in conscious processing. These thoughts include thoughts heard by both the person verbalizing and hearing thoughts from another person. Level 2 processing requires much more cognitive effort because of the attempt to handle three-way incoming thoughts from the unconscious, the person's own verbalizations, and the thoughts being received from the other person. "How do I know what I think until I hear what I've said?" (see Weick, 1995) is a question that reflects the idea that a person interprets her own thoughts after verbalizing them.

Level 3 mental processing is the surfacing of unconscious thoughts into conscious processes (i.e., "spreading activation" of concepts held in "working

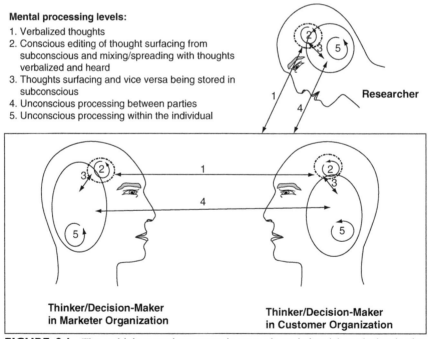

Mental processing levels:
1. Verbalized thoughts
2. Conscious editing of thought surfacing from subconscious and mixing/spreading with thoughts verbalized and heard
3. Thoughts surfacing and vice versa being stored in subconscious
4. Unconscious processing between parties
5. Unconscious processing within the individual

Researcher

Thinker/Decision-Maker in Marketer Organization

Thinker/Decision-Maker in Customer Organization

FIGURE 2.1 The multiple mental processes in research on industrial marketing–buying thinking.

memory" as well as moving of some thoughts involved in conscious process-ing into unconscious storage). Level 3 processing is automatic. An individual is often unaware of how the thoughts came to the surface or what process occurred that moved her conscious mind to focus on a new topic.

Level 4 mental processing includes unconscious processes between two or more persons that do not surface into conscious processes. Each person's nonverbal communications influence, and may attract or repel, the other per-son in ways unrecognized by both. "I don't know why, but I don't trust that guy" is a verbal commentary of level 4 processing.

Level 5 processing reflects a spreading activation within the unconscious of an individual. This includes completing automatic thought and action routines without surface recognition of the process. Level 5 mental process-ing may lead to behaviors that the individual is unable to recognize or report performing (Bargh, 2002; see Bargh, Chen, and Burrows, 1996, for an empir-ical study that relates to this observation), and behaviors not done that the individual reports doing (see Woodside and Wilson, 2002).

Figure 2-1 depicts that the five mental processes also occur for the researcher as the researcher attempts to observe and interpret the mental processes involved between the two principals. Figure 2-1 illustrates the researcher's limited ability to understand all five processes occurring for the two principals, as well as within the researcher herself.

Thus, the researcher's perspective of her five mental processes would ben-efit from explicit discussion and surfacing efforts in the form of introspec-tions (see Wallendorf and Brucks, 1993, for recommendations on how to improve introspection studies in consumer research). The dominant theory-in-use for research on industrial marketing/buying processes relies on the assumption most likely held implicitly, and not explicitly, by researchers that a deep understanding of such processes can be acquired using answers from direct questioning across many firms of one respondent per firm within a marketing or buying organization. Researchers rarely stop to ask introspec-tively, what are my unconscious processes that are influencing the design and execution of my study? How can I surface unconscious thoughts held by me? Is acquiring informants' answers to closed-ended questions enough for a deep understanding of the thinking and doing processes that I am studying?

The process of answering questions always involves a degree of intro-spection and "autodriving" (see Heisley and Levy, 1991) by an informant. The person answering questions must retrieve some bits of information stored in long-term memory, organize and edit the bits, and create a verbal or written response in a form that she believes that the researcher is able to understand. If the findings from research in the mental processing literature are accurate that most mental processing is unconscious and informants have very limited ability in surfacing unconscious thoughts, then acquiring a deep understanding of industrial marketing/buying processes from conscious responses to direct questions from one respondent using a single question-naire must be supplemented by using alternative data collection methods.

Autodriving indicates that the interview is "driven" by informants who are seeing and hearing their own behavior. Autodriving addresses the obtrusiveness and reactivity inherent in consumer behavior research by explicitly encouraging consumers to comment on their consumption behavior as "...photographs and recordings represent it" (Heisley and Levy, 1991, p. 257). However, autodriving relates implicitly to all informants' attempts to retrieve, organize, edit, and report answers to questions. Asking the informant to collect, organize, and describe photographs of themselves or to use other pictures (e.g., via Zaltman's metaphor elicitation technique, ZMET) to describe a context or themselves embodies explicit autodriving tools that can be useful for bringing up unconscious processes (e.g., Christensen and Olson, 2002). The researcher observing a marketer/buyer meeting, and subsequently asking one of these two parties to describe the meeting that just occurred, is another example of autodriving.

DEEP UNDERSTANDING: THE PRINCIPAL OBJECTIVE OF CASE STUDY RESEARCH

Any combination of the following purposes may serve as the major objective of CSR: description, understanding, prediction, or control. However, we propose that *deep understanding* of the actors, interactions, sentiments, and behaviors occurring for a specific process through time should be seen as the principal objective by the case study researcher. Deep understanding in CSR includes: (1) knowledge of "sensemaking" processes created by individuals (see Weick, 1995) and (2) systems thinking, policy mapping, and systems dynamics modeling (e.g., Hall, 1991)—what might be labeled appropriately as meta-sensemaking.

Sensemaking is how the individual (i.e., person, group, and/or organization) make sense of stimuli. Sensemaking foci include: (1) focusing on what they perceive; (2) framing what they perceive; (3) interpreting what they have done, including how they solve problems and the results of their enactments (including the nuances and contingencies in automatic and controlled thinking processes). Because gaining "thick description" (see Geertz, 1973, pp. 5-6; Sanday, 1979; and Arnould and Wallendorf, 1994) can be restricted to varying levels of depth and detail, thick description alone is not enough. The resulting data and information from a thick description may focus on surface details only, for example, describing the physical characteristics of the environments, actors, and their conversations. To learn (1) the subjective significance of persons and events occurring in a case study, and (2) the linkages and underlying (or, influence) paths among concept variables identified in a case requires deep understanding.

RESEARCH STEPS REQUIRED TO ACHIEVE DEEP UNDERSTANDING

Achieving deep understanding in CSR usually involves the use of multiple research methods across multiple time periods (i.e., triangulation; see Denzin, 1978). Triangulation often includes: (1) direct observation by the researcher within the environments of the case, (2) probing by asking case participants for explanations and interpretations of "operational data" (Van Maanan, 1979), and (3) analyses of written documents and natural sites occurring in case environments (see Figure 2-2).

The category of operational data includes spontaneous conversations of participants in a case, activities engaged in and observed by the researcher, and documents written by the participants. "Presentational data" are the appearances and answers to inquiries that informants strive to establish and maintain "in the eyes of the fieldworker, outsiders and strangers in general, work colleagues, close and intimate associates, and to varying degrees, themselves" (Van Maanan, 1979, p. 542).

> Data in this category [presentational] are often ideological, normative, and abstract, dealing far more with a manufactured image of idealized doing than with the routine, practical activities actually engaged in by members of the studied organization. In short, operational data deal with observed activity (the behavior per se) and presentational data deal with the appearances put forth by informants as these activities are talked about and otherwise symbolically projected with the research setting. (Van Maanan, 1979, p. 542)

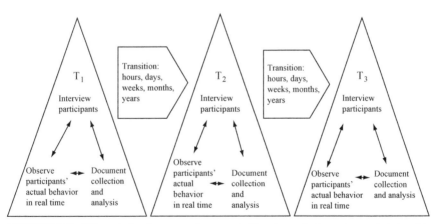

FIGURE 2.2 Triangulation in case study research. Showing only three time periods is arbitrary; the key point is that the case study researcher often prepares narratives of his or her interviews, direct observations, and document analyses, and then these narratives are presented to selected participants in the following time period to verify that the narratives include the details reported, observed, and found in the previous time period. For examples, see Nutt (1993) and Howard and Morgenroth (1968).

Gaining deep understanding often includes research to learn the "mental models" (Senge, 1990; Huff, 1990) of the participants. A mental model is the set of propositions a participant in a case understands to be reality—that is, an accurate portrayal of the causes, events, and outcomes relevant in the case. Each person studied in a case has a set of related but unique mental models describing

(1) The "typical" steps (i.e., persons, conversations, behaviors, and events) that occur in the process being studied by the researcher.

(2) The steps that should occur in the typical process (i.e., the participant's normative mental model).

(3) What actually occurred in a given process, for example, the most recent process completed or a completed process "strategically" important for the organization.

(4) The participant's perceptions of how another specific person or others in the organization, in general, understand the details of the process being examined.

Senge (1990) makes a number of telling points about decision-makers' mental models. Here are three of his points particularly worth noting for CSR. First, the mental model of any one person interviewed in a case study often fails to match closely with the direct observations made by the researcher or other persons interviewed (taken individually); the perceptions and beliefs expressed both by the interviewee and formed by the researcher from direct observation are likely to miss important details and depth of understanding. Second, mental models are rarely made explicit and tested by participants in the case; they are formed tacitly; participants often assumed their mental models to accurate views of: (1) what has occurred and (2) why it has occurred (or what should and should not occur) and why. Third, important feedback relationships among variables (i.e., "loops," such as increases in variable A leads to decreases in variable B that leads to further increases in variable A) go unrecognized by the participants in the case being studied. Hall (1978; 1984) provides detailed illustrations of all three of these points.

The mental model of a participant in a case study is an emic representation of reality. For example, an emic report is the verbatim "sensemaking" comments made by the individual under study in a case. The interpretation of the same process provided by the case study researcher is an etic representation of reality.

Etic representation in CSR often includes description and explanation of emic meaning as well as building composite accounts of the process based on data from triangulation. Thus, the collection of emic mental model accounts from interviews represents one set of data for the case study researcher.

Collecting operational, as opposed to presentational, data is a core strength of CSR. A core proposition within the mental models of most case study researchers is that operational data often vary widely from presentational data. Thus, case researchers seek a deep understanding by directly observing in "real time" (Arnould and Wallendorf, 1994) and (when possible) asking case participants, "What exactly is happening right now? What were the triggering events leading up to what happened? What is the meaning of what just happened to the case participants? What is going to happen next because of what has just happened?"

A distinguishing belief embraced by case study researchers (often implicitly) is that participant verbal reports of conversations, behaviors, and events distort and fail to include details necessary for deep understanding of the processes under study. "Rich as I believe these [respondent] interviews are, they are frozen in time, individual statements only vaguely anchored in the social and historical context that created them" (Wolf, 1990, p. 351). As Arnould and Wallendorf (1993) conclude, "Because of the inherent inconsistencies and ellipses in oral reports, verbal data alone are not regarded as sufficient for developing ethnographic interpretation. The preferred corrective for these limitations is combining verbal report data with data from long-term participant observation in cultural context." If long-term participation is impossible, the alternative includes adopting multi-method procedures, for example, interviewing all parties participating in conversations and events under study, and the collection of documents and additional unobtrusive measures (see Webb and Weick, 1979; Webb, Campbell, Schwartz, and Sechrest, 1966).

THE CORE CRITICISMS OF LARGE SAMPLE SURVEY RESEARCH AND CASE STUDY RESEARCH

The core criticisms made by case study researchers of large sample surveys (i.e., n > 100) of one person in a household, informal group, or organization include:

(1) The failure to confirm reported conversations, behaviors, and events, independent from the one person surveyed.

(2) The failure to collect the necessary detail for gaining deep understanding of the mechanics and reasons embedded in the processes examined. These criticisms are countered by critics (i.e., researchers using large samples persons in identified populations) to CSR by a core criticism of their own: CSR results are not generalized to a population, the particular case included in a given case study is so unique that it represents a one-off context.

Briefly, we offer the following observations related to this debate. First, we advocate adopting the view (i.e., mental model) that any one respondent is severely limited in reporting the details necessary to learn to deeply understand the process being studied—some use of triangulation of methods and multiple informants is necessary to confirm and deepen information. Second, the objective of CSR is not to generalize findings to a population but to probe theory (i.e., one or more explicit mental models related to the processes being examined; see Campbell, 1975; Yin, 1994). Third, the criticism can be directed at any one study as being idiosyncratic in its selection of population, data collection procedures, data handling and analysis, and selection of subjects for study from the population; labeling a study as being idiosyncratic is one step to concluding that the data collection procedures used and findings made can not be replicated—a false conclusion given that no one study can be replicated perfectly. Fourth, several case studies can be completed and fixed samples of cases may be drawn; case studies are not limited to n = 1; multiple cases, or multiple behaviors and events within one case study, can be examined to deepen understanding of patterns and contingencies related to theory (see Nutt, 1993, for an example of a large sample case study and McCracken, 1988, for a defense of multiple case sampling for identifying patterns across cases).

Our objectives do not include attacking large-sample, one person per household or organization, one-time survey research studies. However, the substantial amounts of respondent reporting of events that did not occur, and the absence of reporting events that did occur in such studies (see Farley and Howard, 1975), as well as the absence in such studies of details necessary for deep understanding of processes being studied, are additional motivators for adopting CSR methods.

In an essay on "Organizational Performance as a Dependent Variable," March and Sutton (1997, p. 702) bemoan the fact that the bulk of research on identifying the causes of organizational performance rely on cross-sectional data and retrospective studies: "These studies may actually tell us less about the determinants of performance than about the ways performance information affects memory, cognitive processing, and story telling." Retrospective bias may be the telling weakness of most empirical studies on measuring the performance of new product introductions specifically and, in general, on most studies measuring other areas of organizational performance.

> Performance information itself colors subjective memories, perceptions, and weightings of possible causes of performance. Informants exist in a world in which organizational performance is important. That world is filled with widely believed conventional stories about the causes of good and poor performance. As a result, retrospective reports of independent variables may be less influenced by memory than by a reconstruction that connects standard story lines with contemporaneous awareness of performance results. (March and Sutton, 1997, p. 701)

March and Sutton (1997) also fault theory building that includes not viewing organizational performance as an independent variable: "... the theoretical ideas and analytical models that are normally used [e.g., by the majority of organizational and inter-organizational researchers] ignore a variety of feedback loops that are likely to be important." Organizational behavior as a series of feedback loops is a suggestion stressed by Senge (1990) as one central for shifting research paradigms from linear thinking to system thinking. The importance of building and testing complex models is critical to capture the impact feedback loops on performance demonstrated empirically by Hall (1976; 1984).

The crucial point here: deep understanding of the multiple perceived realities that occur through time in organizations and households requires the use of multiple data collection methods across several time periods. Meta-sensemaking—the researcher's pursuit of a vision of reality lying outside the social beliefs of one person interviewed per organization or household—requires that additional data be collected (e.g., interviews of other persons involved in the behavior being examined; direct observation; and the analysis of documents and other unobtrusive measures).

DATA COLLECTION AND ANALYSIS METHODS USEFUL FOR CASE STUDY RESEARCH

While CSR is often associated in the literature with using qualitative research methods, we advocate viewing CSR as *not* being restricted to one set of research methods. Quantitative methods, including statistical hypotheses testing, are appropriate for many CSR studies. Also, the value of most CSR reports may be enhanced considerably by using multiple tools, both qualitative and quantitative methods, in the same study.

The value of most CSR reports increases with the use of dissimilar, multiple research methods and the inclusion of multiple study objectives (e.g., see Pettigrew, 1995). One of our objectives for this book is to provide insights for achieving useful descriptions and explanations and to go beyond these objectives—to describe the additional, possible objectives of predicting and controlling case study behavior.

THEORY BUILDING AND THEORY TESTING USING CASE STUDY RESEARCH

CSR is often associated in the literature with theory building as opposed to theory testing (Dyer and Wilkins, 1991; Eisenhardt, 1989). However, examples of theory testing reports using CSR are available. The quality of a CSR report often may be increased dramatically by designing the study to include *both* theory building and theory testing (e.g., see Howard and Morgenroth, 1968; Gladwin, 1989). We advocate the broader view: CSR is often appropriate for both theory building and theory testing. Several examples of successfully doing theory building and testing by CSR scholars are described in this book.

THE OBJECTIVES OF CASE STUDY RESEARCH

CSR is appropriate for several research objectives: description, explanation, prediction, and control of the individual process, animal, person, household, group, or organization. Thus, we advocate that CSR is often appropriate for several research objectives going beyond description and explanation. **Description** in CSR is the attempt to answer who, what, where, when, and how questions. **Explanation** in CSR is the attempt to answer the why question. Sometimes CSR explanations include reports provided by: (1) the direct participants in the case; (2) informed third-party observers to the case; and, (3) the case study researcher. **Prediction** in CSR includes forecasting near-term and/or long-term psychological states, behaviors, or events that will follow within the individual case and/or similar cases. **Control** in CSR includes attempts to influence the cognitions, attitudes, and/or behaviors occurring in an individual case. Control is a relevant objective in experimental studies of single cases (see Hersen and Barlow, 1976), for example, in studying the efficacy of alternative methods for achieving behavioral changes desired by: the participants (e.g., subjects, clients, or patients) in a case; an organization (e.g., a product/service marketer, a government lobbyist); a non-profit organization or society (e.g., a department of social work; a school or university).

Each of these four research objectives can be viewed beneficially as orthogonal to the other three objectives (see Figure 2-3). Thus, we advocate embracing the mental stretch that case description is possible without explanation; and, explanation without description is also possible. Also, every possible four-way combination shown in Figure 2-3 occurs in CSR.

Objectives		Prediction			
		No		Yes	
		Control			
Description	Explanation	No	Yes	No	Yes
No	No	1. Abstract (Art)	2.	3.	4.
No	Yes	5.	6.	7. Building in degrees of freedom	8. Dynamic causal modeling
Yes	No	9. Naïve observation	10.	11.	12.
Yes	Yes	13. Participant observation	14. Action research	15. Ethnographic decision tree modeling	16. Clinical (psychology, psychiatry)

FIGURE 2.3   Classifying case study research by research objectives.

Let's concentrate on a few of the cells in the figure to demonstrate the possibilities. Cell 1 is the null CSR report: no information relevant to describing, explaining, predicting, or controlling is included in the study; an abstract artist rendering of a case study is illustrative of Cell 1.

Cell 7 includes attempts to "build-in degrees-of-freedom" (Campbell, 1975) in a theory of behavior that may be relevant to a given category of cases. Creating a set of 10, 20, or 30 propositions that the case study researcher proposes as typical of decision-making and behavior for a given case theory is illustrative of building-in degrees-of-freedom. Such theory building may be content-free of a specific case, that is, the theory may be formed deductively.

Weick's (1969; also see Weick, 1979; Bougon and Komocar, 1990) dynamic causal modeling of organization and change is an example of a content-free theory for explaining, predicting, and controlling case behavior without starting with a description of a particular case. Several propositions are included in dynamic causal modeling that these researchers believe useful for achieving effective, long-lasting change (i.e., control) in a social system (i.e., a given case). Here is an example proposition:

> A social system's identity nodes and loops are typically over determined by the pattern of the whole and are almost impossible to change directly (e.g., Warwick, 1975) or in a piecemeal fashion (e.g., Miller, 1982). Thus, within a holistic approach, when the nodes and loops of interest to strategic change coincide with the social system's identity nodes and loops, the solution to strategic [long-lasting] change is indirect. The solution is to focus change efforts on peripheral loops rather than on those directly responsible for system identity. (Bougon and Komocar, 1990)

Cell 9 is a description without explanation, prediction, or control: a naïve report of events in a case by a reporter totally unfamiliar with what is occurring in the case. Andy Griffin's (a U.S. actor/comedian) humorous portrayal of a backwoodsman reporting the first-time observance of an American football game illustrates Cell 9.

Representative of cell 13 CSR, most participant observation studies include the objectives of providing thick descriptions and deep explanation of the processes and events occurring within a specific case; developing models to predict outcomes or future events and designing change strategies to influence (i.e., control) case behavior are not primary objectives in such studies. *Qualitative inquiry* is an example of a scientific periodical with a primary focus on thick description and deep understanding in CSR.

Participatory action research reports are representative of cell 14 CSR because the objectives of such studies include thick description, deep understanding, and attempts to influence the design and outcomes of behaviors occurring in a case, without attempting to build predictive models for estimating values of proposed dependent variables (e.g., see Whyte, 1990; 1991).

Ethnographic decision tree modeling (EDTM) does not include attempts to influence outcomes by the researcher but do include model building to predict estimates of values of specific dependent variables. Thick description and deep understanding provide the foundation for EDTM; thus, EDTM is illustrative of cell 15 in Figure 2-3. The *Journal of Contemporary Ethnography* is an example of a scientific periodical with a primary focus on such research reports.

Applied theory development in social work and clinical psychology/psychiatry illustrates cell 16 CSR—the aims of the researcher include thick description, deep understanding, prediction of outcomes, and control of behavior exhibited in a specific case. The *Journal of Applied Behavioral Analysis,* the *Journal of Clinical Psychology*, and *Behavior Therapy* are scholarly publications related to this category of CSR.

SUGGESTIONS REGARDING SELECTION OF CASE STUDY RESEARCH OBJECTIVES

Our aim does *not* include the claim that moving away from cell 1 toward cell 16 is always best. We do suggest greater awareness of the possibilities of planning to accomplish multiple objectives in CSR. Also, different CSR tools (i.e., research methods) are relevant for achieving different objectives. For example, EDTM is useful in particular for building theory for predicting outcomes occurring naturally in cases and action research is useful in particular in designing strategies to change behaviors and outcomes in cases. Thus, skill building in learning research tools relevant for case studies across a wide range of objectives should complement your training in advanced CSR.

CORE PROPOSITIONS IN CASE STUDY RESEARCH

Several core propositions in CSR are summarized visually in Figure 2-4. Briefly, twelve of these propositions are described here. (1) Time is recognized explicitly in modeling behavioral processes in CSR. For example, in the studies of n = 1, the possibility of variability in responses (i.e., events or outcomes) is built into the study by observing behavior of the respondent across several time periods.

(2) In many case studies, multiple individuals participate in different conversations and behaviors within one time period in the case. Conversational analysis is the primary focus of many case studies. (3) Individuals are members of identifiable households, groups, or organizations. (4) Much like actors appearing in different scenes in a play, different individuals in the same group may participate in conversations and behaviors in different time periods; for example, note in Figure 2-4 that individual 6 is found in conversations in T1 and T3.

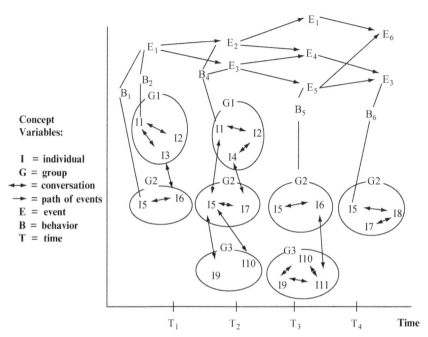

FIGURE 2.4 Concepts and propositions in case study research. Adapted from Calder (1977), Figure 14.2, p. 198.

(5) When examined deeply, most cases involve three or more informal groups or organizations that affect the process and outcomes under study. The involvement of "third-parties" in interorganizational case studies has been the focus of several studies in supply-chain management (e.g., see Biemans, 1989).

(6) Identifiable individuals and groups engage in identifiable behaviors leading to identifiable events (i.e., outcomes). (7) Specific events influence the occurrence of other events. (8) Some events are repeated, for example, E1 to E2 to E1 in Figure 2-2. (9) The presence of certain events (e.g., E5) changes the influence of another event; for example, E6 occurs in T4 following E1, given that E5 has occurred. Thus, CSR and theory building often includes contingency propositions of complex relationships. (10) Not all members of a group communicates with every other member in the same group; for example, in Figure 2-2 I1 talks with I2 and I3 in Group 1 in T1, but I1 does not talk with I2. (11) Participation in the case of identifiable groups occurs only in a limited number of time periods; for example, G1 is found in T1 and T2, and G3 is found in T2 and T3. (12) Conversational contacts within a group may increase or decrease from one period to the next within a case; for example, witness the increase in contacts in G3 between T2 and T3 in Figure 2-2.

Additional variables described in most case studies are not included in Figure 2-4. For example, the display of emotions, such as showing anger, approval, and trust (see Homans, 1974), is not included. Events shown in Figure 2-4 include decisions, performance outcomes, and revelatory incidents—Figure 2-4 does not include the attempt to distinguish among these three categories of events.

Different streams of CSR focus on different concept variables shown in Figure 2-2. For example, policy mapping is the attempt to diagram, explain, and predict recurring relationships among events in a case study (e.g., Hall, 1976, 1984, 1991; Howard and Morgenroth, 1968). Decision systems analysis is the attempt to diagram and explain (but not to predict) relationships among non-recurring events in a case study (e.g., Howard and Morgenroth, 1968).

The CSR methods appropriate for a given study depend on the nature of the process being examined, as well as the interests of the researcher. For processes being repeated with adjustments, such as managing a newspaper business or pricing gasoline, policy mapping is an appropriate research tool. For one-off processes, such as an individual or organization adopting a new technology, decision systems analysis and EDTM are appropriate research tools. While many different CSR methods are available, all include the recognition of the core concepts summarized in Figure 2-4.

SUMMARY

CSR is an inquiry focused on describing, understanding, predicting, and/or controlling the individual (i.e., process, animal, person, household, organization, group, industry, culture, or nationality). Any combination of the following purposes may serve as the major objective of CSR: description, understanding, prediction, or control. However, we propose that deep understanding of the actors, interactions, sentiments, and behaviors occurring for a specific process through time should be adopted as the principal objective by the case study researcher and that the researcher makes use of explicit autodriving tools to aid in bringing up unconscious mental processes among informants.

A mental model of a process provided by a participant interviewed in a case study is an emic representation of reality. The interpretation of the same process provided by the case study researcher is an etic representation of reality. Etic representation in CSR often includes description and explanation of emic meaning as well as building composite accounts of the process based on data from triangulation. Triangulation includes: (1) direct observation by the researcher within the environments of the case, (2) probing by asking case participants for explanations and interpretations of operational data, and (3) analyses of written documents and natural sites occurring in case environments.

The core criticisms made by case study researchers of large sample surveys consisting of interviews of one person per household, informal group, or organization include: (1) the failure to confirm reported conversations, behaviors, and events, and (2) the failure to collect the necessary detail for gaining deep understanding of the mechanics and reasons embedded in the processes examined.

The core variables in CSR include individual and group behaviors through time resulting in a sequence of paths of events (decisions, performance outcomes, and revelatory incidents). Beliefs and sentiments held by individuals and groups are additional core variables sometimes studied in CSR. No one CSR method is appropriate for all studies.

3

MAPPING CONTINGENT THINKING BY B2B MARKETERS AND CUSTOMERS

Synopsis

Given that planned marketing strategies and observable behaviors are often contingent on buyer and third-party (e.g., competitor) responses, deep understanding and descriptions of the thoughts and actions of marketers need to reflect the dynamic interplay of such contingencies. The same view applies to planned organizational buying strategies and observable behaviors: buying behavior adapts through time based on information that is learned and marketers' responses to requests made by the customer organization. Consequently, a two-way, or multiple-party, approach to theory construction is useful in particular for mapping the "if/then" responses of the marketer's thoughts/actions linked with the if/then responses of buyers' thoughts/actions through several time periods. Using in-depth interviews and case histories of one marketing organization and 28 buying organizations related to the office furniture industry, the chapter illustrates descriptive modeling of the contingency dynamics in the thoughts and actions of the multiple parties involved in marketing/buying interactions.

INTRODUCTION: ONLY CONTINGENT ALGORITHMS

Loewenstein (2001, p. 503) stresses, "People do not seem to have all-purpose algorithms for deciding how to behave. Instead, they often seem to behave according to a two-stage process in which they first attempt to figure out what kind of situation they are in and then adopt choice rules that seem appropriate for that situation." Similarly, Herbert Simon provides the metaphor of a pair of scissors for thinking about rational behavior: one blade has to do with the psychology of the organism and the other with the structure of the environment (reported in Goldstein et al., 2002, p. 173). To achieve deep understanding of the process and outcomes of the multiple meetings occurring over weeks, months, and sometimes years in organizational marketing/buying relationships, the metaphor needs to be expanded to include two or more sets of scissors. This point builds on the contingent nature of effective selling behavior (Weitz, Sujan, and Sujan, 1986) and the contingent relationships observed in buying behavior (Woodside and Wilson, 2000).

Two points follow from this expanded view. First, each party to the marketing/buying interaction likely would benefit from understanding the nature of contextual influences on the other's decisions and behaviors. Second, contexts change and evolve, and consequently, "behavior will change abruptly and radically when the individual's construal of the situation she is in does change" (Loewenstein, 2001, p. 503).

In business-to-business (B2B) marketing/buying behavior, members of a marketing organization and a buying organization are likely to interact among themselves and with the other organization over several days, week, or months. Consequently, how members in each organization view the context of their interactions and related problems/opportunities likely evolves and/or changes abruptly. Cyert, Simon, and Trow (1956) provide one of the first detailed reports of such contextual dynamics. In their case study covering an 18-month period, the buying committee in the organization that they described became unable to cope with the task of buying because of the increased risk they felt in purchasing. By the end of the case, the decision was made not to buy from any supplier—to flee from the problem.

This chapter illustrates the use of decision systems analysis (Hulbert, Farley, and Howard, 1972) to construct an inductive model of middle range (Merton, 1957) for organizational marketing/buying processes that occur frequently for office furniture and design services. The study is based on in-depth case histories in 28 organizations, each engaged in buying office furniture at the time of the research, and one marketing firm interacting with each of the 28 buying organizations over time.

A middle-range theory attempts to generalize beyond a particular case history but not beyond one set of circumstances (e.g., industry setting). Previously, most industrial marketing research reports that have included the use of decision system analysis (DSA) focused on just one decision process (for example, Cyert et al. (1956) and Woodside and Vyas (1983)) or several decision processes limited to one firm (e.g., mapping the decision process of price-point shifts done by Howard and Morgenroth (1968)).

An exception to this observation is the inductive model of industrial supplier choice summarized by Vyas and Woodside (1984) that was developed by studying several decision processes of six industrial firms in five disparate industries. Such an overall model may be useful as a general outline or map, but likely lacks the inclusion of nuances valuable for understanding organizational marketing/buying strategies within a specific industry.

The basic premise for the present study is that a four-step research sequence is useful, particularly for constructing inductive models of industrial purchasing (and marketing). Step one involves the preparation of several (n > 20) in-depth case histories of the purchasing process applicable to one industry for several different buying problems (i.e., new task, modified, and straight rebuys for small, medium, and large firms) (Robinson, et al., 1967). Step two constructs a middle-range theory in an attempt to summarize the streams of interactions/behaviors and decisions of buying firms for one industry. Step three collects additional case study data for generalizing by testing the accuracy of the contingencies in the process, as well as the outcomes, predicted by model. Step four involves repeating steps one and two for several industries, until similar patterns of industrial buying processes are observed among two or more industries.

The outcome of step four is a comprehensive model of industrial purchasing strategy consisting of a limited number of middle-range models. Whereas all industrial buying processes include unique events, sequences, and interactions of buying center participants, it may be possible to catalogue most marketing/buying processes as belonging to one of a few middle-range models. This basic proposition applies at the micro (step one) level: most micro-models, case histories, of industrial buying processes may be very similar to one of a limited number of patterns of behaviors/decisions/interactions. If this is true, developing a composite, or summary, of the relevant patterns of industrial purchasing strategies across several firms for one industry may be useful for theory and recommendation. The evidence reported here, based on the examination of 28 purchasing case histories from one-industry, supports this basic proposition. The following report constructs a model covering the joint contingent nature of marketing/buying behaviors (steps one and two). A limitation of the study is not being able to collect additional data beyond what is used for inductive model building. Completing steps three and four are necessary for testing the nomological validity of the model and to generalize the model across industries. The suggestion is that future research studies might perform these additional steps by collecting additional case data to test the validity of the process model described in the following sections.

Method

The organizational marketing/buying processes involved in the office furniture industry were selected for the study for several reasons. Organizational purchases of office furniture are pervasive; nearly all organizations buy or rent office furniture.

The manufacturing and marketing industries for office furniture and design are medium-sized ($60 billion in the U.S. in 2002), and one manufacturing or distributing firm does not dominate these industries. Over 70 percent of the office furniture marketed in the U.S. is sold through office furniture distributors. Most of these distributors offer office design, credit, warehousing, installation and repair, as well as ordering and transporting services to their customers. No single distributor has a dominant market share (i.e., none hold a 50% plus market share in any state in the U.S.), although a few (4 to 8) large competing distributors have most of the available business within specific standard metropolitan statistical areas (SMSAs). (These industry characteristics are based on information from personal interviews with marketing representatives working in the office furniture manufacturing and distributor industries, completed in 1985 through 2002).

From the 1970s to the 1990s, two technological developments created new task buying problems for many office furniture customers. "Modular" office furniture, the "open system," was introduced in most U.S. markets in the late 1960s and was adopted by many large corporations during the 1970s. Modular office furniture consists of metal, wood, and fabric-covered partitions with attached desk-to-work areas, hanging overhead cabinets, and lighting and storage spaces with wiring for communications built underneath or overhead into the partitions. This relatively new office furniture technology was still replacing wood and metal freestanding desks in large office work areas in many organizations in the mid-1980s when the initial wave of data for the study was completed.

Modular furniture applications offer several distinct advantages over the typical arrangements of rows of desks in large open office areas that were found most often in American industry in the 1950s and 1960s: larger work areas, less noise, more "work stations" in the same available office space, and a greater degree of privacy. The installation of modular furniture often involved design costs—a major investment in changing over several (typically 4 to 100) office work stations at one time. Such costs represent a capital expenditure for many firms. The changeover from freestanding wood or metal desks to "cubicle" workstations met with some office worker resistance in the 1960s, and such cubicles are still the subject of jokes in management cartoons in the twenty-first century (e.g., Dilbert comic strips). Design improvements (e.g., adding sound reduction materials to the panels) have reduced such resistance.

The addition of personal computer work and storage spaces has been a second technological advance, creating the need for design and new task office furniture and equipment purchases. The widespread adoption of personal computers in offices through the 1980s helped speed up the changeover to modular open office systems.

Thus the study of office furniture marketing and purchasing strategies permits the possibility of constructing inductive models about marketing product designs new to customers, which some customers classify as new task buys and other customers classify as modified rebuys. Both small (under $100,000) and large (over $100,000) purchases occurred within the marketing and buying processes that were examined. Members of most buying organizations permitted a review of documents (e.g., bid proposals and recommendations to senior management) relevant to their office furniture purchases.

The marketing manager and sales reps of two office furniture distributorships were willing to describe their interactions with customers and strategies in preparing bids. After several meetings with the marketing manager, and traveling with the sales reps to visit customers, two days of sales calls were completed by the researcher with each of five distributor sales reps in each of two distributorships. Because of the extensive length of time involved in data collection, the cooperation of only two office furniture dealerships was sought for the study—one in the mid-1980s and a second during the late 1990s. A possibly surprising finding (because of Internet marketer/buyer communications) from comparing the findings for the two time periods is the continuing reliance of local area dealers by manufacturers in the twenty-first century; manufacturer sales reps, distributor product managers, and office furniture customers interviewed in 2001 all expressed the view that dealers continued to be important due to a combination of reasons: the design, inventory, credit, and related services that they provide that manufacturers and customers find difficult to get elsewhere.

Data Collection

The data collected in the study were the sequences of events, decisions, and meetings of people involved in making recent or current office furniture purchases among 28 organizations. A total of 30 organizations were requested to participate in the study on how organizations buy office furniture; two firms refused to participate. Managers in the 28 cooperating firms agreed to participate by allowing one to three members of their office furniture buying centers to be interviewed. During the resulting face-to-face interviews, the respondents were asked to provide examples of written bid requests, dealer proposals, and interdepartmental memoranda, if available, as examples of information used during the buying process. These documents were reviewed with the members of the buying centers to verify the sequence of activities and decisions reported by respondents and to serve as an "external memory" (Bettman, 1979) to evoke additional thoughts and insights from the respondents.

At least two information sources were used to verify the key events and decisions reported by members of the 28 buying centers. For example, requests for bid proposals (RFPs) were examined and compared to bid proposals received to verify the product categories purchased, and the expenditure level reported by a respondent. Each respondent was asked to clarify discrepant or unclear data when information from the two or more sources varied. When relevant, the sales reps and sales manager of the cooperating office furniture dealer were asked to comment on bid proposals, purchase orders, design work, installation, and repair work for a customer pertaining to the buying process described by the respondents.

The managers in one of the 28 organizations were willing to provide only general information concerning office furniture purchasing processes.

This organization was not included in the final data analyses. The 27 buying organizations participating fully in the study included 13 manufacturing plants, seven financial firms, three hospitals, two national headquarters operation centers, and two colleges. In most of the 27 cases, data from two separate interviews were collected, along with examinations of relevant documents and tours of the newly installed furniture. For 11 of the 27 cases, data from two separate interviews were collected, along with examinations of relevant documents and tours of the newly installed furniture. For 25 of the 27 cases, a sales rep and/or sales manager of the participating office furniture dealer was able to provide additional details, and verify specific events and decisions related to the purchasing processes.

For each case study, most of the data collected covered two or more time periods spread over weeks, and in five cases, two or more months. For example, the researcher was able to observe the preparation of bids in response to RFPs and then learn, three weeks later, if the proposal was successful (a contract was awarded by the buying firm to the office dealer). In five cases, interviews with buying firms were scheduled after interviews had been completed with the office furniture manager responsible for sending bids to these buying firms. This method permitted data collection of the corresponding thought and decision processes of persons in both the buying and selling organizations.

Participants in the buying centers were asked to describe the sequence of events, decisions, and meetings of persons in their organizations (and with sales reps) related to the recent purchase of office furniture. The participants were first asked to describe an office furniture purchase that first came to mind. If the purchasing process was completed more than twelve months ago, the participants were requested to describe a more current buying process, or one completed during the past few months. The interviews required 90 minutes to two hours to complete. For ongoing buying processes, second interviews with the same people were scheduled. Weekly interviews with one or more sales reps and sales managers of the participating office furniture dealer were held throughout the study period.

Consequently, a triangulation of data points (i.e., separate interviews with one or more persons in both the buying and the selling organization, and reading matched RFPs and bid proposals, see Denzin, 1978) confirmed several epiphanies in most of the cases. For example, members of both the buying and the selling organization confirmed the purchase order size in dollars; whether or not a formal RFP was prepared or if the job was awarded to a favored dealer without seeking a second bid; whether a bid was submitted and, if so, when it was submitted; and the name of the office furniture dealer awarded the contract. Also, how well the reasons matched between persons in the buying and selling organizations for awarding and rejecting bids could be examined. When conflicts and paradoxes did arise on specific data points from different sources (e.g., sales rep versus buyer, sales manager versus sales rep, dollar amount on the bid proposal versus dollar amount reported by the sales manager), additional questions were asked at a following meeting with the sales rep, sales manager, buyer, manufacturer sales rep, or delivery/warehouse worker.

A Theoretical Note on Epistemology, Ontology, and Axiology for Collecting Data on Organizational Marketing/Buying Decision Processes and Resulting Behaviors

Figures 3-1 and 3-2 depict theory for collecting data that guided the fieldwork for this study. Related to epistemology (i.e., the nature of knowing), Figure 3-1 reflects the splits occurring within a subject (Holbrook, 1995, p. 183) among:

- Unexpressed unconscious knowledge (F_4 in Figure 3-1).
- The S's unconscious knowledge expressed during the interview (automatic retrievals triggered during the interview, e.g., F_1 in Figure 3-1).
- Conscious knowledge that is verbalized (e.g., a_1) as well as not verbalized (a_4) during the interview.
- Knowledge that consists of interactions from unconscious and conscious beliefs (e.g., c_1, Bargh, 2002).
- Prior knowledge held only for brief periods by S that is unavailable (G) except if learned again via encounters from external sources (e.g., g_1 in Figure 3-1).

Figures 3-1 and 3-2 reflect several ontology (i.e., the nature of reality) assumptions. For example, S may believe that specific truths exist related to answering the questions posed by I—truths contingent on situational configurations that S believes are too complex to describe during the interview. Consequently, S tends to verbalize answers that are more socially desirable (e.g., area D in Figure 3-1, also Bandura, 1977) than S knows to be true in any specific situation. S intends such verbalized answers to appear to be sane, reasonable, logical, and enabling for the conversation to come to closure so that S might get back to work—rather than answers that are accurate and fitting a specific situation that falls within the topics being studied. Thus, for learning contingent-bound truths held by participants in B2B marketing/buying processes, attempts by I to learn such truths need to include asking S to describe situational contingencies that take such processes into alternative and multiple realities. Thus, reporting multiple truths for multiple, contingent realities is required if the research objective is deep understanding of marketing/buying processes. Data collection for such reporting requires moving beyond the following possibilities:

- I interviews S only once.
- I interviews only one S per organization.

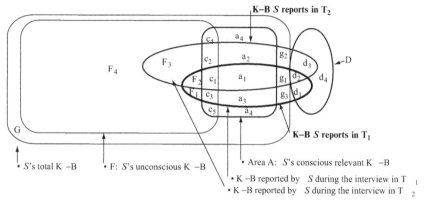

FIGURE 3.1   Knowledge–beliefs (K–B) and report of subject related to process understudy by the interviewer (I).

Categories of data:

- a_1: conscious K–B expressed verbally or written reports by S to the interviewer, I, repeated in both interviews
- a_3: conscious K–B expressed verbally or in written reports by S to the interviewer, I, only in the first interview
- a_4: thoughts that S is consciously aware but does not think to report and/or the I did not ask about
- F_1: unconscious K–B thoughts learned, and reported by S during the the first interview (S learning what she thinks while she is talking)
- F_4: unconscious K–B that S does not become aware and does not report during the interview
- c_1: interactive unconscious and conscious thoughts S expresses during the interview
- c_2: interactive unconscious and conscious thoughts S generates but does not express during the interview
- D: thoughts that S thinks about consciously and knows not to be relevant or accurate but reports (e.g., d_1 during first interview) or does not report (d_4)
- G: K–B no longer accessible/retrievable by S without external (e.g., detective) work (e.g., names of all vendors calling on S in her first year on the job) but S is able to confirm (e.g., g_1 in prompted by showing S documents created months or years ago that are shown by I during questioning)

- I interviews persons from only one side of a marketing/buying process.
- I fails to seek independent confirmation of some specific truths that S expresses for some specific situations by reading related documents and direct observation of some of these situations (Mintzberg, 1979).

The following discussion summarizes relevant theoretical propositions (P_i). P_1: the knowledge–beliefs (K–B) that a subject (S) reports (i.e., the K–B area in the boldest portion in Figure 3-1) in an initial face-to-face interview is a small portion of the K–B available to S that is relevant to the marketing/buying processes being examined. P_2: the report by S includes shares of K–B consciously held (e.g., a_1 in Figure 3-1), unconsciously held (e.g., F_1 in Figure 3-1), and combination (e.g., c_1) of conscious and unconscious K–B; and thoughts that S reports that S "knows" not be relevant or accurate in regards to the case study—for example, d_1 of area D (Ericsson and Simon, 1993; Bargh 2002). P_3: most Ss' K–Bs are held unconsciously (area F in Figure 3-1) by S (i.e., $F > A$); for support see the studies reviewed by Bargh (2002) and the review by Wegner (2002). "Indeed, the more experienced people are with respect a particular cognitive task, the more they seem to lack insight into their own mental processes or strategies" (Hogarth, 1987, p. 56). Learning processes to accomplish tasks become "automatized as one gains experience, and thus ultimately inaccessible to introspection" (Hogarth, 1987, p. 56). P_4: because rapport and trust usually build during an interview, the total amount of K–B that S reports during a second interview is greater than the amount S reports during the first interview. In Figure 3-1, the larger area enclosed representing the K–B that S reports in the second interview versus the area enclosed representing the K–B that S reports in the first interview illustrates P_4. P_5: overlap occurs in the K–B that S reports across multiple interviews, that is, S tends to repeat some K–Bs as well as provide K–Bs unique to each interview.

This discussion provides only a partial development of data collection theory relevant to interviewing participants in marketing/buying processes across organizations. The discussion here is intended not to elaborate a full theory on the topic. One objective is to emphasize the severe limitations of collecting data by written mail surveys of one respondent per organization for such data, self-editing likely occurs always before responding and the likelihood of learning K–B automatic retrievals held by Ss is very low. Another objective: the discussion illustrates the value of multiple face-to-face, verbal interviews with the same S spread over days, weeks, and months to enable additional K–B information to be learned as well as to confirm data collected in the initial interview.

Another noteworthy proposition: (P_6) the K–B reports collected from multiple Ss overlap in contents but each S reports some data unique from other Ss. Expanding Figure 3-1 into a mental picture of two sets of overlapping Venn diagrams would be messy but representative of P_6.

Figure 3-2 illustrates that the study of B2B marketing/buying processes at least implicitly focuses on the interactions of participants within and among three or more organizations. Figure 3-2 shows four layers of participants per organization displayed by levels of authority, job titles, and functions. Figure 3-2 exemplifies the most frequently found organizational designs and that occur the most frequently within and between organizational interactions in the study described in this report.

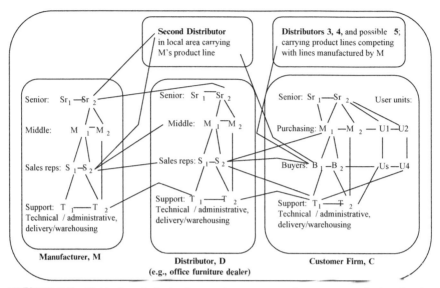

FIGURE 3.2 Field of study for business-to-business research: persons usually found to be actors in one or more stages of the marketing–buying process and examples of principal communication flows. These are the high-impact vertical and horizontal communications found within and between organizations. Manufacturer M sales reps talk face to face with persons in two levels at least of dealer firm. Dealer sales rep often has communications with three levels in customer organization.

Figure 3-2 illustrates several additional propositions. For example, P_7: communications by middle managers represent a gate-keeping role—a role first reported in-depth by Pettigrew (1973, 1975). That is, senior managers rarely talk with sales reps or technicians beyond saying hello or communicating in formal meetings held once to four times annually; senior managers talk directly and frequently only with each other and with middle managers. P_8: talk occurs at more than one level between organizations, but such talk most often occurs on a one-on-one basis; in some specific instances, talk occurs in the form of formal presentations by a manufacturer's (or dealer's) sales rep made to middle managers and sales reps (or buyers). P_9: extended continuing (weekly or often daily) talking occurs most often within organizations; weekly or monthly communications (usually by telephone) occur between major manufacturing principals' and local distributors' middle managers.

P_{10}: talking occurs rarely that spans two organizational levels and especially diagonally across two organizational levels. P_{11}: consequently, some participants are isolated from most other participants in the marketing/buying process, for example, Figure 3-2 depicts Sr_1 having only one communication link in each of the three organizations. P_{12}: infrequently, a usually astute senior manager recognizes the naturally occurring isolation surrounding her organizational position and creates "unnatural links," to investigate K–Bs of other participants across organizations.

For example, Sam Walton, founder and chairman of Wal-Mart Stores, reports,

> "I'll bet I've been in more Kmarts than anybody—and I would really envy their merchandise mix and the way they presented it. So much about their stores was superior to ours back then that sometimes I felt that we couldn't compete. Of course that didn't stop us from trying." (Walton with Huey, 1992, p. 81)

Figure 3-3 illustrates an Sr_1, such as Sam Walton, reaching out across organizations horizontally and diagonally to directly observe and talk to participants in marketing/buying processes. Regarding creating such boundary-spanning relationships, Lee Scott, another senior Wal-Mart executive, reports that for a long, long time, Sam would show up regularly in the [truck] drivers' break room at 4 a.m. with a bunch of donuts and just sit there for a couple of hours talking to them.

> He grilled them. "What are you seeing in the stores? Have you been to that store lately? How do the people act there? Is it getting better?" It makes sense. The drivers see more stores every week than anybody else in this company. And I think what Sam likes about them is that they're not like a lot of managers. They don't care who you are. They'll tell you what they really think." (Walton with Huey, 1992, p. 210)

The last two sentences by Lee Scott reflect the need to get beyond surface, socially and politically acceptable, answers to questions and how to go about acquiring deeper K–Bs held by participants. Also as mentioned by

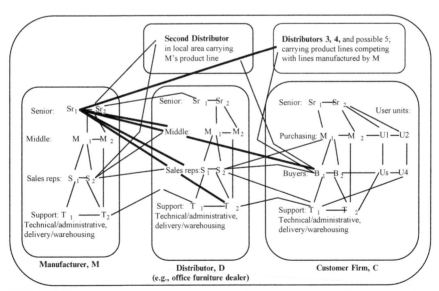

FIGURE 3.3 Example of senior executive (e.g., Sam Walton) creating "unnatural ties" to learn actions and outcomes associated with interorganizational relationships.

Scott, "show up regularly" and "just sit there" are concepts that reflect the need for multiple face-to-face interviews to acquire deep (unconsciously held) K–Bs of participants.

Axiology refers to the nature and types of values underlying research. Axiological discussions frequently emphasize that research can never be value free but must reflect the value judgments of the investigator concerning what topics are interesting, what approaches are worthwhile, and what results are important. "Here, the best we can hope for is that researchers make their values explicit and reveal any personal biases so that readers of their work can take these into account" (Holbrook, 1995, p. 185). In this spirit, the present study advocates replacing the dominant logic of most B2B research. The current B2B research dominant logic relies mainly on:

- Responses to closed-end questions (e.g., 1-7 Likert scales).
- Mail surveys completed by one participant at one organizational level (e.g., senior executives).
- Among marketers only or buying organizations only.
- Data files with less than 30 percent useable responses.
- Explicates few details into the contingencies in inter-organizational marketing/buying processes.

In part, the present study is meant to showcase the now subordinate logic of using open-ended questions, asked repeatedly to the same persons in two, and often multiple, face-to-face settings, in multiple organizations, in both marketing and buying organizational units. In particular, European scholars advocate such a paradigm shift to greater adoption of direct research (e.g., see reports by members of the IMP Group, such as Hakansson and Wootz, 1975; Hakansson, 1982; Möller, 1983). The research reported here illustrates combining face-to-face questioning with direct observation of meetings between sales reps and middle managers, middle managers and senior managers, middle managers and technicians, and sales reps and buyers, as well as "just sitting there" while riding in cars with sales reps.

Results

The 27 completed case histories were categorized into six contingent streams of marketing/purchasing strategies according to key events, similarities, and major differences among the cases. Table 3-1 summarizes the six streams. Figures 3-3 to 3-5 provide details of contingent paths relevant to the six purchase streams. The following method was used to identify the six streams shown in the table and the figures. After writing a summary description and flow diagram of the behavior/decisions/interactions for each case, two case analysts[1] worked inde-

[1] The research support by David Samuel and Niren Vyas in examination of these case analyses is acknowledged with appreciation.

TABLE 3.1 Contingent Streams of B2B Marketing-Purchasing Strategies for Office Furniture

	Stream	Direction	Local Dealer Bids	Order Size
(A)	National contract	1-3-5-7-9-10 in Figure 3-1	No	$100,000 +
(B)	Intensely competitive large purchase	1-3-5-11-13-14-15-16-18-20-21-19 in Figure 3-1 and 22-23-25-27-28-31-33-34-37-38-39-40 in Figure 3-2	Yes	$50,000 to $100,000 +
(C)	Competitive large purchase	1-3-5-11-14-15-16-18-20-21-19 in Figure 3-1 and 22-23-29-28-31-33-38-39-40 in Figure 3-2	Yes	$20,000 to $10,000 +
(D)	State government contract	1-3-5-11-12 in Figure 3-1 and 1–6 in Figure 3-3	No	$1,000 to $10,000
(E)	Competitive small purchase	1-3-4-5-11-12 in Figure 3-1 and 1-2-7-9-10-11-14/13 in Figure 3-3	Yes	$3,000 to $20,000 +
(F)	Non-competitive small purchase	1-3-4-5-11-12 in Figure 3-1 and 1-2-4 in Figure 3-3	No	$500 to $20,000 +

pendently to study each case and list up to ten key events and turning points that might be relevant in classifying the cases. The two lists of key events and turning points were compared; eight items appeared on both lists. Both lists were used to flow diagram the "emerging strategies" (Mintzberg, 1979) in the sequences shown in Figures 3-3 to 3-5.

Two sales reps and the sales manager of the office furniture dealership participating in the study were also interviewed about how they would classify types of buying situations. The three considerations mentioned by all three were: (1) expenditure level; (2) specifications; (3) amount and type of competition. These three considerations were included as part of the ten key events and decision turning points in the purchasing strategies for classifying office furniture purchasing strategies. The other seven considerations included the following items: (4) whether or not the purchasing requirements could be met by a national contract; (5) whether or not design work was required; (6) if it was required, would the dealer offer a design proposal; (7) whether formal bids would be sought or the contract would be negotiated with one dealer; (8) whether formal bids would be sought or the contract would be negotiated with one dealer; (9) whether customers would attempt to renegotiate bids; (10) whether a state government contract would be used to purchase the required products.

Limitations

Before specific findings are described, some limitations of the study should be noted. The research method is limited to reporting the sequences of events and decisions in the buying processes for office furniture among 27 organizations. This small sample may not be representative of the purchasing behavior of other organizations and time periods.

Substantial details of the individual buying processes are not included, as an attempt is made to generalize across the 27 cases. As in the case of a road map, the loss of detail of the immediately surrounding terrain is necessary to learn the major intersections—turning points—and direction being taken across the cases. The resulting maps of the major arteries of purchasing strategies are broad summaries only of the sequences of events, decisions, and interactions that are likely to be found. Some "direct research" (Mintzberg, 1979; Van Maanen, 1979) involving participant observation is necessary to gain an in-depth understanding and explanation of real-life organizational purchasing strategies.

Substantial agreement occurred among members of the research team on the key turning points and major branches in the observed purchasing streams. For example, the availability and use of a national contract relates to a series of interactions and behaviors strikingly different from the purchase of office "seating" (chairs) for four work stations. However, some differences occurred in interpreting the sequence of events and the importance of specific

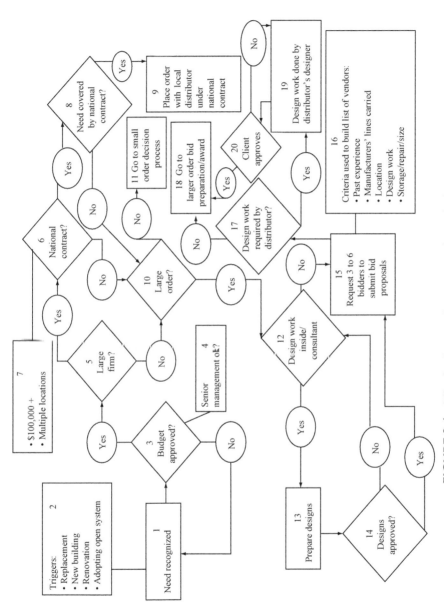

FIGURE 3.4 Office furniture contingent streams in purchasing processes.

49

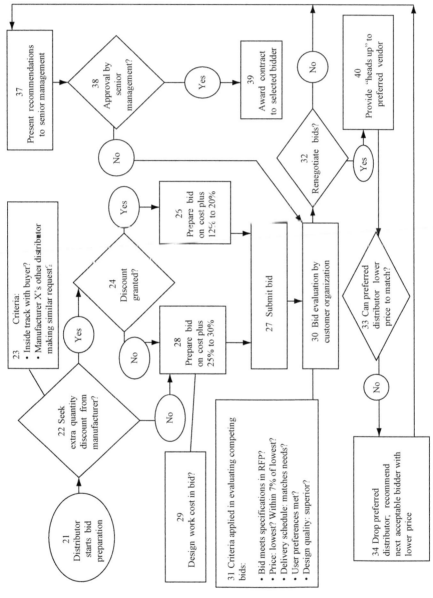

FIGURE 3.5 Contingency model of large order marketer bid preparation and buyer award process.

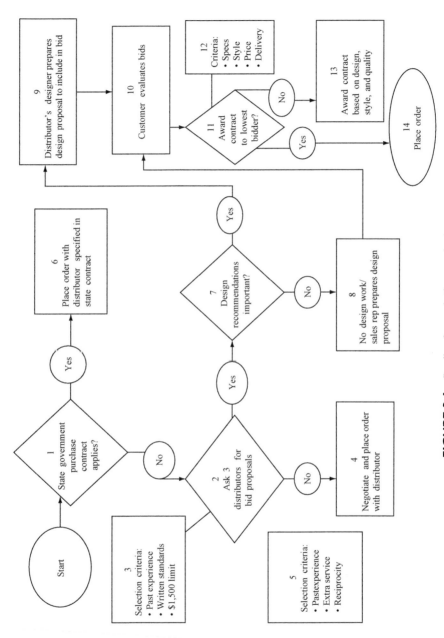

FIGURE 3.6 Small order marketing–purchasing process.

actions in analyzing the 27 cases. Thus, different teams of researchers would be unlikely to produce identical maps of the same purchasing strategies.

Some details of each of the six contingent purchasing strategies are provided in the following sections. Implications for developing a behavioral theory of industrial purchasing and marketing strategies and prescriptions for managers are provided in each section.

National Contracts

Some of the ten considerations were relevant only under specific scenarios, for example, national contracts involving several customer plant locations and national headquarters were relevant only for organizations with large annual expenditures in office furniture. National contracts were negotiated at the national level by "national account marketing managers" (Barrett, 1986). They represented the office furniture manufacturer, and corporate buying officers represented the headquarters and other locations of the buying organization (Woodside and Sammuel, 1981). Such office furniture contracts set price discount schedules and local dealers to be used by state and city for office and plant locations of the buying organization.

Several major benefits are provided by the use of national contracts. For the marketing firm, national contracts can represent substantial shares of total sales; competitors are prevented from gaining substantial sales volume among major customers; the accuracy of sales and production forecasts may increase; local distributors servicing local plants and officers of a national corporation may receive substantial purchase order without working up detailed bid proposals. Steelcase Corporation, the office furniture–manufacturing firm with the largest market share in the U.S., was cited most often by members of the buying centers studied as being the office furniture manufacturer most aggressive in marketing national contracts.

Deep price discounts, improved delivery schedules, and rapid response to service and repair requests were the three benefits cited most frequently by buying center members for participating in national contracts. Most national contracts do not require local buyers to participate in the contract. However, purchases of other manufacturers' product lines outside a national contract are difficult to justify; such justification is usually required for annual purchasing audits. The reported price discounts were very substantial for office furniture purchased under a national contract, for example, cost plus 12 percent. An important benefit of national contracts for the purchasing organization is the standardization of multiple office locations using one manufacturer's product line. When using modular furniture, it is important for all office locations to purchase the same product line, because competing products cannot be combined physically. For example, Steelcase modular furniture does not connect with Herman Millar or Westinghouse product lines. Thus, a major combination of offices between or within plant locations would create added costs and storage if competing furniture lines were used. A manufacturer's design changes/improvements in modular furniture have been known to cause serious problems in the offices of large organizations, when the old and new designs are incompatible. The marketing strategy of Herman Miller, a major modular furniture manufacturer competing with Steelcase, is to offer major design improvements (e.g., sound-deadening features) while maintaining compatibility with previous Herman Miller lines. Herman Miller follows a high-price, high-product quality marketing strategy compared with Steelcase.

One Example of a National Contract

A few details of the decision process and key events in the stream of behavior follow for the purchase of office furniture under a national contract. The purchase was made for the new headquarters building and regional office centers of a large financial firm, Colonial Life Insurance Company. The planned move to a new 350,000 square foot headquarters building was the catalyst in the "building committee's" decision to adopt the open office system (modular furniture). The building committee included seven senior executives of the company, and was chaired by the company's chief executive officer.

The buying center also included a full-time inside designer, Ann Platt, who worked on an independent contract. She was in charge of all interior design work. Dennis Lobby, the purchasing officer, was responsible for seeking and evaluating bid proposals from national office furniture manufacturers. The vice president for services was a fourth entity in the buying center; the VP for services, Lobby, and Platt met to evaluate the bids received and prepare a formal proposal to present to the building committee.

Lobby described this stage: "By that time the proposal was a formality because we knew which line would be best and they (the building committee) had to approve my recommendations and okay the terms of the master contract." Approval of the bid selected and local distributor recommended by Lobby, Platt, and the VP was granted by the building committee, as predicted by Lobby. This specific evaluation/recommendation/ratification decision process supports the hypothesis developed by Hill and Hillier (1979) that senior management often serves first to define the buying problem and set initial parameters (e.g., budget), while other members of the buying center are more involved in making product and vendor selection decisions.

Four manufacturers were asked to bid: Steelcase, Herman Miller, E.F. Houserman, and Westinghouse. Lobby first checked to ensure that a full-service distributor (offering installation, repair, delivery, design, and storage) representing each manufacturer was available in the local area. Lobby required that each manufacturer carry both complete lines of modular and traditional (wood and metal desks and cabinets) furniture: "This type of purchase system would ensure a consistent design and color scheme in all work areas. Another important attribute is that it would establish the rank of employees. For example, everyone at one position would get a certain type desk, chair, etc. All managers would receive another model. All department heads receive a third type, and at each higher level the furniture would be of higher quality or aesthetic value."

Prior experience with local distributors affected the selection of a manufacturer for this national contract. Lobby described the award of the contract to both Steelcase and Hines McWaters, the local distributor carrying Steelcase products. "They [Steelcase] gave us the best price, discounts, and delivery. I have also had good experience with Hines McWaters repair crews and that was another plus for them. We did not go with Herman Miller furniture because we felt the price was a bit high. Houserman was not chosen because they did not have a local dealer at the time." This manufacturer/dealer selection process reflects the use of a phased decision rule–conjunctive followed by disjunctive heuristics. Carrying complete lines of modular and traditional furniture, offering acceptable prices and quality discounts, as well as good delivery schedule and a reputable local dealer, were basic requirements for serious consideration. Manufacturer/dealer combinations that did not meet minimum levels of performance on these choice criteria were eliminated. The manufacturer/dealer combination that excelled on one or more of these criteria was selected.

"Add-on" business, additional sales of office furniture related to but not covered by the initial contract, was an additional advantage of a national contract for the manufacturer and dealer. For example, Lobby mentioned that a large follow-up order was made of office furniture matching the furniture purchased in the national contract, and this follow-up order was also placed with Hines McWaters. "We needed to refurbish four top-level executive offices, and we gave Hines McWaters the contract. No other vendors were trying for the order because they were not notified." Lobby reported that Hines McWaters did all the design work at no extra charge. This and additional add-on business was expected to total more than 40 percent of the original national contract of $145,000.

Figure 3-3 depicts a bare-bones summary of the national contract buying process: steps 1-3-5-7-9-10. Only four of the 27 cases (15 percent) involved national contracts. In summary, national contracts by definition include negotiations directly between manufacturers and large, multiple location, buyers. For office furniture national contracts, the buyer's perceptions of local dealer capabilities and levels of performance may influence the buyer's selection of a manufacturer's product line.

Large Purchase Order Streams

Figure 3-3 includes two additional office furniture purchasing streams. One stream leads to a large bid preparation and award (box 19). The second stream leads to a small order decision process (box 12).

The large purchase order (but not via national contract) stream accounts for 11 percent of the research cases on office furniture buying. Two major branches occurred in the large purchase order stream in Table 3-1 (in Figure 3-4 from 23 to 25-27-28); the second branch is labeled the "competitive, large purchase order stream" in Table 3-1 (in Figure 3-4 from 23 to 29-28).

Whether the dealer sought an extra quantity discount from a principal manufacturer (diamond 23 in Figure 3-4) was dependent on the dealer's answers to two questions (box 24). If dealer X's sales rep believed that dealer X had the "inside track" (was strongly preferred by the larger customer), and the manufacturer of the product line preferred by the customer was unlikely to grant an extra discount to a competing dealer (carrying the same line) for this specific customer, then dealer X's sales manager would not request an extra quantity discount from the manufacturer. The sales manager preferred not to request additional quantity discounts from a principal manufacturer for two reasons: (1) additional quantity discounts reduced the dealer's trade discount and (2) these discounts hurt the dealer's reputation in the minds of the principal manufacturer—the dealer was perceived as being able to compete only on price, not quality service.

Most major office furniture manufacturers do not offer their distributors exclusive contracts within a city or at the state level. For example, Herman Miller has relationships with two or three dealers; each dealer has offices in each of the major cities within the same state. For a given customer and large purchase order situation, one dealer may ask the manufacturer for an extra quantity discount, while another dealer may not make the same request. The dealer granted the extra discount might quote a lower price to the customer, causing the customer to reject the bid of the second dealer. The bids received are often made public information by customers making large purchase orders; and the second dealer with the higher bid often resents the rejection, which resulted from the principal granting the special price concession to the competing dealer without informing the second dealer.

A manufacturer often does grant the extra quantity discount as requested by the dealer if one of three conditions were met (box 26): (1) if the dealer's potential customer involved in seeking the extra quantity discount was prestigious in the state, e.g., a major bank with 80 or more branch locations (such customer could serve as a referral for additional business from other customers); (2) Steelcase was competing for the account—Steelcase was known to be very competitive on price and the other major manufacturers wanted to prevent Steelcase from increasing its market share; or (3) substantial add-on business was potentially available from the dealer's prospective customer (an incentive for granting the extra quantity discount to receive future purchase orders, possibly at higher prices).

Renegotiating the Bids

Note in Figure 3-4 that some instances of permitting dealers a second chance to bid occurred for large purchase orders (diamond 33). This decision was made when dealer X's submitted design or product line was judged to be superior, but dealer Y's bid did not meet the specifications required and dealer Y's bid was lower by 10 percent or more (box 41). The preferred dealer (X) might be asked to submit a lower bid, if possible (box 34). Dealer X often complies with this request, or agrees to comply if the customer is willing to accept some lower price/quality substitutes on traditional office furniture lines (box 36). Attempts to renegotiate bids were uncommon; only two instances were found among the 27 cases. In both instances, the preferred bidder did receive and the low bidders did not receive purchase orders. The need to be aware of possible processes for the renegotiation of bidding among some large purchase order buyers, and to be able to develop contingency plans to encourage or respond to bid change requests, are marketing strategy implications of bid renegotiations.

Senior Management Buying Center Participation

Note that senior management is involved in ratifying (or rejecting) the bid recommendation of other members of the buying center (box 38). Thus, senior management involvement is found most often near the beginning (box 4 in Figure 3-3) and near the end of the buying process. Senior management participated in the final approval of all large purchase order cases in the research study. Such participation has been found in several research studies on buying center behavior (Spekman and Stern, 1979; Lilien and Wong, 1984). Large purchases ($100,000+) that include the adoption of modular office furniture represent a new task problem-solving situation for capital equipment for organizations. Thus, the early initial buying center participation of senior management is not surprising. Such early buying center participation is not found often for purchases of production items (e.g., Lilien and Wong, 1984).

The Preference for Bidding Through the Local Dealer

Most respondents (8 out of 12) of the large purchase order cases reported a preference for buying through a local dealer when possible. Several rationales were provided. "We like to go through the local dealer because it helps his business and also we can't afford to warehouse the furniture until it can be installed." The preceding is the response of the general service manager for the state-wide bank, commenting on buying through local dealers even though purchase requirements were "in such large quantities that we could deal directly with the manufacturer." This particular respondent appeared to be unaware of the possibility that national contracts for office furniture are usually written to include warehousing, installation, and repair work done by local dealers. Two other reasons were given for making large purchases through local, versus nonlocal, dealers or directly from manufacturers: (1) the desire to maintain and increase local goodwill and reciprocity and (2) timely response to repair and other service requests.

User Involvement in the Buying Center

Department managers in large organizations were involved in approving design layouts when the purchase involved the widespread adoption of the modular office furniture. In traditional furniture purchases for senior executives, these users were given the opportunity to select one of the two or three product lines, but not to search through several other product lines. Thus, some limited options were made available to department managers, key executives, and office supervisors after the search process had been narrowed to one to three design and product line alternatives. This step was done by the person (usually a purchasing manager or buyer) most involved in face-to-face meetings with dealer sales reps. Three buyers in different organizations made comments similar to the following, concerning user involvement in the adoption process of modular furniture. "I would do some things differently (if I could do it over again). I would have gotten the department managers to put their layout approvals in writing. We are having a few problems with some managers who deny ordering the furniture that they chose a few months earlier. Some dissatisfaction is being expressed with the color scheme of the seating and panels purchased in the open office departments. It is very frustrating because we went through so much planning beforehand."

Buying Centers for Large Purchase Orders

The buying centers for large purchase orders of office furniture involved three to six job functions and seven to 30 people. These included the organization's CEO; chief financial officer (CFO), the purchasing officer; a senior buyer or the purchasing officer's secretary; a full-time designer, design consultant, or a team of interior design engineers; and senior executives who would be using new modular furniture work stations. As described by Webster and Wind (1972), and found by Spekman and Stern (1979) and others (Woodside and Vyas, 1983), buying centers were informal, cross-sectional decision units whose membership compositions changed through time, and by phases in the buying process.

Small Purchase Order Streams

Figure 3-6 summarizes three small purchase order streams that were observed. Small purchase orders ranged from $500 to $20,000 in all three small purchase order streams.

The buying centers in two organizations made purchase awards using a "state contract pricing agreement," even though the organizations were not state governmental units or agencies. For example, a country hospital purchased $18,000 of conventional steel desks, cabinets, chairs, and carpeting using the state contract. The state contract was negotiated by the senior state purchasing official and office furniture manufacturers. The contract included provisions that other government-related organizations could buy office furniture at the prices specified in the state contract, if they decided to do so. For the country hospital, no search was conducted for product lines or a local dealer, because the state contract specified Steelcase. The hospital had employed a design consulting firm three years earlier; this firm had made specific recommendations on office layout and manufacturer's product lines. The hospital was continuing to adopt all of the major recommendations made by the consulting firm.

This county hospital case is a useful illustration of the power of consulting firms in influencing organizational buying behavior, even when such firms are no longer interacting actively with members of the buying center. For additional evidence of such influence, see Choffray and Lilien (1980). Also, state-level governmental contracts may enable manufacturers and local dealers to increase market share with relatively lower marketing expenses than those incurred when marketing to other organizations even though low or no direct profits may result. Steelcase appears to be the most aggressive manufacturer in seeking state-level government contracts. The sales manager and sales reps of the office furniture dealer participating in the study all believed that state government business was worthwhile for local dealers. A small dealer margin was gained from such business; an increase in visibility in the local business community resulted from servicing such governments accounts and the dealer's marketing and service departments maintained high activity levels (e.g., install and repair crew were working eight-hour days).

Other Small Purchase Order Streams

Most (67 percent) of the nine remaining small purchase order buying strategies involved the use of formal request for proposals (see box 2 in Figure 3-6). Whether such buying centers attempted to induce competitive responses from dealers using a formal bidding process depended on three criteria (box 3 in Figure 3-5). A "negotiated strategy" was used if the purchase amount was very small (< $1,500), the small purchase involved modular furniture additions and the buying organization had standardized its buying requirements on one product line, and precedence (past experience) in vendor choice was a decision rule—"We always buy from dealer X, that's just the way we do things." A "negotiated strategy" was used when a member of a buying center met with one or two competing sales reps to describe the organization's purchase requirements, and to acquire information on product lines, prices, delivery, and service. No formal bids were requested in negotiated buying processes. The office furniture sales reps interviewed all preferred negotiated, as opposed to bid-on, buying processes. One sales rep reported that he continued to meet two to three times per month with members of the buying center of his most important customer (with annual sales of more than $500,000 for a large complex of buildings). Thus, he felt that the buying process was more like negotiation than bidding, since he had so much inside information on the buying process, even though formal bids were used to meet internal purchasing policy and audit requirements within the buying organization. This information was provided after six formal and informal interviews with the sales rep. Such nuances must be considered in classifying buying processes into formal bid versus negotiation categories.

Design Work

Note in Figure 3-6 that even for buying streams involving small purchase orders, the design recommendations of the dealer's designers may be critical in that dealer being awarded the contract. If design recommendations are important, and the dealer's designer submits a superior design, the dealer may receive the contract award even when the dealer is not the lowest bidder.

Delivery Requirements

In two cases, delivery requirements of the buying center were the most important considerations in awarding the contracts between the three and four vendors requested to submit proposals. One senior buyer reported, "Any lead time greater than four weeks is absurd." He was responsible for searching for product lines and meeting dealers in the purchasing process for four executive chairs. He reported that he was dissatisfied with the delivery schedules of any of the dealers, "But that is not entirely their fault—part of the problem is created by the manufacturer." The practice of maintaining very low product inventories seems to be widespread among office furniture manufacturers, because of the large financial costs involved, the extended length of time taken by organizations in buying office furniture, and the inability to predict demand changes due to economic expansions and recessions. Consequently, dealers often quote delivery times of eight to twelve weeks in bid proposals. The sales manager and sales reps interviewed in the study all sided with the manufacturers' inventory cost problems; most (but not all) customers were willing to wait up to three and four months for delivery of major purchases of office furniture.

Influences of Situational Contexts

Specific situational influences were noted in the buying behavior of those making small as well as large purchase orders. In one case involving the purchase of $18,000 worth of lobby furniture by a small, private women's college, the college's business manager had used a negotiated buying process; this resulted in awarding most of the college's purchase to the same dealer for over 15 years. Bids from other firms were not sought. However, there was a serious fire in one building on the college campus. A donation to help with the repairs was requested from the dealer; this was the only time a donation had ever been requested. The dealer made a donation of $50. The college business manager commented, "After years of being a very good customer, we were disappointed. We knew we were paying higher prices than we could have gotten elsewhere." The business manager used a bid procedure in awarding the contract for the new lobby. Two dealers bid on the job; the dealer perceived to offer the best design was awarded the contract.

Learning such "hidden agendas" in specific buying processes requires gaining the trust of buying center respondents, and investing substantial time in following up leads or clues offered by the respondents during face-to-face interviews. For example, one might ask if any one particular dealer had been used often over the years. Was this dealer being asked to quote on jobs this year? If not, why not?

Reciprocity influenced making a small purchase order ($20,000). See box 5 in Figure 3-5. The buying center of a national consulting firm was required by its corporate executives to buy from a specific local dealer that was a substantial client ($50,000 contract) for an accounting and management audit completed three years earlier.

THEORETICAL AND MANAGEMENT IMPLICATIONS

This chapter presents a phenomenological, middle range model of organizational marketing/buying of office furniture. This major proposition of the study was supported, that is, the specific cases of organizational marketing/buying behavior could be categorized into a few meaningful contingent streams of realized strategies.

The key variables that appear to influence the path taken in the marketing/buying processes include organizational size, expenditure level, need for design work, the amount of dealer competition for the purchase requirements, and whether a formal bidding process is used. The described marketing/buying processes for office furniture included several separate decisions. The decisions and behavior of dealers, manufacturers, and buying center members, and the interactions of participants that occurred early in (and in some cases before) the buying process, influenced events and decisions occurring in later stages.

No attempts by the office furniture dealer or buying center participants to use game theory, critical path analysis, or other management science methods were observed or reported during the study. On the buying side, discussions on how decisions should be made were not found to occur during the course of the study, e.g., the questions of what vendor attributes and product features should and should not be considered, and what decision rules should be used were not determined before the decisions were made. The buying decision processes were simplified and segmented into a series of small, localized options with a clear preference for evaluating a few choices observed. Thus, requesting three or four vendors for bid proposals was preferred, not five, six, or ten vendors; a limited number (three to five) of choice criteria were used in making selections; and phased, two-staged, decision rules were used (e.g., conjunctive followed by disjunctive heuristics).

Depending on customer size and the lifetime value of the customer firm (expressed qualitatively by one or more members of the selling group), the marketing manager, sales reps, and/or manufacturer sales rep often raised issues of how communication, design work, and product prices should be configured in approaching customers and preparing quotes. These marketers often raised questions among themselves about the accuracy of their vision of customers' views of requirements and buying processes. Members of the buying group less often consciously questioned downstream implications of how their own actions would lead to responses by the dealer that the buying group would later regret having initiated. Thus, at least in this one industry and one study, marketers rather than buyers more often asked about the downstream-unintended consequences of our actions. However, such self-questioning occurred infrequently between both sides of the observed exchanges.

Analogous to a statewide road map, much local detail is not included in the streams of marketing/purchasing strategies summarized in Figures 3-3 to 3-5. The summaries in the figures are intended only as a medium-scale view of likely directions of the buying processes for office furniture.

As advocated by organizational and social researchers (Denzin, 1983; Geertz, 1973) and humanistic scholars (Hirschman, 1986), "thick descriptions" of the behavior, decisions, and interactions were collected on the observed buying processes. An attempt was made to "crack the code" of the phenomenon (Hirschman, 1986, p. 243) by presenting a comprehensive picture of the whole, that is, a gestalt view of the phenomenon. While perfect correspondence between two research teams' interpretations of the "same" phenomenon is never possible, research and inductive, middle-range model building by other research teams is necessary before concluding that the streams of buying processes reported here are a reliable construction of the phenomenon. Such additional research for building middle range theories is worthwhile for generalizing beyond the individual case study.

PART II

TOOLS FOR ILLUMINATING THE UNCONSCIOUS AND CONSCIOUS MIND

4

BALANCED AND UNBALANCED UNCONSCIOUS–CONSCIOUS THINKING: A JEWISH COUPLE BUYS A GERMAN CAR AND ADDITIONAL TRANSFORMATION STORIES

Synopsis

Consumer researchers often describe Heider's (1958) balance theory without showing how the theory relates to recent theoretical developments in consumer behavior. Empirical examination of the theory is also lacking in consumer psychology literature. This chapter updates Heider's balance theory in consumer behavior by developing the theory's links to perceptual, attitudinal, and automatic (unconscious) behavior theories, controlled (conscious) thinking (see Bargh, 1994; Bargh, Chen, and Burrows, 1996), and cognitive/experiential self-theory (Epstein, 1994). Propositions essential for applying balance theory to consumer psychology link automatic/controlled memory retrievals and story-telling of unbalanced (i.e., paradoxical) situations that stimulate further thinking and action. Using storytelling (e.g., see Fischer, 1999; Shank, 1990) research methods has aided in examining these theory developments empirically.

INTRODUCTION

This chapter illustrates what happens when a customer's conscious thinking declares war on her unconscious thinking—how do you convince yourself to do what your heart tells you is wrong? First, consider the core literature on balanced and unbalanced mental states. The work by Fritz Heider (1958) is particularly helpful.

One of Heider's (1958, p. 210) central "working hypothesis ... is a tendency toward balanced states in human relationships." Heider demonstrates that this hypothesis extends to consumer psychological perspectives, such as product ownership:

> *p* owns *x* induces *p* likes *x*, or *p* tends to like something he owns. Irwin and Gebhard (1946) concluded from their experiments with children that a clear majority of them "expressed a preference for an object which was to be given to them as compared with an object which was to be given to another child" (p. 650), and, "the results may illustrate some general principle whereby ownership enhances the value of an object to the owner" (p. 651). Ownership might be considered "one form of nearness" (p. 651). (Heider, 1958, pp. 194–195)

Solomon (1999, pp. 217–218) convincingly argues that balance theory may be applied to understand consumer behavior and design effective marketing strategies. However, Heider's contributions until now have not been integrated into recent theoretical and empirical work in consumer psychology. Chapter 4 makes two contributions. First, the chapter demonstrates how balance theory is theoretically useful for linking modes of thinking and behavior (see Bargh, 1994; Bargh, Chen, and Burrows, 1996; Epstein, 1994). Second, the chapter describes empirical examinations in consumer research of balance theory hypotheses. Chapter 4 bridges past and present theoretical literature streams relevant to consumer researchers interested in how individuals resolve psychological unbalanced states and maintain/achieve balanced states.

The first section is a brief review of balanced and unbalanced states. The second section links balance theory and recent advances in multiple psychological processing theories. The second section includes a binary-flow model based on balance theory and theories on automatic to controlled thinking. The third section explores the use of the storytelling research paradigm (see Shank, 1990) for examining balance theory hypotheses in consumer behavior contexts. The final section covers limitations and suggestions for theory and research extending balance theory.

FOUNDATION KNOWLEDGE OF BALANCED AND UNBALANCED MENTAL STATES

Heider (1958, Chapter 7) distinguishes two types of relations between separate entities: unit and sentiment relations. "Separate entities comprise a unit when they are perceived as belonging together. For example, members of a family are seen as a unit; a person and his deed belong together" (p. 176). "U denotes the cognitive unit between two entities, and notU the fact that the two entities are segregated" (p. 201). A sentiment relation refers to the positive (L or +) or negative (DL or −) feelings or valuation that one gives to an entity, such as a person, activity, or object.

These relations may be for dyads, triads, or more complex cases, but all relations are from the perceiver's subjective point of view. Thus, while a brand may possess a given attribute or provide a specific benefit, if a consumer perceives the opposite, a notU relation results between brand and attribute/benefit.

Heider describes the two relation concepts to result in four possibilities between two entities: "U, notU, L, and DL." While being one of these four relation states might be viewed as excluding the other three, he emphasizes:

> By a balanced state is meant a situation in which the relations among the entities fit together harmoniously; there is no stress toward change. A basic assumption is that sentiment relations and unit relations tend toward a balanced state. This means that sentiments are not entirely independent of the perceptions of unit connections between entities and that the latter, in turn, are not entirely independent of sentiments. Sentiments and unit relations are mutually interdependent. It also means that if a balanced state does not exist, then forces toward this state will arise. If a change is not possible, the state of imbalance will produce tension. (Heider, 1958, p. 201)

While unit and sentiment relations are non-orthogonal, they represent independent theoretical and empirical constructs grounded in cognition (i.e., units) and affection (i.e., sentiments). When tension caused by imbalance arises in the mind of the individual, then the individual is likely to exercise some mental and physical effort to eliminate the tension.

> Unbalanced situations stimulate us to further thinking; they have the character of interesting puzzles, problems which make us suspect a depth of interesting background.... Stories in which the stress is laid on unbalanced situations are felt to have a deep psychological meaning. Dostoevski, for instance, describes again and again feelings full of conflict resulting from just such situations. (Heider, 1958, pp. 180–181)

The work of several scholars in consumer behavior (e.g., Arnould and Wallendorf, 1994; Hirschman, 1986) and related fields of human inquiry (Bruner, 1990; Mitroff and Kilman, 1976; Orr, 1990; Zukier, 1986) supports the proposition that, "... people think narratively rather than argumentatively or paradigmatically" (Weick, 1995, p. 127). Research on storytelling (e.g., see Arnould and Wallendorf, 1994; Fourier, 1998; Shank, 1990) is useful because it helps clarify and deepen knowledge of how people resolve paradoxes triggered in their minds by unbalanced states. Learning stories enables the researcher to perceive the complexity often associated with initial balanced states becoming unbalanced and the steps taken to achieve old or new balanced states. Storytelling research enables holistic views into initial balanced states becoming unbalanced and the steps taken to achieve the old or a new balanced state. Also, for the person doing the (un)conscious thinking, stories serve as "guides to conduct" by facilitating the interpretation of cues turned up by that conduct (Weick, 1995, p. 127).

Most of Heider's (1958) presentation on balanced/unbalanced states builds on "...the assumption that the relation U and L can be treated as positive relations, and notU and DL as negative relations" (p. 201). However, this proposition is not to imply that positive sentiment links always with a unit (U) relation, and a negative sentiment links always with notU. Self-perceptions of disliking oneself or a family member are examples of a DL and U combination. Heider (1958, p. 209) points out that, "...If I dislike what I own [a negative sentiment toward an object belonging (U) to a person] I may either begin to like it (change in sentiment) or sell it (change in unit relation)." When a situation is balanced, no tension is felt. Heider (1958, p. 214) recognizes that conscious thinking need not occur: "In this connection, it is important to emphasize that the action which brings about one's own pleasure need not presuppose conscious and calculating means-end reasoning nor that the person is selfishly oriented."

Displayed for consumer-brand-attribute contexts, Figure 4-1 summarizes four sets of relationships in triads resulting in balanced states: (a) all three relations are positive and (b, c, and d) two relations are negative and one is positive. In Figure 4-1a, the relation between person and the attribute is positive, that is, the consumer likes the attribute. For example, a consumer likes a manual transmission in automobiles. The unit (U, shown as + in Figure 4-1a) relation is positive between brand and the attribute; for example, the brand is available with manual transmission. The person likes the brand. Consequently, the three relations are harmonious in Figure 4-1a. Other contexts are appropriate for consumer psychology perspectives, for example:

- person (P) - product (X) - person (O)
- person (P) - product (X) - benefit (B)
- person (P) - activity (A) - person (O)

Imbalance occurs when two of the relations are positive and one is negative. Figure 4-2, parts a, b, and c, depicts the parallel unbalanced states for person with respect to brand and attribute. The case of three negative relations (Figure 4-2d) is somewhat ambiguous and reflects associations that are unlikely to influence balance or unbalanced states.

The story of a Jewish couple buying a German car reported later in this chapter reflects the transformations from a balanced state (depicted as Figure 4-1c) to an unbalanced state (depicted as Figure 4-2b) to new balanced state (depicted as Figure 4-1a and partially as Figure 4-1b). The discussion of the study describes the transformation and these states in detail.

Heider (1958) is careful to emphasize that relations between entities are not always symmetrical: (p L o) does not necessarily imply (o L p). However, he proposes that such relations tend to become symmetrical. For example, "We want people we like to like us, and we tend to like people who like us—and the parallel is true for negative sentiments" (p. 205). Proposing non-symmetrical situations in consumer psychology is useful for extending Heider's theory. Doing so helps to achieve Becker's (1998) and Ragin's (1987) recommendation that theory and data "sampling ought to be conducted so as to maximize the possibility of finding what you hadn't even thought to

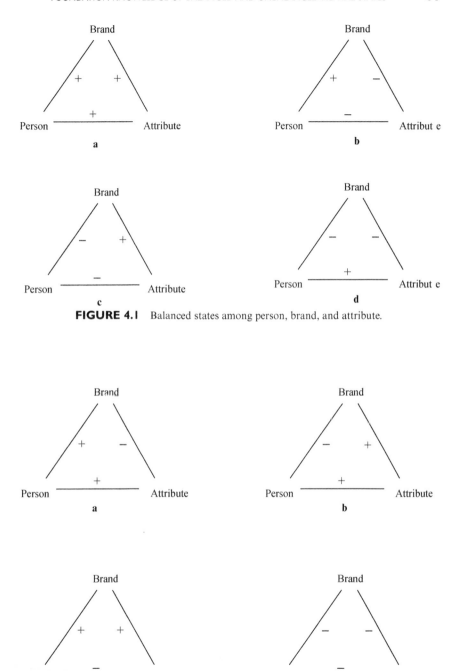

FIGURE 4.1   Balanced states among person, brand, and attribute.

FIGURE 4.2   Unbalanced states among person, brand, and attribute.

look for" (Becker, 1998, p. 164). A case study of a non-symmetrical affective relation between a brand and a person is described later.

Two additional sets of propositions from Heider need to be explored more fully in consumer psychology. First, "the possibility of a negative attitude toward the self (p DL p) must also be considered. If p dislikes himself he might reject a positive x as too good for him; a negative p and a positive x do not make a good unit" (Heider, 1958, p. 210). This view reflects the argument that using a very attractive model in advertisement may backfire because the intended customer perceives a positive relation with himself or herself and the model could not occur.

Second, Heider describes the possibilities of a neutral attitude and a disunion unit relation (1958, pp. 201–202). While stereotypical thinking and affective responses occur automatically (see Bruner, 1986; Epstein, 1994), exposure to unknown entities may generate neutral attitudes and noncategorization at least momentarily. A disunion relation is categorizing an entity as not belonging, being different; while the absence of a unit relation is not yet categorizing the entity as unit or disunion. Neutral affective states and an unknown unit relation equate with a consumer's very fleeting initial exposure to a product or brand.

RECENT ADVANCES IN MULTIPLE PSYCHOLOGICAL PROCESSING THEORIES

Beliefs (i.e., associations between entities), attitudes, and even behaviors frequently become activated automatically on the mere presence of an entity, without conscious intention or awareness (i.e., pre-consciously) (see Bargh, 1989; Bargh, Chen, and Burrows, 1996; Epstein, 1994; Fazio, 1986, 1990; Holden and Lutz, 1992; Holden, 1993; Woodside and Trappey, 1992). Several scholars have proposed and empirically supported the view that two fundamentally different modes of processing information exist. This is what Epstein (1994) refers to as rational and experiential. These two thinking modes can conflict with each other. "The experiential system can override the rational system even when subjects know the appropriate rational response. The experiential system is more responsive to concrete than to abstract representations" (Epstein, 1994, p. 718).

EXPERIENTIAL (PRECONSCIOUS) VERSUS RATIONAL THINKING

Characteristics of experiential versus rational thinking systems include the following propositions (adapted from Epstein, 1994):

- Encoding reality in concrete images, metaphors, and narratives versus encoding reality in abstract symbols, words, and numbers.

- Rapid automatic processing oriented toward immediate action versus slower processing oriented toward delayed action.
- Crudely differentiating; stereotypical thinking versus highly differentiating.
- Experienced passively and preconsciously versus experienced actively and consciously.
- Self-evidently valid perspectives versus trying to think logically and by justifying.
- A holistic view versus an analytic view.

AUTOMATIC AND UNAWARE THINKING AFFECTING BEHAVIOR

In a series of intriguing experiments, Bargh *et al.* (1996) were able to show that subjects can be primed by completing simple tasks to exhibit behaviors automatically. For example, subjects asked to create sentences from words relating to the elderly stereotype (e.g., rigid, bitter, helpless) versus subjects who used control words walked more slowly after the study was completed compared to subjects in the control condition. In a final debriefing, "no subjects expressed any knowledge of the relevance of the words in the scrambled sentence task to the elderly stereotype. Furthermore, no participant believed that the words had an impact on his or her [walking speed] behavior" (Bargh *et al.*, 1996, p. 237).

Related to Bargh's work on preconscious automatic thinking and behavior, and within consumer-marketer influence contexts, Zaltman (1997) and his colleagues (Zaltman and Coulter, 1995; Braun and Zaltman, 1998) provide compelling evidence that consumers' memory processes are sometimes frail. "Consumers might be influenced to misremember or refabricate information from their own past experiences, attitudes, or expectations" (Braun and Zaltman, 1998, p. 33). Thus, a requirement arises to go beyond self-reporting by consumers for estimating the impacts of marketing influences. A key finding in the work of Zaltman and his colleagues is that consumers may greatly underestimate their use of external information in making purchasing decisions (LaDoux, 1996; Russo, Johnson, and Stephens, 1989).

BALANCE THEORY AND PERIPHERAL/CENTRAL ROUTES TO PERSUASION

Substantial research findings support the related proposition in consumer psychology that mere exposure can change attitude and cause purchase choices (see Krugman, 1965; Zajonc and Markus, 1982; Fazio, Powell, and Williams, 1989; Petty, Unnava, and Stathman, 1991; Woodside, 1994).

Consequently, peripheral advertising persuasion (i.e., low involvement processing following the mere exposure to advertising) can affect attitude and brand choice. Discussions of peripheral routes to persuasion match well with Heider's view of entities in a balanced state. Little to no controlled thinking is likely to occur in such situations.

Heider (1958) predicts the circumstances when automatic thinking and behavioral effects are most likely to be overridden: when a person perceives tension that an imbalanced state exists. The active mental steps (i.e., controlled thinking) occurring to reduce tension and achieve balance is analogous to Petty and Cacioppo's (1986) central route to persuasion assumptions. Within the central route to persuasion, consumers actively acquire additional information and create heuristics to resolve dilemmas (e.g., purchase versus non-purchase and brand choice selection).

While not relating his work to Heider (1958), Bargh (1989) develops similar views expressed by Heider (1958, p. 214) that much of thinking, "need not presuppose conscious and calculating means-end reasoning." Also, Bargh (1989) develops a detailed model on how automatic and controlled thinking processes are contingent and related rather than separate and unique processes, "Thus, attention, awareness, intention, and control do not necessarily occur together in an all-or-none fashion. They are to some extent independent qualities that may appear in various combinations" (Bargh, 1989, p. 6). Heider advocates a similar view when he identifies circumstances when imbalance replaces balanced states.

In consumer contexts, order of attribute/benefit-to-brand retrieval reflects strength of cue/object link: a strong positive link facilitates top-of-mind automatic retrieval of the object upon presentation of the cue (Cohen, 1966; Farquhar, Herr, and Fazio, 1990; Holden and Lutz, 1992; Woodside and Trappey, 1992). Positive and unit dyads and triads are readily accessible for consumers reflecting associate-to-brand accessibility as well as consumer-brand-purchase thoughts (see Axelrod, 1968, 1986; Haley and Case, 1979). Thus, a spreading activation (Collins and Loftus, 1975) of entities, all or nearly all in balanced relations occurs automatically among attributes, benefits, brands, and (purchase/use) behaviors.

A CONTINGENCY VIEW OF THINKING PROCESSES AND BALANCE THEORY

Figure 4-3 builds on Heider's (1958) assumptions to summarize the conditional relationships between automatic and controlled thinking. Box 2 in Figure 4-3 reflects the proposition that unaware perceiving of entities and features in environments do occur. Such unaware perceiving can lead automatically to unconscious beliefs, attitudes, and behaviors (boxes 3, 4, and 5 in Figure 4-3). Such unconscious processing occurs often for balanced states.

One example: "I've been a faculty member here for 28 years and I have never seen a problem [with gender discrimination]," a statement made by a male faculty member, 60 years old, at a business school faculty meeting in 1996. This expressed view was followed by contradictory views expressed by all female faculty members (two persons) who had been on the same faculty for ten years each.

Figure 4-3 steps from 2-7-8-10-11 are the spreading activation in automatic thinking resulting from a balanced state. A person noticing a dyad or triad linkage in the environment resulting in an imbalanced state (box 9) causes tension and activates controlled thinking to achieve the original balanced state or to transform cognitions/affections/behaviors to reach a new balanced state (box 12). Because of the tension and substantial cognitive efforts involved in resolving imbalanced states, the original balanced state has a natural advantage over alternative and novel balanced states. Thus, several strong and new linkages with new entities may need to be formed to overcome the automatic relations among entities retrieved automatically for the original balanced state. The narrative of a Jewish couple buying a German car illustrates this proposition.

STORYTELLING RESEARCH PARADIGMS

"Stories are crucial for sensemaking" (Weick, 1995, p. 120). Shank (1990, p. 12) proposes that, "Human memory is story-based. Not all memories are stories. Rather, stories are especially interesting prior experiences, ones that we learn from." Heider (1958, p. 181) views stories that stress unbalanced situations as having deep psychological meaning. Storytelling-related studies in consumer research are extensive though rarely related to the work of Heider (see Fourier, 1998, for a partial review of this literature). Fourier (1998, p. 366) expresses the usefulness of the approach:

> A critical insight emerging from this analysis concerns the holistic character of consumer/brand relationship phenomena and, by extension, the perspective that is required for their study. The data submit the important point that deep knowledge of the consumer/brand relationship is obtained only through consideration of the larger whole in which that relationship is embedded....This study makes a strong case for understanding the broader context of people's life experiences as a basis for anticipating the constellation of brands with which relationships are likely to develop.

Shank (1990) and Shank and Abelson (1977) provide useful tools for collecting and understanding other people's stories: in order to understand a story, it needs to be broken down into the conceptual actions underlying the events. These actions are then understood in terms of the "scripts, plans, goals, and themes" to which they refer. A script is a set of expectations about

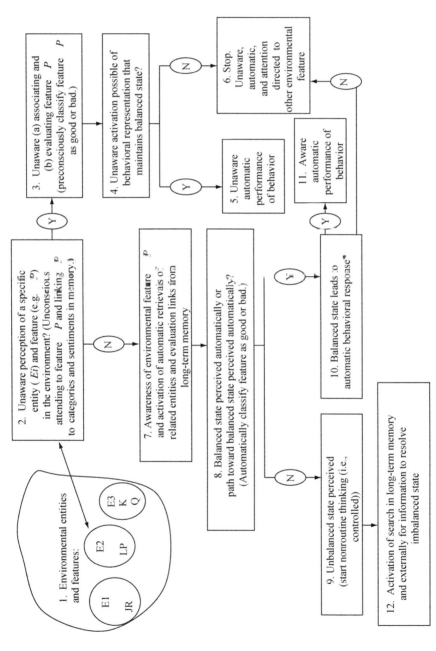

FIGURE 4.3 Modeling unaware perceiving, automatic perceiving, judging, and preconscious links of environmental features and behavior.

what will happen next in a well-understood situation. "My contention here is that when results, especially unexpected results [e.g., imbalanced states], are added to the package of themes, goals, and plans, an inherent prediction is added that allows a story to be found [by person in his/her memory] by looking at the structures that were involved and the results that were obtained. Attached to this package is a **lesson**—in essence the abstraction of the contents of a story uniquely derived from that story" (Shank, 1990, p. 93, bold added). A lesson sometimes implies that a paradox presented in a story has been resolved. For example, "a Jewish couple buys a German car," might suggest that the entities, Jewish couple and German car, represent an imbalanced dyad; the lesson may be that some justifications are possible for the couple to buy the car.

The dynamic paradigm of transformation from balanced to imbalanced to balanced states is a storytelling approach. This approach includes reaching beyond box 12 in Figure 4-3 to describe how the main actors in the story resolve the tension that is felt by the imbalanced state. Thus, describing the three acts in such stories include (1) an initial balanced state generated automatically following aware or unaware perceiving of an object; (2) active (i.e., controlled thinking) noticing of an entity and relation that causes an imbalanced state; (3) mental and behavioral steps taken to reduce or eliminate the tension of the imbalanced state. Examples of such three-act stories follow.

A Jewish Couple Buys a German Car

Appendix 4-1 is an abridged story written by the husband (Posner, 1998) in the Jewish couple buying a German car. Figure 4-4 includes the thoughts appearing to come to mind automatically for Posner shown as three, balanced triad states. Each triad includes two negative and one positive relation.

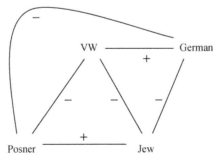

FIGURE 4.4 Original balanced state for Posner and VW case study. The relationship between the person, Posner, and the attribute, Jew, is a unit relationship, that is, what Posner perceives as belonging together; unit relationships are often positive sentiment relationships as well. The other two relationships shown are sentiment relationships, that is, positive or negative feelings or valuations that the person assigns to connect the entities: Posner and German car as well as Jew and German car.

Figure 4-5 includes additional entities retrieved without effort and automatically from long-term memory and reported in Posner's story. Note that all triads are balanced states in Figure 4-5: three positive relations or two negative and one positive relation. The currency of some of the relations is apparent in a 1999 Associated Press news story entitled "Volkswagen Sued for Holocaust Acts" (Chilsen, 1999). The lawsuit says that up to 400 children were killed from maltreatment and poor conditions in a nursery near a Volkswagen plant where their parents were forced to build munitions and the "Beetle."

As shown in Figure 4-6, seeing the "New Beetle" VW car creates an imbalanced state in the Posners' minds: two positive relations and one negative relation. There may be several ways available to resolve this imbalance. For example, (a) the Posners may develop negative sentiments toward the New Beetle, replacing the initial positive sentiments they hold; (b) the Posners may try to break the unit relation between the New Beetle and German car by learning about VW manufacturing plants in other countries and convincing themselves that VW is really not a German enterprise any longer; (c) Gerald Posner may try to emphasize that he is "only half-Jewish" and that no family member died in the Holocaust, to disconnect with the Jewish unit relationship shown in Figures 4-5 and 4-6. How did the Posners resolve the imbalance?

The mental battle seesawed between the original balanced state and creating a new balanced state. Figure 4-7 depicts entities supporting the original balanced state: Holocaust survivors file class-action lawsuits and see the movie *Saving Private Ryan*. Four entities that support a balanced state and

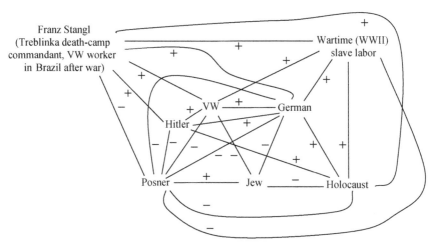

FIGURE 4.5 Extended original balanced state for Posner and VW case study. All three-way relationships shown are balanced states: sets of three positive relationships and sets of two negative and one positive relationships. Figure 4-4 is only a partial representation of relationships described in Posner's story. Less central relationships are not included in Figure 4-4, for example, Adolf Eichmann working as a foreman at an Argentine Mercedes factory after the war.

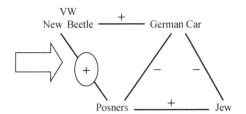

FIGURE 4.6   Activation of conscious thinking by Gerald and Trisha Posner. The Posners' positive sentiment toward the VW New Beetle creates state of imbalance and activates cognitive efforts to resolve stress and achieve (possibly new) balance. References by the Posners to the original extended balance state (see Figure 4-4) would support transforming them into a negative sentiment.

that occurred before the Posners bought the New Beetle are shown in Figure 4-7. This new balanced state includes transforming the Posners-and-German-car relation from a negative to a positive sentiment. The acceptance of this transformation is confirmed by the support received from Trisha Posner's mother for the entity of buying the New Beetle.

While the view may be expressed that the outcome of this story is a self-fulfilling prophecy, the act of buying the VW car is uncertain even toward the end of the story. Certainly the possibilities of outcomes other than the Posners' purchase are plausible. The need for the presence in working memory of several new entities and relations to transform an initial balanced state into a new balanced state is a central conclusion from analyzing the story. The recognition by senior VW management of the firm's war crimes, or other similar acts, appears to be a necessary entity in transforming the Posners to a new balanced state in which they would buy the New Beetle.

Moving to and from Finland

Appendix 4-2 tells the amusing story of moving to and from Finland in a diary format. The global entity, "Scenic beauty," summarizes the third entity between the diarist and Finland in the initial balanced state (see Figure 4-8). Note that unit relations (U) are shown between snow and snowplow and snow and shoveling snow in Figure 4-8a; positive sentiments are never indicated in the story for the snowplow or shoveling snow.

In Figure 4-8b several new entities occur that transform the balanced state into an imbalanced state. The two positives and one negative in the main triangle in Figure 4-8b indicate the imbalanced state.

The new balanced state includes a negative person and Finland relation, replacing the initial positive relation. Note also that "Scenic beauty" is no longer an entity in the new balanced state. A key conclusion is that transformations between original and new balanced sates may involve learning new core entities in relations and eliminating older ones.

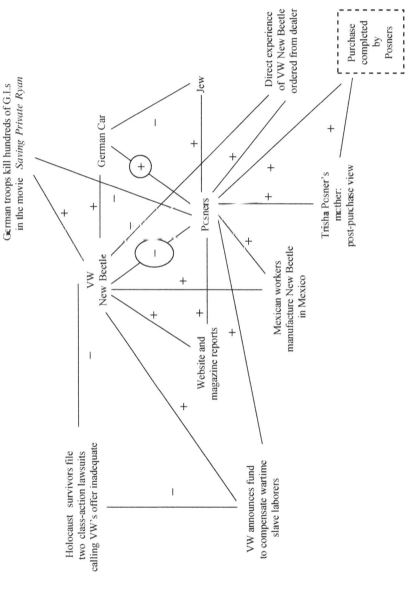

FIGURE 4.7 Information search, conscious thinking, and applied preconscious thinking by Gerald and Trisha Posner to achieve a new balanced state.

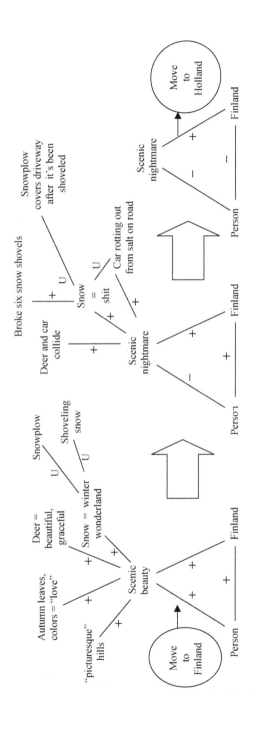

FIGURE 4.8 Moving to and from Finland. U, unbalanced.

a. Original balanced state.

b. Unbalanced state.

c. New balanced state.

A Parent Buys Barq's Root Beer

Figure 4-9 summarizes the final story: a parent of a teenage son buys Barq's Root Beer. The customers targeted for Barq's are teenage boys (Koerner, 1998). Before the Coca-Cola Company purchased the firm, Barq's sponsored heavy metal music to build a unit relation between the brand and an entity known to be liked by the target market. Consumer research indicated that one of the reasons teenage males liked heavy metal music was that they knew their parents disliked such music. Acts related to the music are a way to establish independence and to rebel against parental authority. Note the positive and negative sentiments expressed between parent and teenage son in Figure 4-9, capturing family love and authority dislike.

This story illustrates a non-symmetrical relation between two entities: parent and Barq's. Parents of teenage boys are not the intended targets. More pointedly, the story illustrates how anthropomorphizing brands may be occurring in creating images. The consumer researcher might expect to hear the teenage son saying, "Hey Dad, you're not suppose to like Barq's."

The initial imbalanced state in Figure 4-9 may be transformed into a balanced state in several ways, including: (a) the company embraces parents as customers and (b) the parents start to dislike Barq's to demonstrate acceptable parental behavior to their sons.

Barq's targets males because of prior positive responses to promotional activities among males and little response among females. Also, teenage

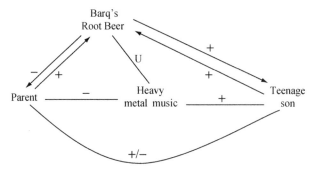

FIGURE 4.9 Possible non-symmetrical relationship between person and brand. The chief marketing officer (CMO) for Barq's Root Beer is successful in establishing a positive symmetrical relationship with the customer targeted for Barq's: teenage males. The CMO creates a unit relationship with heavy metal music in the minds of the targeted customers by sponsoring heavy metal concerts. A non-symmetrical relationship occurs when a parent likes to drink Barq's; the parent is an undesirable customer. The heavy metal sponsorship helps in two ways: builds positive sentiments with a desired customer and negative sentiments with an undesired customer. The teenage son has both positive and negative sentiments with respect to his parent. U, unbalanced.

females are found to accept a drink alternative suggested by males more often than the reverse (Koerner, 1998).

LIMITATIONS AND SUGGESTIONS FOR THEORY AND RESEARCH

This chapter is intentionally limited to describing the value of Heider's theory in consumer research. The case studies generalize to the theoretical views presented earlier and the cases are not intended to be representative of any human populations.

Heider's (1958) views on balanced and imbalanced states offer useful insights for understanding consumers' automatic and controlled thinking processes. Basic assumptions in his theoretical work help to explain how balanced states occur, how imbalanced states occur, and the actions taken to achieve a new balanced state. Bargh (1998) in particular describes how much of what we call thinking includes elements of automatic and controlled processes. Such views are grounded in the assumptions and predictions described by Heider.

Heider's work helps to solve the dilemmas of when and how balanced and imbalanced states occur in product and brand purchase situations. His work is also useful in understanding how consumers resolve imbalanced states.

Relating balanced and imbalanced transformations, interpretive research methods such as autodriving (see Heisley and Levy, 1991), Zaltman's (1977) metaphor-elicitation procedure, and participant observation studies (see Arnould and Price, 1993) are useful for learning the stories that consumers retrieve from memories. While valuable, researchers should go beyond data based on consumers' self-reporting of automatic retrievals resulting in balanced states. Our knowledge is scant on preconscious processing by consumers that they are never aware of, as well as on how consumers reach and resolve imbalanced states.

The question is not, therefore, how often automatic thoughts, attitudes, and behaviors occur, but whether and how often they are controlled or overridden by some conscious intention and purpose. "Control over automatic influences requires three things: (a) awareness of the [automatic] influence or at least the possibility of the influence, (b) motivation to exert the control, and (c) enough attention capacity (or lack of distractions) at the time to engage in the control process" (Bargh *et al.*, 1996, p. 241). Heider's propositions on thinking being stimulated by moving from balanced to unbalanced situations are insightful precursors supporting Bargh's conclusions.

APPENDIX 4-1. VW DAY: SOMETIMES BUYING A CAR MEANS BURYING THE PAST

By Gerald Posner (*New York Times Magazine*, Sunday, October 4, 1998)

Why would any Jew buy a BMW, Mercedes, or Volkswagen? It was my mantra, repeated frequently to friends, especially those with Jewish surnames and a German car. Before anybody could answer, I'd cite the wartime slave labor used by all three firms and that their factories fueled the Nazi effort. My worst vitriol was reserved for lowly Volkswagen. The "people's car" was conceived by Hitler, who reportedly helped with the original design.

Even after the war, there were links with unsavory characters. Adolf Eichmann was a foreman at an Argentine Mercedes factory before the Israelis tracked him down in 1960. Franz Stangl, the Treblinka death-camp commandant, worked for Volkswagen in Brazil before he was found in 1967.

I am 44 years old and Jewish–Catholic. No family members died in the Holocaust. My heartfelt objections are purely emotional—not necessarily reasonable—and grew from my research for two books about the Third Reich and war criminals. My anger was deep-set, and while I realized the new generation bore no guilt for its parents' crimes, I did not want my hard-earned money going to companies that were even tangentially connected to the Nazi war effort.

My wife, Trisha, an English Jew, encouraged my unusual sentiments. Yet most disagreed. My Jewish father thought my position too extreme. Friends pointed out that the Israelis used Mercedes army trucks. I was not impressed. An English Jew who was a ranking officer of BMW asked, "Would you buy an Italian car?" Yes. "What about clothes from Spain?" Yes. "Well then, your objection to buying German cars is strictly based on time. A succession of Roman Emperors tried to wipe out every Jew in the empire, and the Spanish had the Inquisition. Your objection to Germany is because it was so recent." He was right, but if I were to boycott all countries that had at some point institutionalized anti-Semitism and sanctioned killing Jews, there would be few things to buy. Reason be damned, it was Germany that had earned my wrath.

Then a strange thing happened. Last spring, while strolling in Washington, I passed a car of which I was immediately enamored—Volkswagen's New Beetle. Trisha was with me and shared my enthusiasm for the startling design. We actually began debating whether we might one day want one. It was the first crack in my "boycott German cars" veneer. I started visiting dozens of New Beetle Web sites and read magazines that gave it kudos. But buying one was no easy step. We were proud not to have owned a car during 20 years in New York. And we asked all the practical questions: Do we need the extra responsibility for only a few trips out of the city? What about upkeep? A fortune for insurance? And, of course, the fundamental obstacle—it was German.

Trisha and I flip-flopped frequently. Yes, it was a great car, and it was time to bury the past. No, we didn't need it, and would probably be happier in 20 years if we put the $20,000 into a mutual fund. Maybe the long waiting lists were a sign the car was not for us. The desire for one might just be a mid-life crisis, and if we were patient, it would pass.

I told some friends of my unexpected Beetle obsession. "Didn't you feel like scratching a Mercedes after you saw *Schindler's List?*" asked one. "What about VW's failure to pay war reparations?" asked another. The reparations obstacle seemed resolved when Volkswagen abruptly reversed itself in early July and announced it would finally establish a fund to compensate wartime slave laborers. The angst returned when Holocaust survivors filed two class-action lawsuits contending that VW's offer was inadequate.

In late summer, a dealer in upstate New York called. The car I wanted— in silver—would soon arrive. The next day we saw *Saving Private Ryan* and watched uncomfortably as German troops mowed down hundreds of GIs on the beaches of Normandy. We almost canceled the order.

The car arrived just before Labor Day. It is thoroughly captivating. And whenever I have second thoughts about driving a German car, I calm myself with the reminder that Mexican workers south of the border manufacture the New Beetle.

When Trisha telephoned her 85-year-old mother in London, a conservative Jew, and told her we had bought the Beetle, the answer was quick. "Congratulations, darling. Maybe the war is finally over."

APPENDIX 4-2. MOVING TO AND FROM FINLAND

Author Unknown (Received from Koll, 2000).
Dear Diary.
Aug. 1. Moved to our new home in Finland. It is so beautiful here. The hills are so picturesque. Can hardly wait to see them covered by snow. God's country. I love it here.

Oct. 14. Finland is the most beautiful place on Earth. The leaves are turning all different colors. I love the shades of red and orange. Went for a ride through some beautiful hills and spotted some deer. They are so graceful, certainly they are the most beautiful animals on Earth. I can't imagine anyone wanting to kill such an elegant creature. The very symbol of peace and tranquility. Hope it will snow soon. I love it here.

Dec. 2. It snowed last night. Woke up to find everything blanketed in white. It looks like a postcard. We went outside and cleaned the snow off the steps and shoveled the driveway. We had a snowball fight (I won). When the snowplow came by we had to shovel the driveway again. What a beautiful place. Mother Nature is perfect harmony. I love it here.

Dec. 12. More snow last night. I love it. The snowplow did his trick again (that rascal). A winter wonderland. I love it here.

Dec. 22. More of that shit fell last night. I've got blisters on my hands from shoveling. I think the snowplow hides around the corner and waits until I'm done shoveling this driveway. Asshole!

Dec. 23. "White Christmas" my busted ass! More friggin snow. If I ever get my hands on that son-of-a-bitch who drives that snowplow, I swear I'll castrate the dumb bastard. Don't know why they don't use more salt on the roads to melt this fucking ice.

Dec. 28. More white shit last night. Been inside since Christmas day except for shoveling out the driveway every time "Snowplow Harry" comes by. Can't go anywhere. Got buried in a mountain of white shit. The weatherman says expect another 25 cm of shit tonight. Do you know how many shovels full of snow 25 cm is?

Jan. 1. Happy Fucking New Year, The weatherman was wrong (again). We got 34 cm of white shit this time. At this rate it won't melt before July. The snowplow got stuck up the road and shithead had the balls to come to the door and ask to borrow MY shovel. After I told him I had broken 6 shovels already shoveling all the shit he pushed into my driveway, I broke my last one over his fucking head.

Jan. 4. Finally got out of the house today. Went to the store to get food and on the way back a Goddamn deer ran in front of the car and I hit the bastard. Did about 9000 Finmarks damage to the car. Those fucking beasts ought to be killed. Wish the hunters had killed them all last November.

May 3. Took the car to the garage in town. Would you believe the thing is rotting out from all that fucking salt they keep all over the road. Car looks like a piece of shit!

May 10. Moved to Holland. I can't imagine why anyone in their friggin mind would ever want to live in that Godforsaken country of Finland.

5

ADVANCING UNDERSTANDING OF CUSTOMERS' MEANS–END CHAINS: ERIC DRINKS TWELVE CANS OF BEER AND TALKS TO GIRLS

Synopsis

Means–end chain (MEC) theory proposes that knowledge held in consumers' memory is organized in a hierarchy with concrete thoughts linked to more abstract thoughts in a sequence progressing from means (i.e., brands and product features) to psychological and social consequences and finally to ends (i.e., fulfillment of personal values). This chapter proposes several advances in the theory. First, specific buying and consumption situations serve as frames of reference when consumers are thinking about products and alternative features of products and brands. Second, states of psychological imbalance may occur in consumers' minds among linkages retrieved automatically for features/consequences and consequences/values; thus, Heider's balance theory incorporates MEC theory and research. The theoretical and practical usefulness of means–end research increases by asking consumers to name an acceptable alternative to the product and brand used in a recent consumption situation, as well as an unacceptable option and to describe the features/consequences/values of these options. Consequently, Fournier's alternative relationships of consumer/brands (e.g., casual friendships, marriages, enmities) becomes relevant for MEC theory. To examine the propositions empirically, this chapter describes psychological schemata for four MECs that combine two consumers' recent consumption situations with personal values.

INTRODUCTION: ASSOCIATING BRAND/FEATURES/ CONSEQUENCES/BENEFITS/VALUES

In consumer research on MECs, the meanings that a consumer associates with a product, service, or specific brand are represented hierarchically. The lowest level depicts an object's attributes—those that are physical or concrete, and those that are abstract (e.g., a brand's image). The remaining levels are consumers' outcomes including functional and psychosocial consequences, followed by consumers' instrumental and terminal values (see Gutman, 1997).

Laddering is a research method frequently used for electing MECs. Traditionally, laddering is a metaphor representing a respondent's answers to a series of "Why?" probes, typically starting with the attributes that distinguish more desired from less desired alternatives. Asking for successive elicitations creates a chain of elements leading from a product's attributes to one or a few terminal values: each successive concept learned becomes a sub-goal for the final goal. Gutman and Reynolds (1978) illustrate a resulting ladder elicited from a respondent in a study of breakfast cereal: crunchy → has body → stays with me → avoid snack → aids weight loss → improves appearance → romance.

In the empirical research described in this chapter, the questions, "What makes you say that?" and "What does that lead to?" are used in place of "Why" probes. Becker (1998) emphasizes that "Why?" requires a "good" answer, one that makes sense and can be defended. Such answers are unlikely to reveal logical flaws and inconsistencies. Becker recommends using, "How?" questions.

> When I asked them, [such questions] people gave more leeway, were less constraining, invited them to answer in any way that suited them, to tell a story that included whatever they thought the story ought to include in order to make sense. They didn't demand a "right" answer, didn't seem to be trying to place responsibility for bad actions or outcomes anywhere. (Becker, 1998, p. 59)

The scientific literature is compelling because most thinking is unconscious and consumers typically are unable to bring up and report unconscious processes (unconscious processes often drive behavior that consumers are unaware that they performed; e.g., see Bargh, 2002; Zaltman, 2003). Advancing theory and research that inform knowledge of consumer unconscious processes is worthwhile.

The value for consumer theory and research of MECs and the laddering method relates only implicitly to unconscious mental processes—and how laddering may help to surface unconscious thoughts. For example, direct questioning of how a cereal being crunchy aids a consumer's love life may cause a scoffing response from the consumer. Asking the consumer a sequence of probing questions is a form of "autodriving" (Heisley and Levy, 1991); research may enable the consumer to surface unconscious thoughts that rarely enter conscious processing.

Surfacing unconscious processes may result in tension and stress because unbalanced associations occur among concepts now in a consumer's working memory (Heider, 1958). The thought, "A Jewish couple buys a German car" (see Figure 5-1 and Woodside and Chebat, 2001) implies an example of such stress resulting from the surfacing of negatively valued concepts and images—

some held unconsciously—with the positive experiences associated with buying a car highly prized for its design features. Advancing Heider's balance theory to person, brand, and attribute (and attribute to benefit to instrumental and terminal values) enables more robust MEC laddering research because the resulting ladders may uncover and display stress and stress resolution, as well as harmonious associations.

Pieters *et al.* (1988) advocate following an alternative empirical method for MECs rather than the better-known laddering approach that Gutman and Reynolds (1978) demonstrate. Peiters *et al.* (1988) elicit people's reasons for wanting to do something or to pursue a goal rather than to name concrete features that they associate with a product. Bagozzi and Dabholkar (2000) apply Peiters *et al.*'s approach for mapping people's cognitive schemata regarding a specific target, President Clinton. While Pieters *et al.* (1998) and Bagozzi and Dabholkar (2000) refinements are useful for describing how specific schemata accurately predict attitudes and intentions regarding future events, the following advances focus on framing means–end theory and research by consumers' recent experiences.

HEIDER'S BALANCE THEORY

Heider (1958, Chapter 7) distinguishes two types of relations between separate entities: unit and sentiment relations. "Separate entities comprise a unit

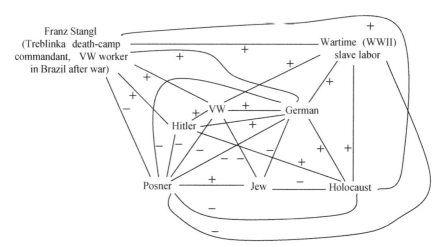

FIGURE 5.1 Extended original balanced state for Posner and VW case study. All three-way relationships shown are balanced states: sets of three positive relationships and sets of two negative and one positive relationships. Figure 4-4 is only a partial representation of relationships described in Posner's story. Less central relationships are not included in Figure 4-4, for example, Adolf Eichmann working as a foreman at an Argentine Mercedes factory after the war. Adapted from Woodside & Chebat (2001).

when they are perceived as belonging together. For example, members of a family are seen as a unit; a person and his deed belong together" (p. 176). "U denotes the cognitive unit between two entities, and notU the fact that the two entities are segregated" (p. 201). A sentiment relation refers to the positive (L or +) or negative (DL or −) feelings or valuation that one gives to an entity, such as a person, activity, or object.

These relations may be for dyads, triads, or more complex cases but all relations are from the perceiver's subjective point of view. Thus, while a brand may possess a given attribute or provide a specific benefit, if a consumer perceives the opposite, a notU relation results between a brand and such an attribute or benefit.

Heider (1958) describes the two relation concepts to result in four possibilities between two entities: "U, not U, L, and DL." He emphasizes:

> By a balanced state is meant a situation in which the relations among the entities fit together harmoniously; there is no stress toward change. A basic assumption is that sentiment relations and unit relations tend toward a balanced state. This means that sentiments are not entirely independent of the perceptions of unit connections between entities and that the latter, in turn, are not entirely independent of sentiments. Sentiments and unit relations are mutually interdependent. It also means that if a balanced state does not exist, then forces toward this state will arise. If a change is not possible, the state of imbalance will produce tension. (Heider, 1958, p. 201)

Unit and sentiment relations represent independent theoretical and empirical propositions grounded in cognitions (i.e., units) and affections (i.e., sentiments). When tension caused by imbalance arises in the mind of the individual, then the individual is likely to exercise some mental and physical effort to eliminate the tension.

> Unbalanced situations stimulate us to further thinking; they have the character of interesting puzzles, problems which make us suspect a depth of interesting background.... Stories in which the stress is laid on unbalanced situations are felt to have a deep psychological meaning. Dostoevski, for instance, describes again and again feelings full of conflict resulting from just such situations. (Heider, 1958, pp. 180–181)

ADVANCING MEANS–END CHAIN LADDERING RESEARCH WITH HEIDER'S BALANCE THEORY

Figure 5-2 summarizes the application of Heider's balance theory and related extensions to MEC laddering research. Note that the grounding in Figure 5-2 includes "prequel to action" to emphasize that if consumer research focuses on existing consumer/brand relationships (Fournier, 1998), such relationships depend on specific purchase or use situations. A situation is defined as a

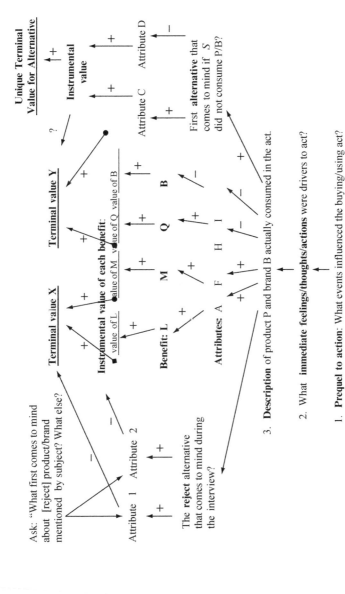

FIGURE 5.2 Means–end laddering research: updating the theory and data collection method.

conjunction of time, place, objects and person(s). Consequently, the experiences, attributes, and benefits that a consumer identifies (to herself and the interviewer) are contingent on the structure of the situation leading to brand purchase or use. Consequently, the situation informs the attributes/benefits/value associations.

The implication for research design is that MEC data for a given respondent should be collected for multiple situations (some of which may be relevant to the focal brand). A focal brand is defined as the one that the consumer names as used most often or identifies as the one used most recently; alternatively, a focal brand may be defined as the specific target chosen by the researcher—the primary focus of the study for which the researcher asks a respondent to describe—its product features and consequences in experiencing such product features and how these experiences relate to personal values. Asking informants individually to identify a focal brand for a given product category is a less reactive procedure; the researcher naming a target brand indicates possible self-validation problems—informants report perceptions about the brand mentioned by the researcher that may not relate much to the informants' past or future lives (Feldman and Lynch, 1988). Thus, asking the informant to report on her most recent consumption behavior and collecting means–end data with respect to situation X as well as for situation Y may be more relevant for the informant and reduces the occurrence of self-validity problems.

Figure 5-2 includes the assignment of sentiments (positive and negative signs) to associations in the resulting laddering steps. In Figure 5-2, note that product P and brand B associate negatively with attribute I and lack of I relates negatively with the benefit B (e.g., assume benefit B is an informant's comment, "good tasting mouthwash," for a mouthwash attribute I). Figure 5-2 advances MECs by suggesting collecting data on the first alternative that comes to mind for the consumer for the recent experience in the focal situation. For example, "If you had not consumed brand B in situation X, what might you have consumed instead?"

Figure 5-2 also asks for reject alternative information and implies the proposition that the respondent is able to easily remember a product/brand that would have been unacceptable for consumption in her recent experience. Such brand rejection data are then followed by means–end probes to bring up brand/attributes/values associations for unacceptable alternatives for use in the given situation. The brand strategist might ask here: how often, and for what situations, does my product and brand surface as the reject alternative? And when rejection occurs, what attributes and personal values surface in the respondent's mind?

FOURNIER'S CONSUMER/BRAND RELATIONSHIP TYPOLOGY

Fournier (1998) extends the two-party social relationship metaphor to encompass the consumer and brands. She develops the consumer/brand relationship proposition, including anthropomorphizing the brand as an active relationship partner—at the level of consumers' experiences with their brands. Her proposal of 15 consumer/brand relationships includes arranged marriages, casual friends, marriages of convenience, committed partnerships, best friendships, compartmentalized friendships, kinships, rebounds, childhood friendships, courtships, dependencies, flings, enslavements, enmities, and secret affairs.

ADVANCING MEANS–END CHAIN LADDERING RESEARCH BY APPLYING FOURNIER'S CONSUMER/BRAND RELATIONSHIPS

Use of the advanced MEC laddering research that Figure 5-2 summarizes serves to complement and inform Fournier's consumer/brand relationship typology: Multiple consumer-brand relationship types are uncovered by collecting data within given situations of consumer/brand experiences, acceptable alternatives to these lived experiences, as well as rejected alternatives. Equally valuable are the data uncovering association streams of the three laddering paths (done, alternative, and rejected) to terminal values.

APPLYING THE ADVANCES IN MEANS–END CHAIN LADDERING RESEARCH

The following four case studies illustrate applications of advances in MEC laddering research. The four cases report two experiences for each of two subjects (Ss).

Method

In order to collect the data to examine the propositions, two subjects, Eric and Peter, were chosen to participate in two separate interviews each. Each subject is a senior in college, in his early twenties, living in an apartment on-campus at a large university in the eastern U.S. The interviews were conducted at the residences of the respondents at two different times during the day. The two situations under consideration for this study were the consumption of a beverage in the morning after waking up and the beverage consumption between eight o'clock and midnight on a Friday night. For the MEC laddering process described previously, each respondent was asked a series of 34 questions for each situation. The questions were designed to elicit responses that would provide the perceived attributes, benefits, and consequences of the products consumed.

The respondents were also asked to provide alternative products that they might have chosen in each situation as well as rejected products that would not be considered. The subjects were also asked questions pertaining to prior actions to the consumption of the beverage and about the situation itself, such as where it occurred and if anyone else was around. With the responses gathered from each subject, an extended MEC was created for each subject in each situation using the theoretical model shown in Figure 5-2.

The extended MEC begins at the bottom with the prequel to the action discussed. This prequel is the event(s) that is believed to influence the action to occur. From this prior event there must be some sort of recognition, or immediate feelings or thoughts that act as drivers to act. Stemming from the driver is the action itself, or the product usage. The consumer's description of the product (what it was, how much was consumed, and what brand) as well as a brief description of the situation (when and where the action occurred, others present at the time). Completion of these steps results in completion of MECs, including the identification of terminal values.

Identifying a specific consumption experience and situation provides theoretical ground for developing MECs based on the proposition that the consumption of a specific product and brand is acceptable in only certain situations. In fact, the same brand and product form may associate positively to one situation and negatively to alternative situations for the same consumer. Also, different attributes and benefits may come to mind for a consumer for the same brand depending on the usage situation that the consumer is thinking about (Bearden and Woodside, 1978; Belk, 1974). Consequently, resulting MECs may be expected to vary contingent on the focal situations being described in consumers' experiences.

From the description of the product and the situation comes the three distinct series of the extended MEC. On the left is the reject alternative and on the right is the alternative that would be considered. The center of the model focuses on the product that was actually used or consumed. The separate attributes of the product or brand are laid out in order to get an idea of the benefits or consequences of each. This same questioning process is used to collect information for the alternative and reject products. The benefit of the attributes is where the MEC begins to probe for the instrumental beliefs and values of the respondent. These beliefs are often unconsciously stored thoughts that the consumer may not connect but that actually play a role in the decision-making process. Some benefits may lead to the same values and benefits from the alternative and the reject products can also tie into these same values. The model shows that the alternative and reject products may tie in with the entire MEC, which is why they should be considered when looking at unconscious thinking of consumers. Finally, the chain concludes with terminal values or their core values and beliefs in the S's life.

FINDINGS

Beverage Consumed On Monday Morning

For this situation each respondent answered questions about the first beverage they consumed on the day that the interviews took place. Eric went to bed around one in the morning and did not have anything to drink before going to sleep. After waking up at ten o'clock on Monday morning with a dry mouth and morning breath, he went down to the kitchen in his apartment and poured a 16-oz. glass of Tropicana orange juice. Eric proceeded to have another glass of orange juice while he ate a bagel alone at the table. The attributes that he associates with Tropicana orange juice are that it tastes sweet, kills morning breath, and contains vitamin C (see Figure 5-3).

No benefit was linked with the sweet taste, but sweet taste is an attribute that Eric remarked that he prefers. The benefit of killing morning breath was having better breath throughout the day, which was also a benefit that he did not believe any alternative drinks offered. Eric explained that his mother had always told him that he should drink a lot of orange juice to prevent getting a cold, which is a benefit of a product containing vitamin C. By preventing illness he believes that he will not have to visit the doctor (which was a positive relationship, because he does not like paying the extra money or dealing with doctors in general). As an alternative Eric suggested that he also likes to drink Gatorade because it quenches his thirst and keeps him hydrated. Again, by staying hydrated he believes that he will be able to stay in better shape and remain healthier, which ties in with the benefits of the vitamin C in orange juice.

Having good breath is important for Eric because one of his main goals is to feel comfortable in his surroundings. By not having bad breath he felt that he could socialize with others and not worry about others smelling his breath.

Coffee is the product that Eric reports that he rejects because of caffeine, calories, and causing him to have to go to the bathroom. The consequences of all of these attributes negatively connected with the value of feeling comfortable because each one posed a problem with comfort.

Interestingly, there were two other benefits that surfaced in this interview stemming from staying healthy and staying in shape. As a result of staying in shape Eric felt that this would make him more attractive to females, which seemed to be a common theme with the four different situations. Saving money came up as a core value because in the interview he explained that he bought Tropicana orange juice even though it tended to be more expensive. He was willing to pay the price premium for the brand but overall he is looking to save money.

Peter spent Sunday night watching movies and eating popcorn with his girlfriend until about 2 a.m., when they went to bed. When he woke up around 11 on Monday morning, his mouth was very dry from the popcorn and he had bad breath. He got out of bed and went to the refrigerator in the bedroom and pulled out the gallon jug of orange juice. He drank three 10-oz. servings directly from the jug while his girlfriend and roommate were asleep in the room. Peter does not recall the brand because he bought whatever was cheapest at the store, but he does know that it was not a major brand like Tropicana. His alternative product was apple juice, and the rejected product was cranberry juice (see Figure 5-4).

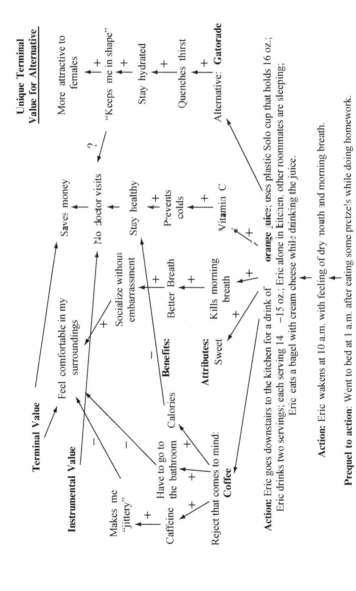

Terminal Value

Unique Terminal
Value for Alternative

More attractive to
females

"Keeps me in shape"

Stay hydrated

Quenches thirst

Alternative: **Gatorade**

Feel comfortable in my
surroundings

Saves money

No doctor visits

?

Socialize without
embarrassment

Stay healthy

Prevents
colds

Vitamin C

Instrumental Value

Calories

Better Breath

Benefits:

Makes me
"jittery"

Have to go to
the bathroom

Kills morning
breath

Attributes:
Sweet

Caffeine

Reject that comes to mind:
Coffee

Action: Eric goes downstairs to the kitchen for a drink of **orange juice**; uses plastic Solo cup that holds 16 oz.; Eric drinks two servings; each serving 14 –15 oz.; Eric alone in kitchen. other roommates are sleeping; Eric eats a bagel with cream cheese while drinking the juice.

Action: Eric wakens at 10 a.m. with feeling of dry mouth and morning breath.

Prequel to action: Went to bed at 1 a.m. after eating some pretzels while doing homework.

FIGURE 5.3 Means–end chain laddering findings for Eric's first beverage on Monday morning.

94

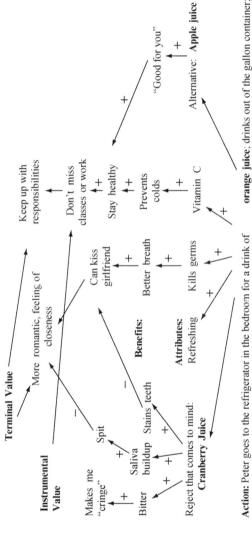

FIGURE 5.4 Means–end chain laddering findings for Peter's first beverage on Monday morning.

Prequel to action: Went to bed at 2 a.m. after eating popcorn and watching a movie with his girlfriend.

Action: Peter awakens at 11 a.m. with feeling of dry mouth and bad breath.

Action: Peter goes to the refrigerator in the bedroom for a drink of **orange juice**; drinks out of the gallon container; Peter drinks three servings; each serving ≈ −10 oz.; girlfriend and roommate are asleep in the room.

Terminal Value

Instrumental
Value

Keep up with
responsibilities

Don't miss
classes or work

Stay healthy

Prevents
colds

Vitamin C

Alternative: **Apple juice**

"Good for you"

More romantic, feeling of
closeness

Can kiss
girlfriend

Better breath

Kills germs

Refreshing

Benefits:

Attributes:

Makes me
"cringe"

Spit

Saliva
buildup

Stains teeth

Bitter

Reject that comes to mind:
Cranberry Juice

The attributes that Peter described for the orange juice were that it was refreshing, it killed germs, and it contained vitamin C. In the interview he remarked that he was not sure if the orange juice actually killed germs but this was what he guessed gave him better breath after drinking it. As a result of having better breath he said that he would actually be able to kiss his girl-friend because she did not like to taste his bad breath. Besides the fact that Peter does not like the taste of cranberry juice in general, he also felt that it stained teeth with its red coloring, and caused saliva buildup, which made him spit. These consequences can be negatively linked with Peter's being able to kiss his girlfriend. All of this leads up to the core value of romance and the feeling of closeness that Peter believes is important.

Peter mentioned that he believed that vitamin C prevents colds and would help him to stay healthy. He also felt that the alternative, apple juice, could help him to stay healthy because it is "good for you." Staying healthy is important to Peter because another core value is that he likes to keep up with his responsibilities in life. He does not like to fall behind in schoolwork or to miss days at his job.

Both respondents chose the same beverage for quite similar reasons, but it did not turn out that their core values were also the same. There was the similarity of staying healthy, but that is one of the only similarities. Also, each respondent had a different relationship with his brand of choice. Using the relationships developed by Fournier (1998), Eric is in a "committed partner-ship" with the Tropicana brand, while Peter is a "casual friend/buddy" with his brand of orange juice. Eric is in a long-term, voluntary union with Tropicana even though it is higher priced because it is a brand that he knows and trusts. Peter buys more based on price. As long as a certain brand is the cheapest, he will continue to purchase it, but if a competitor suddenly becomes cheaper, he will buy that brand. There is no long-term commitment in the brand relationship.

Beverage Consumed Last Friday Night Between 8 P.M. and Midnight

Both Eric and Peter are self-described heavy drinkers, drinking ten beers on average four or five nights a week. This consumption has increased somewhat over the last couple of years, but all throughout they have been "beer drinkers." Eric's situation on Friday night began when he invited friends over for pizza and to watch the game on TV (Figure 5-5). He had gone out earlier and bought two 30-packs of Busch Light for the evening and his friends were expecting to drink when they arrived. As the night progressed the group began to play drinking games and consume even greater amounts of beer. By midnight Eric recalls having about 12 cans of beer before going to sleep.

The attributes suggested for Busch Light beer are a smooth taste, it con-tains alcohol, and that it contains calories. The fact that the beverage contained alcohol seemed to be the most prominent reason for consuming

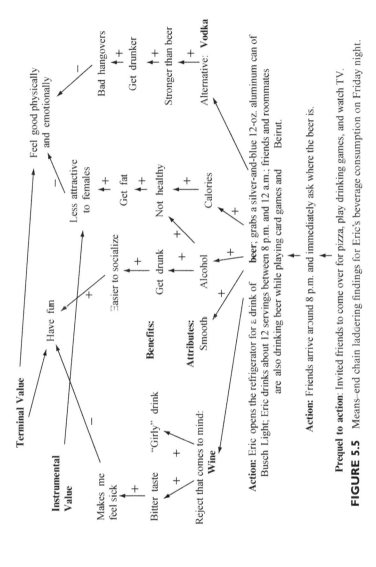

Terminal Value

Feel good physically
and emotionally

Bad hangovers

−

+

Get drunker

**Instrumental
Value**

+

Stronger than beer

+

Alternative: **Vodka**

Have fun

Less attractive
to females

−

+

Get fat

+

+

Not healthy

+

Calories

−

Makes me
feel sick

+

Easier to socialize

+

Get drunk

+

+

Bitter taste

"Girly" drink

Benefits:

Alcohol

+

+

+

Reject that comes to mind:
Wine

Attributes:

Smooth

+

Action: Eric opens the refrigerator for a drink of **beer**; grabs a silver-and-blue 12-oz. aluminum can of Busch Light; Eric drinks about 12 servings between 8 p.m. and 12 a.m.; friends and roommates are also drinking beer while playing card games and Beirut.

Action: Friends arrive around 8 p.m. and immediately ask where the beer is.

Prequel to action: Invited friends to come over for pizza, play drinking games, and watch TV.

FIGURE 5.5 Means–end chain laddering findings for Eric's beverage consumption on Friday night.

the beer. The benefit of the alcohol is that it gets the person drunk, which makes it easier to socialize, but much like the calories in the beer, the alcohol is also not healthy. The calories lead to getting fat and being less attractive to females. The alternative product to drink on a Friday night for Eric was vodka. Vodka was an alternative because it was stronger than beer, which would get him drunker, but this leads to having a hangover. The negative consequence of being so very drunk leads to being unattractive to females and goes against his core values of feeling good both physically and emotionally.

The rejected product for Eric was wine, no specific brand, just wine in general. He reports not liking the taste of wine and he also perceives wine as a "girly" drink. The bitter taste of the wine causes him to feel sick to his stomach, which has a negative relation to the core value of feeling good physically. The alcohol in beer, which makes it easier to socialize, has a positive relationship with the value of having fun. Eric stressed that at his age he was more concerned with having a good time than with worrying about too many responsibilities but he did see this mentality changing in the near future because of graduation.

The situation for Peter was different because of the setting, but for the most part the MEC looked similar to that of Eric. Peter had taken a test earlier in the afternoon that he did not believe had gone very well. After the test, he went down to the local bar, Mary Ann's, for "happy hour." He met up with friends at the bar and they began to drink beer. By 8 p.m. Peter was still at the bar and he was still drinking bottles of Busch Light beer. He had about eight beers between 8 p.m. and the time he left the bar at 10 p.m.

The attributes that Peter describes in Busch Light beer are that it is carbonated, and that it contains alcohol and calories. He could not explain what he thought the benefits of carbonation are, but this could be investigated in a follow-up interview if one were to be performed. Alcohol was the major attribute that Peter described in beer. The alcohol led to getting drunk and acting immature, which was negatively related to his core value of thinking rationally and responsibly. Peter mentioned rum as the rejected beverage because of a bad experience that he had in the past. Due to this bad experience he cannot drink any rum because it makes him vomit.

Calories were not a major concern for Peter but he did acknowledge that they are not healthy. Because of this he would need to work out to be more attractive to females. Wine was given as an alternative to beer as a beverage to consume on a Friday night. Peter felt that wine is more of a sophisticated drink and makes him look more mature. He felt that this would make him more attractive to females—in this case, one of his core values.

The brand relationships between both Peter and Eric and Busch Light beer are about the same. Both respondents remarked that Busch Light beer was popular with them because it was cheaper than most beers, but that it was not the cheapest. This is a "casual friendship/buddy" type of relationship because there is not a long-term commitment to the brand. The consumers

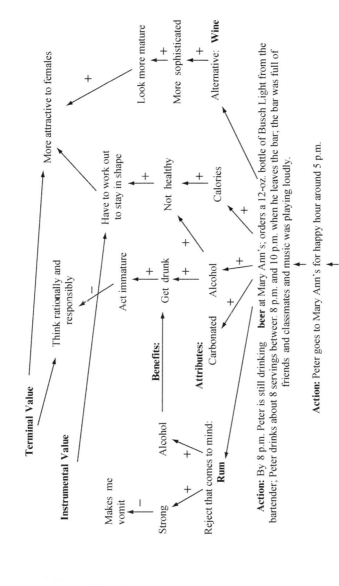

FIGURE 5.6 Means–end chain laddering findings for Peter's beverage consumption on Friday night.

Action: By 8 p.m. Peter is still drinking **beer** at Mary Ann's; orders a 12-oz. bottle of Busch Light from the bartender; Peter drinks about 8 servings between 8 p.m. and 10 p.m. when he leaves the bar; the bar was full of friends and classmates and music was playing loudly.

Action: Peter goes to Mary Ann's for happy hour around 5 p.m.

Prequel to action: Had a test earlier that afternoon that didn't go so well.

are loyal but they do buy other brands and will likely not stay with this brand after graduation because of their increased financial situation. Another brand relationship can be seen between Peter and rum. This is an "enmities" relationship because he has a desire to avoid the product due to its negative effects.

APPLYING ADVANCED MEANS–END CHAIN LADDERING TO LEARN UNCONSCIOUS PROCESSES

Research on consumer thinking processes (see Zaltman, 2003) indicates multiple levels of mental processing. Figure 5-7 summarizes five levels of thinking processes that demonstrate MEC laddering research.

Level 1 represents conscious thinking that is verbalized between two or more parties. Level 2 thinking includes conscious handling of thoughts before and after verbalizing thoughts and surfacing thoughts. Level 3 thinking includes surfacing thoughts that are mostly not under conscious control. Level 4 thinking represents unconscious thinking between two or more persons. Level 5 thinking represents unconscious processing including spreading

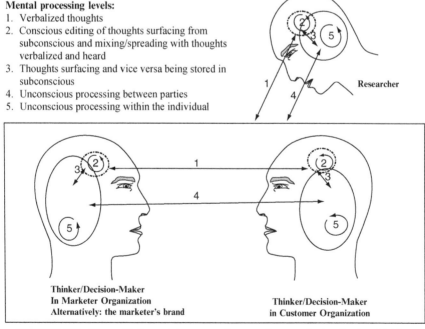

Mental processing levels:
1. Verbalized thoughts
2. Conscious editing of thoughts surfacing from subconscious and mixing/spreading with thoughts verbalized and heard
3. Thoughts surfacing and vice versa being stored in subconscious
4. Unconscious processing between parties
5. Unconscious processing within the individual

Researcher

Thinker/Decision-Maker
In Marketer Organization
Alternatively: the marketer's brand

Thinker/Decision-Maker
in Customer Organization

FIGURE 5.7 The multiple mental processes in research on marketing–buying thinking.

activation of relationships among concepts that the individual is unaware are occurring.

Other empirical findings (see Bargh, 2002; Wegner, 2002) support a core proposition about how the mind thinks: the most processing occurs unconsciously (indicated by the thicker line 5 in Figure 5-7). Such unconscious thinking influences consumers' actions in ways mostly unknown to the consumers' themselves.

Such observations are likely to cause stress among consumer researchers who mainly apply the current (early twenty-first century) dominating logic of asking closed-ended (e.g., 7-point scale items) questions because such questioning mostly reaches only level 1 processing, that is, verbalized thoughts (Zaltman, 2003). Some deeper form of questioning is necessary to reach into level 2 to 5 mental processing. The advances in MEC laddering research that Chapter 5 discusses may help achieve this objective.

LIMITATIONS AND SUGGESTIONS FOR FUTURE RESEARCH

The four MEC laddering cases serve to inform theory development and are not intended as representative of college students in general or for specific segments of beverage consumers. This report is limited by not taking the step of describing the results in follow-up interviews with the two case study Ss and having the Ss confirm and elaborate on the researcher's interpretations (Hirschman, 1986, argues for such a validation step). Such an additional "autodriving" step will likely prove useful for achieving further advances in MEC laddering theory and research.

The author gratefully acknowledges the data collection by Eric Goodwin of Boston College on the four cases described in this chapter.

6

ADVANCING FROM SUBJECTIVE TO CONFIRMATORY PERSONAL INTROSPECTION

Synopsis

Research findings support the view that a multiple-methods approach is necessary to surface the substantial amount of relevant thinking processes that occur both consciously and unconsciously within different phases of consumer decision-making. This chapter advocates viewing all studies that ask informants questions as representatives of researcher/informant introspections. Because answers to questions differ substantially depending on how they are framed, applying multiple, explicit question frames to acquire conscious and unconscious thoughts in researcher/informant introspections is helpful. This chapter reviews multiple methods, including metaphor elicitation of unconscious thinking useful for achieving and confirming thick descriptions of conscious and unconscious thinking associated with informants' deep-seated beliefs and observable actions.

INTRODUCTION: CREATIVELY DESTRUCTING DECISION-MAKING

A substantial body of consumer research now supports a "creative destructive" (Lowenstein, 2001) view of consumer decision-making (see Bargh, 2002; Zaltman, 2003). Such a view proposes that in actuality consumers have far less access to their own mental activities than marketers give them credit for. A number of studies support the conclusion that informants are able to only partially retrieve and report the reasons for their actions (for a review see Woodside and Wilson, 2003). "Ninety-five percent of thinking takes place in our unconscious minds—that wonderful, if messy, stew of memories, emotions, thoughts, and other cognitive processes we're not aware of or that we can't articulate" (Zaltman, 2003, p. 9).

Consequently, this chapter offers a workbench model of informant's thinking related to interpreting and answering questions that the informant asks herself or is asked by another researcher (e.g., another person address-ing a question to an informant). Chapter 6 suggests the use of a combination of introspective conscious and unconscious thought-retrieval elicitation tech-niques to achieve three objectives: (1) confirming both the beliefs/evaluations held consciously and unconsciously by the informant; (2) confirming the exis-tence of experiences and related outcomes as described by the informant; and (3) achieving a deep understanding of how consumers become aware of their own desires (see Belk, Ger, and Askegaard, 2003) that affect their search behavior, purchases, and how they use products and services.

Figure 6-1 portrays multiple issues related to thinking about an issue raised by a researcher—regardless of whether the researcher is the same or a person different from an informant. Table 6-1 summarizes some of the research concerns and findings that relate to the first nine issues in Figure 6-1.

Given that dominant logic in consumer research continues to rely on ask-ing questions that require introspection (i.e., interpreting the questions, retrieving information from memory, editing, and reporting), Levy's (1996, p. 172) views represent a sound defense for advancing introspection research methods:

> In a casual sense, introspection is an inevitable part of consumer research, used by all research workers, as it means looking within one's self to know one's ideas and feelings. That is, introspection is another word for being self-conscious, aware, thoughtful, having ideas, and knowing what they are.

SUBJECTIVE PERSONAL INTROSPECTION

"Subjective personal introspection" (SPI) (see Holbrook, 1986) includes a family of research methods that rely extensively or even exclusively on the researchers' life experiences as data (Wallendorf and Brucks, 1993). Holbrook (1986, 1995, 1999, 2003, 2004) provides a stream of introspective empirical reports focusing on one method of introspection: "impressionistic narrative accounts of the writer's own private consumption experiences" (Holbrook, 2004, p. 3). Holbrook's contributions stimulated the work of other consumer researchers (e.g., Gould, 1991, 1995; Hirschman, 1992; Williams, 1992) and work with a colleague (Holbrook and Kuwahara, 1998).

Wallendorf and Brucks (1993) discern five categories of introspection on the basis of the level of closeness or intimacy between the researcher and introspector:

- Researcher introspection: the ultimate level of closeness in which the researcher is the sole introspector in the study; while several studies are available using this method, "our review of the social science literatures indicates that consumer research may be alone in this regard." (Wallendorf and Brucks, 1993, p. 141)

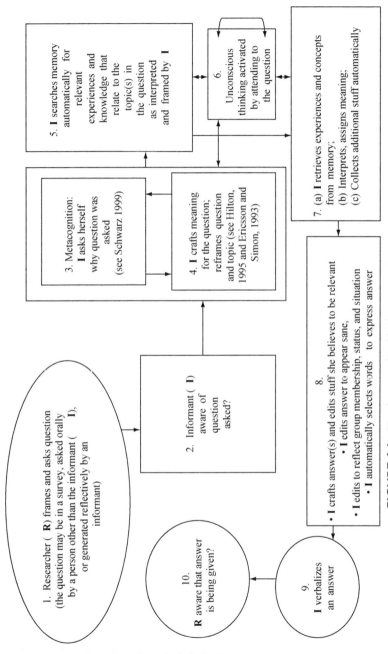

FIGURE 6.1 How introspective thinking occurs when a question is answered.

1. Researcher (**R**) frames and asks question (the question may be in a survey, asked orally by a person other than the informant (**I**), or generated reflectively by an informant)

2. Informant (**I**) aware of question asked?

3. Metacognition: **I** asks herself why question was asked (see Schwarz 1999)

4. **I** crafts meaning for the question; reframes question and topic (see Hilton, 1995 and Ericsson and Simon, 1993)

5. **I** searches memory automatically for relevant experiences and knowledge that relate to the topic(s) in the question as interpreted and framed by **I**

6. Unconscious thinking activated by attending to the question

7. (a) **I** retrieves experiences and concepts from memory;
(b) Interprets, assigns meaning;
(c) Collects additional stuff automatically

8.
• **I** crafts answer(s) and edits stuff she believes to be relevant
• **I** edits answer to appear sane,
• **I** edits to reflect group membership, status, and situation
• **I** automatically selects words to express answer

9. **I** verbalizes an answer

10. **R** aware that answer is being given?

TABLE 6-1 Research Concerns and Findings for Nine Issues Related to Introspection

Issue	Research Concerns and Findings
1. Researcher (**R**) frames and asks question	1. Alternative question frames have large influence on how informant (**I**) interprets and answers the question.
2. Informant (**I**) aware of question asked?	2. **I** may not attend or interpret **R**'s statement as a question
3. Metacognition: **I** asks herself why question was asked	3. Metacognition likely to be an implicit step that **I** does not verbalize unless unsure, not confident, about rationale
4. **I** crafts meaning, reframes question and topic	4. Meaning/interpretation **I** assigns may poorly match with **R**'s framing of the issue and general focus of the inquiry
5. **I**'s search of long-term memory for experiences and knowledge relevant to question as **I** has framed it	5. **I**'s initial search is done automatically; a spreading activation occurs quickly among easily retrieved concepts; evaluations are assigned automatically among concepts retrieved based on unconscious thinking
6. Unconscious thinking activated	6. Most thinking occurs unconsciously; **I** partially able to uncover unconscious thinking by reflection and use of thinking probes (e.g., metaphor elicitations)
7. **I** retrieves experiences and knowledge from memory, interprets own thoughts, assigns meaning	7. **I** automatically and unconsciously decides when to stop retrieving experiences, interpreting, and assigning meaning
8. **I** crafts answers, edits thoughts	8. Crafting and editing done automatically partially and by controlled thinking as well (**I** may ask, "Will I get in trouble if I say what I really think?")
9. **I** verbalizes answer	9. **I** unlikely to provide rationale for beliefs without probing by **R** in order to limit cognitive effort and limit interviewing time

106

- Guided introspection: people other than the researcher are asked to introspect or think aloud about themselves and their actions; answering a written questionnaire is one form of guided introspection.
- Interactive introspection: the researcher assists others in their introspections but the object of the study is the "emergent experiences of both parties" (Ellis, 1991, p. 30). Wallendorf and Brucks comment, "Beyond Ellis's initial discussion, there does not appear to be a social science literature that has used and refined this method. The present study does advance Ellis's perspective and includes an interactive introspection among the triangulation of methods employed."
- Syncretic combinations: the most common form expands the sample beyond the researcher but also incorporates details of the researcher's life experience that s/he is willing to document; unlike interactive introspection, this combination does not have the researcher share his/her introspections with informants (e.g., Freud, 1908).
- Reflexivity within research: ethnographic studies using participant observation and relying on two sources of data: (1) observational and interview material from people in a cultural group being studied and (2) reflexive material that emerges from being a participant studying that cultural group.

ADVANCING TOWARD CONFIRMATORY PERSONAL INTROSPECTION

Employing a syncretic combination of methods likely leads to deeper "sensemaking" than SPI as developed and advocated by Holbrook (1986, 2004). Such a syncretic combination includes two or more of the following methods: (1) researcher self-introspection and written description of an observable stream of behaviors and thoughts occurring while the behaviors occurred; (2) the researcher interviewing any mentors who participated in the behavioral process under study; (3) the researcher interviewing a cohort to learn the cohort's interpretations about the researcher's own understanding of the occurrence of specific acts in the stream of behavior, and the antecedents that lead to each act; (4) the reflective use of decision and conscious processing tools by the researcher to help surface prior conscious metaphors (see Park, Hughes, Thurkal, and Friedman, 1981); (5) metaphor generating tools (e.g., Zaltman, 2003) and the use of experimental research designs (e.g., see Bargh, 2002) to uncover unconscious thinking relevant to the behavioral process being investigated; and (6) the use of independently developed survey schedules to assist the researcher/informant in her introspection.

The objectives of this combination of methods include:

• Confirming the occurrence of milestone behavioral events and decision heuristics used in making choices in specific phases of the behavioral process.
• Uncovering unrecognized paradox and resolutions in differences in opinions held by multiple persons participating in several phases of the behavioral process under study.
• Helping to make explicit the "implicit mental model" (Senge, 1990) relevant to decision-making within the original time frame of the introspection study.
• Surfacing thoughts held unconsciously that are applicable to choices made in the process under study.

In his report of the following incident, Holbrook (2004, p. 11) offers a backhand application (i.e., he is not an advocate of the need for independent assessments of researcher introspections) of syncretic combinations in his interpretive analysis of photographs from his family's archive. "The closest I have come to a member check [an independent assessment of an SPI for accuracy and completeness] has been inviting my ninety-one-year-old mother to attend a conference where I presented some of this material and dutifully made revisions in my comments as she called out occasional corrections from the audience." Note that he reports that his mother's comments helped to revise his incorrect remembrances and her silences imply confirmation of other parts of his narration.

Thus, the attempt here is to illustrate how unique forms of introspective syncretic combinations can be planned that help to (at least partially) overcome Wallendorf and Brucks's (1993) conclusion that researcher self-introspection offers severely limited potential in contributing useful research in consumer behavior.

The application of multiple research methods transforms Holbrook's SPI to achieve a confirmatory personal introspection (CPI) that includes many of the criteria of scientific approaches to research without the loss of the criteria representing the artistic approach (see Brown, 1998, for a review of both approaches). CPI is likely to be found useful for designing products and marketing communications that consumers find desirable and that motivate their purchase behavior. These two views respond to Andreasen's (1985) and Well's (1993) "research backward" guideline to answer the "So what?" question before implementing an empirical investigation.

Given the substantial scientific evidence that most thinking is unconscious (for reviews, see Bargh, 2002; Zaltman, 2003), the research tools to surface unconscious thoughts described subsequently are worthy of attention. Field studies applying CPI may demonstrate the usefulness for working from several complementary literature streams to extend Zaltman's (2003) treatise on how consumers think—including strategies for theorizing from process data (e.g., Eisenhardt, 1989; Langley, 1999); decision plan net theory of individual choice models (see Park *et al.*, 1981); "autoethnography" and other personal introspection methods (Holbrook, 2004; Wallendorf and Brucks, 1993), as well as related views on "sensemaking" (Weick, 1995); and unconscious and automatic influences on consumer judgment, behavior, and motivation (see Bargh, 2002).

In bare-knuckle terms, the view here attacks the current dominate logic in consumer research of learning the reasons for consumer choice of brands or store sites by relying principally on written, self-completed surveys using mostly closed-ended (fixed-point) questions. While most consumers are able to complete the surveys, such a highly cognitive method excludes data collection of most thoughts—embracing the finding that most thinking occurs unconsciously, consumers have only limited accessibility to the unconscious, and "people generally do not think in words" (Zaltman, 2003, p. 13). Behavioral research methods that enable consumers to access their unconscious thoughts need widespread adoption in studies on product and brand knowledge held by consumers. CPI research includes methods designed to reduce the inherent attempts to self-edit and block unwelcome, or socially unacceptable (see Fisher, 1993), thoughts, and to stimulate informants to report reasons for their actions seemingly "too minor to mention" in open-ended written responses.

Subsequent to this introduction, the literature review suggests placing introspection in consumer research within grounded theory (Glaser and Strauss, 1967) and building theories from case study research (see Eisenhardt, 1989; Langley, 1999). In the third section, we urge the adoption of Hirschman's (1986) humanistic inquiry philosophy and method recommendations as much as possible for researcher introspection. The fourth section describes the application of multiple methods focusing on the same empirical ground covered by a researcher's introspection—multiple methods that are useful for surfacing unconscious thoughts and aiding retrieval of conscious thoughts generated during the process being examined. The fifth section offers implications for theory construction that follow from CPI. The final section covers limitations, conclusions, and suggestions for further research.

INTROSPECTION, CASE STUDY RESEARCH, AND CONSTRUCTING GROUNDED THEORIES

Building theories from case study research (Eisenhardt, 1989), the organization decision-making literature (see Langley *et al.*, 1995), and the historical method in consumer research (Smith and Lux, 1993) provides useful theoretical grounding for researcher self-introspection. Eisenhardt (1989) informs us, "The case study is a research study which focuses on understanding the dynamics present within single settings...Moreover, cases studies can employ

an embedded design, that is, multiple levels of analysis within a single study
(Yin, 1994)."

Langley *et al.* (1995) review organizational literature that recognizes
phases in some decision-making that often involves an iterative feedback
process, but nonetheless often reaches some form of choice agreement among
multiple participants in the process followed by action. These authors
emphasize that even when a decision can be isolated the processes leading up
to it rarely can be.

> Thus, most of the literature notwithstanding, we believe that no decision can
> be understood *de novo* or *in vitro*, apart from the perceptions of the actors
> and the mindsets and cultures of the contexts in which they are embedded.
> On the contrary, we shall argue that decision making must be studied *in toto*
> and inspiration, emotion, and memory, and at the collective level to include
> history, culture, and context in the vast network of decision making that
> makes up every organization. (Langley *et al.*, 1995, p. 261)

Several authors in separate but complementary research streams emphasize that subconscious processes play may major roles in decision-making
Thus, Langley *et al.* (1995, p. 268) wish to add to Simon's administrative man,
"insightful man, who listens to the voices emanating from his own unconscious, or perhaps, better expressed, who sights the images that well up in his
own imagination." Smith and Lux (1993) call for the study of unconscious
motives (M_u) in their historical method exposition in consumer research,
"Unlike transparent motives that 'just are,' unconscious motives arise from
social circumstances that do not necessarily have to stand as they are, but of
which the individual may not be consciously aware at the time the act occurs.
Such unconscious motives might be likened to unreflected experience
(Thompson *et al.*, 1989) in that they constitute a ground against which behavior is the figure."

Unconscious processing is an additional observation found in the literature on decision-making and thinking research. "It is often difficult to say
who decided something and when—or even who originated a decision"
(quoted in Quinn, 1980, p. 134, and Langley *et al.*, 1995, p. 265).

CORE PROPOSITIONS FOR EXAMINING THE BUYING PROCESS FOR MAJOR SERVICES

Consequently, the core proposition (CP_1) offered here is that consumer
choice processes include recognizable phases involving several persons participating in one or more phases with conscious and unconscious
thoughts/motives affecting the buyers' beliefs and actions, and that one or all
of the participants may be unable to consciously explain the causes of spe-

cific milestone sub-decisions occurring in the process. However, (CP$_2$) relating to the purchase process for a major consumer durable (e.g., motor vehicle) or service (e.g., the selection of a university to attend for a three or four year degree), one or more phases of the process are likely to include substantial conscious effort and some of the thinking involved, but not all, can be retrieved within a researcher introspective study.

ADOPTING THE HUMANISTIC INQUIRY PARADIGM FOR RESEARCHER INTROSPECTION

Hirschman (1986) provides four criteria appropriate for humanistic inquiry that, if applied, are useful for increasing the usefulness of researcher introspections—including SPIs:

- Credibility—representing the multiple realities of the process examined adequately, possibly by the researcher submitting the interpretation to the scrutiny of the participant in the process who provided some of the original data and seeking responses as to the report's authenticity.
- Transferability—transfer of the resulting interpretation of the process to other contexts, such as the purchase of a major service different from the one being examined (e.g., processes involved in buying a medical procedure versus processes for a university degree).
- Dependability use of multiple human investigators enhances internal stability of measures taken.
- Confirmability—seeking of neutrality and objectivity, possibly by asking outside auditors to confirm or dispute the interpretations of the researcher.

CRAFTING FORMAL SURVEY PROTOCOLS FOR SELF-INTERVIEWS

One step toward increasing credibility in researcher self-introspection is for the researcher to formally interview herself on two or more separate settings. While such a suggestion may seem absurd, calls for further reflection by decision-makers for more useful "sensemaking" of events and causes of these events are made elsewhere (e.g., Weick, 1995). The use of a formal survey protocol for completing by the researcher with her adding and answering additional questions is another suggestion that may improve credibility—thus, the use of a written interview schedule of questions crafted earlier by an informant and others serves to guide, broaden, and deepen emic interpretations during SPIs.

LEARNING WHILE TALKING

One step toward accomplishing confirmability occurs by having two researchers interview one another while interviewing themselves. This method helps operationalize Weick's (1993) famous proposition, paraphrased here as, how do I know what I think until I hear what I have to say. And, how do I know what I've done until I tell aloud what I did. Another step toward confirmability as well as dependability is having an "inside auditor" answer questions that confirm or disconfirm as well as deepen the interpretations reported by the researcher self-introspection (e.g., the corrections offered by Holbrook's mother on his interpretations of her father's behavior).

THE INSIDE AUDITOR

The use of such an inside auditor, as one's mother or another person involved directly in the focus of the introspection, is almost certain to be helpful for clarifying and deepening researcher introspective reports. By using inside authors as well as agreeing with Hirschman's (1986, p. 246) advocacy of an outside auditor, an advance toward CPI was consequently made:

> To assess whether or not the interpretation is drawn in a logical and unprejudiced manner from the data gathered and the rationale employed, humanistic inquiry relies on the judgment of an outside auditor or auditors. These individuals should be researchers themselves, familiar with the phenomena under study.

THE COHORT AUDITOR

To stimulate the mental surfacing of observations about self and the process being examined by the introspection, one can use an additional category of auditor: the cohort auditor. The cohort auditor (CA) is a person living in the same current environment as the researcher completing a self-introspection, who the researcher introspector (RI) asks to comment on the process and outcome under study. Thus, the RI both tells his/her story to the CA and asks for questions and comments from the CA as the story is being told. Besides being a "sounding board," the CA is likely to provide information that triggers retrievals relevant to the focus of the study by the RI that might otherwise not occur.

Park *et al.* (1981) describe the process of creating decision plan nets that identify and link the presence of three product or services feature according to three dimensions:

- Rejection-inducing dimension (RID)—a dimension that leads to immediate rejection of any alternative failing to reach a satisfactory level of that dimension.

- Relative preference dimension (RPD)—a dimension at a level highly desirable but which, if absent, does not lead automatically to rejecting the alternative.
- Trade-off dimension (TD)—a dimension specified in terms of a conditional acceptance in the absence of its satisfactory level requiring an offsetting improvement on another primary or secondary feature (Park, 1978). See Figure 6-2 for an example of a decision-plan net that includes RIDs, TDs, and RPDs.

THE FORCED METAPHOR ELICITATION TECHNIQUE

The forced metaphor elicitation technique (FMET) has goals similar to those of the Zaltman metaphor elicitation technique (ZMET) and Doyle and Sims' (2002) "cognitive sculpting" technique—that is, using metaphor analysis as a research tool to gain a deeper understanding of the unconscious linkages associating with a behavior. Sims and Doyle (1995) illustrate cognitive sculpting research with informants, use of table-top objects as metaphors of what they are saying and have done—resulting in what Sims and Doyle refer to as "explicating knowledge."

Christensen and Olson (2002) provide an application of the ZMET for a study of 15 very highly involved mountain bikers: "Approximately one week prior to the interview, each recruited participant was contacted and given a set of instructions. First, they were asked to think about mountain biking. Then they were told to select eight to ten pictures that represent their thoughts and feelings about mountain biking and bring the pictures to the interview. Each picture is a metaphor that expresses one or more important meanings about mountain biking...Respondents participated in in-depth interviews conducted by three interviewers trained in the ZMET methodology and experienced in conducting ZMET interviews." (See Zaltman, 1997, for further details.)

The FMET (Figure 6-3) is a tool for surfacing metaphors for use in researcher introspection. FMET includes four distinct steps. First, the respondent is asked to draw or select pictures for three sets of two objects each:

- The animal that first comes to mind that the RI believes "represents some aspects of who you are, what you are like."
- The animal that first comes to mind "that you admire, might select to be if you were an animal other than a human."
- The beverage that first comes to mind "that best represents you most of the time during the daytime."
- The beverage that first comes to mind that "best represents you at home or a party on a Friday night."
- The motor vehicle that first comes to mind that "best represents the vehicle you really would most likely be if you were, in fact, a motor vehicle."

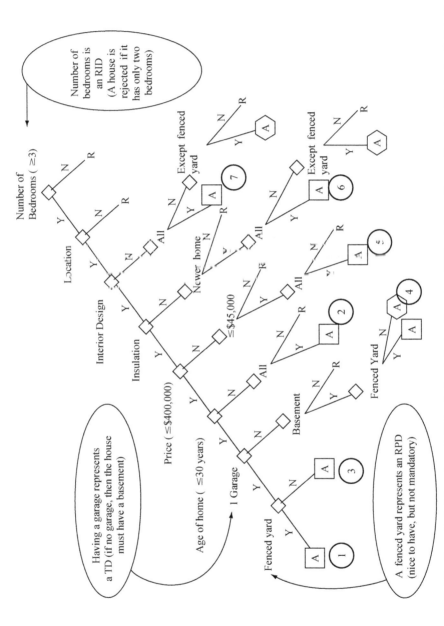

FIGURE 6.2 Example decision plan net. RID, rejection-inducing dimension; RPD, relative preference dimension; TD, trade-off dimension.

114

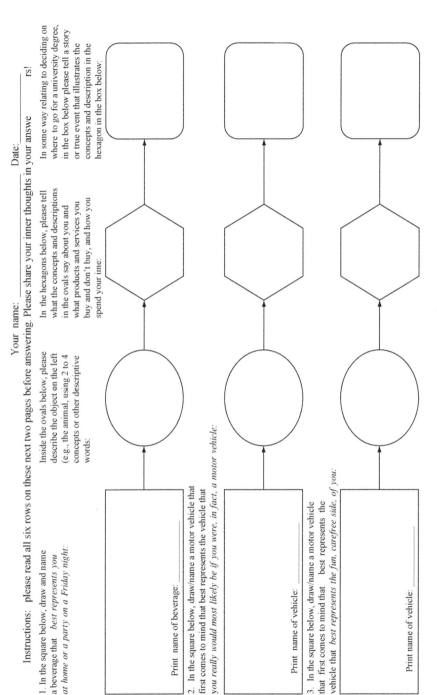

FIGURE 6.3 Metaphor and storytelling exercise: part one.

The text within the figure reads:

Your name: _____ Date: _____

Instructions: please read all six rows on these next two pages before answering. Please share your inner thoughts in your answers!

1. In the square below, draw and name a beverage that *best represents you at home or a party on a Friday night*:

Inside the ovals below, please describe the object on the left (e.g., the animal, using 2 to 4 concepts or other descriptive words):

In the hexagons below, please tell what the concepts and descriptions in the ovals say about you and what products and services you buy and don't buy, and how you spend your ime:

In some way relating to deciding on where to go for a university degree, in the box below please tell a story or true event that illustrates the concepts and description in the hexagon in the box below:

Print name of beverage: _____

2. In the square below, draw/name a motor vehicle that first comes to mind that best represents the vehicle that *you really would most likely be if you were, in fact, a motor vehicle*:

Print name of vehicle: _____

3. In the square below, draw/name a motor vehicle that first comes to mind that best represents the vehicle that *best represents the fun, carefree side, of you*:

Print name of vehicle: _____

115

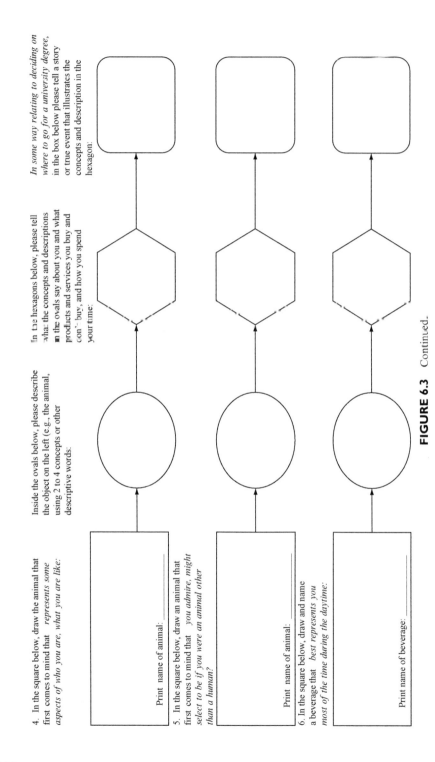

4. In the square below, draw the animal that first comes to mind that *represents some aspects of who you are, what you are like:*

Inside the ovals below, please describe the object on the left (e.g., the animal, using 2 to 4 concepts or other descriptive words:

In the hexagons below, please tell what the concepts and descriptions in the ovals say about you and what products and services you buy and what you buy, and how you spend your time:

In some way relating to deciding on where to go for a university degree, in the box below please tell a story or true event that illustrates the concepts and description in the hexagon:

Print name of animal: _____

5. In the square below, draw an animal that first comes to mind that *you admire, might select to be if you were an animal other than a human?*

Print name of animal: _____

6. In the square below, draw and name a beverage that *best represents you most of the time during the daytime:*

Print name of beverage: _____

FIGURE 6.3 Continued.

- The vehicle that first comes to mind that "best represents the fun, carefree side of you."

Nearly all individuals can identify themselves as more than animal, beverage, and vehicle, depending upon the situation being framed by the question (Dichter, 1985; Woodside, Floyd-Finch, and Wilson, 1986). Thus, the FMET attempts to capture the several unconscious beliefs about the RI. Unlike the ZMET, the FMET does not focus on selecting items in pictures related directly to the behavior being examined—the ZMET is more likely to cause greater cognitive effort and strain in attempting to find pictures that associate with the behavior being examined than the FMET. The ZMET appears to require great cognitive effort and substantial interviewer training and skill for interpreting the pictures selected by the informant; as discussed subsequently, the FMET is designed for the RI to self-interpret how the specific objects selected associate with the choice behavior under investigation.

Second, the FMET asks the RI to say or write the two to four features that first come to mind about each of the six objects in the pictures. Third, the FMET asks the RI to mention the thoughts that first come to mind "what each of these features tells you about yourself." Finally the FMET asks the RI "to tell a story or true event that illustrates the concepts and description" of the features just mentioned about you related to the choice behavior under investigation; Figure 6-4 illustrates the fourth step for the choice of buying a major consumer service—the choice of a university for an undergraduate degree. The RI then has the opportunity to include the results from using the FMET into her interpretation of her service choice.

Figure 6-4 is an example application of one informant's use of the FMET related to the topic of selecting a university or college for an undergraduate degree. Note how the informant's responses in the fourth step help to uncover the matching of personal features within the informant's desires to the features provided by specific brand (in this case, Parma University, Italy).

The pictures include two animals that hunt alone, a motorcycle (a vehicle usually with one rider) and a two-seat sports car, the RI refers to "Independent" to describe the cat and the motorcycle. The RI describes herself as "Independent" as well. Some information is helpful to achieve deep understanding of the motivation to attend a university as far away from her high school friend and her parents as possible—within the felt limits of the reported inadequate transportation system. High need for achievement, independence, freedom, and health via sports are core themes that connect the animal, beverage, and motor vehicle metaphors with the RI's university decision. The FMET results increase understanding of the reasons for the RI's *choice of features* for evaluating and ranking alternative universities.

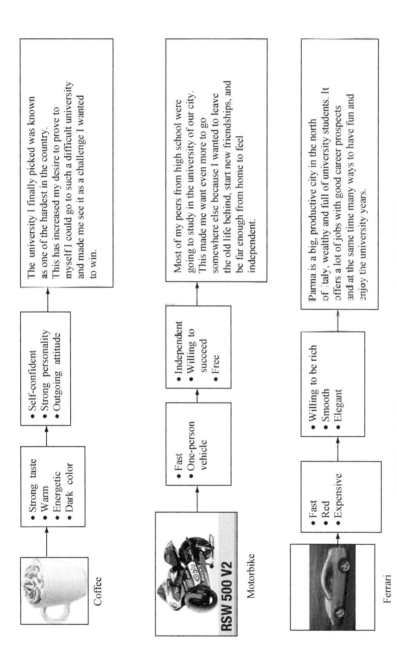

Coffee
- Strong taste
- Warm
- Energetic
- Dark color

- Self-confident
- Strong personality
- Outgoing attitude

The university I finally picked was known as one of the hardest in the country. This has increased my desire to prove to myself I could go to such a difficult university and made me see it as a challenge I wanted to win.

Motorbike
- Fast
- One-person vehicle

- Independent
- Willing to succeed
- Free

Most of my peers from high school were going to study in the university of our city. This made me want even more to go somewhere else because I wanted to leave the old life behind, start new friendships, and be far enough from home to feel independent.

Ferrari
- Fast
- Red
- Expensive

- Willing to be rich
- Smooth
- Elegant

Parma is a big, productive city in the north of Italy, wealthy and full of university students. It offers a lot of jobs with good career prospects and at the same time many ways to have fun and enjoy the university years.

FIGURE 6.4 Metaphor and storytelling. From Nittoli (2003).

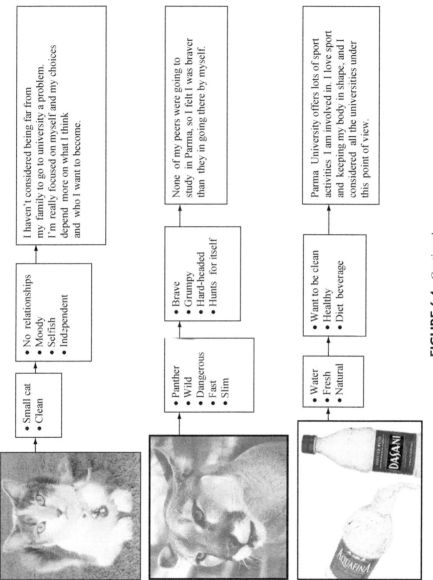

I haven't considered being far from
my family to go to university a problem.
I'm really focused on myself and my choices
depend more on what I think
and who I want to become.

• No relationships
• Moody
• Selfish
• Independent

• Small cat
• Clean

None of my peers were going to
study in Parma, so I felt I was braver
than they in going there by myself.

• Brave
• Grumpy
• Hard-headed
• Hunts for itself

• Panther
• Wild
• Dangerous
• Fast
• Slim

Parma University offers lots of sport
activities I am involved in. I love sport
and keeping my body in shape, and I
considered all the universities under
this point of view.

• Want to be clean
• Healthy
• Diet beverage

• Water
• Fresh
• Natural

FIGURE 6.4 Continued.

119

A CONFIRMATORY INTROSPECTION RESEARCH EXAMPLE FOR EXAMINING POSSIBLE PHASES IN CONSUMER CHOICE BEHAVIOR

Figure 6-5 shows the phase theory used to consider possible sub-decisions that may be involved in the purchase of a major consumer service, in this case, the selection of a university to attend for a three- or four-year bachelor of arts degree. The RIDs, TDs, and RPDs (Park *et al.*, 1981) shown for each decision phase in Figure 6-2 are included merely in order to indicate the possibility of such feature dimensions and not that they always occur for each phase.

This university choice topic is a useful focus for several reasons. First, the selection of a university for such a degree represents the purchase of a major service due to the time and often the financial expenditure for the student and the parents—an important decision made relatively early in life for many persons in many developed nations. Second, based on pre-test interviews, most college students are likely to be able to identify distinct phases in their choice process that include becoming aware of alternative universities; collecting information from family members, friends, and teachers on what attributes to consider in making the decision; selecting universities and colleges to visit; and making the final choice. Thus, the decision is complex and time consuming and one or more phases are likely to include the combination of substantial amounts of conscious and unconscious thinking. Third, for some phases of such an important service purchase, RIDs, TDs, and RPDs are likely to be used. Fourth, this choice decision is relevant to the RI from whom the data were collected: the RI was still attending her chosen university and felt capable of reporting the details occurring in most of the phases of the process.

Figure 6-6 serves to demonstrate the value in using multiple methods in collecting data to confirm and deepen the process under investigation. Note that Figure 6-6 depicts each method as confirming one or more pieces of data learned by one or more other research methods as well as certain amounts of information found unique to a particular method. Also note that not all the information relevant to the process is shown to be captured even when multiple methods are used. Figure 6-6 includes cylinders to indicate that a certain amount of information not directly relevant to the process is recorded. Seemingly non-relevant information may enable the uncovering of information directly relevant to the process under study, for example, an informant may need to talk and say little to get to the point of being comfortable about what she is saying, as well as to learn enough about what she thinks to elaborate deeply on her motivations. Thus, while identifying some data as not relevant directly to the phases in the process, we prefer not to label any part of the data collected as useless information.

P₁: the buying process for a major product – service includes several identifiable phases (e.g., A–E).

P₂: feedback loops (e.g., revised thinking due to new information) occur.

P₃: a few attributes are critical (i.e., RIDs) for each phase, and other attributes are "nice-to-have features" (RPDs).

P₄: different influence sources affect the use of different attributes for different phases of the process.

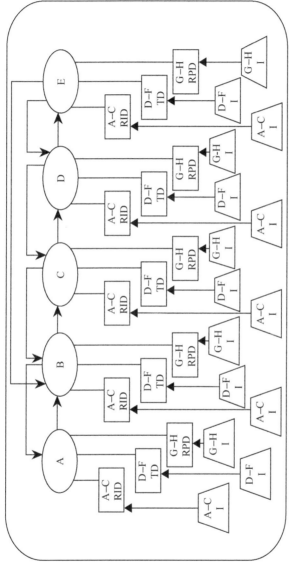

FIGURE 6.5 Propositions (Pᵢ) for the unconscious and conscious thinking–doing process for buying a major product–service. A-E: unconscious-conscious decision phases in thinking-doing process, for example, A = I will attend university; B = I become aware of alternative universities to attend (aware-ness set); C = I select universities to visit (consideration set); D = I select a university to attend; E = I attend the university selected; F (not shown) = I stay or transfer out of the university that I am attending; G (not shown) = I complete university attendance with a degree. The RID, TD, RPD, and each of the A-E phases may or may not be identified consciously by the informant.

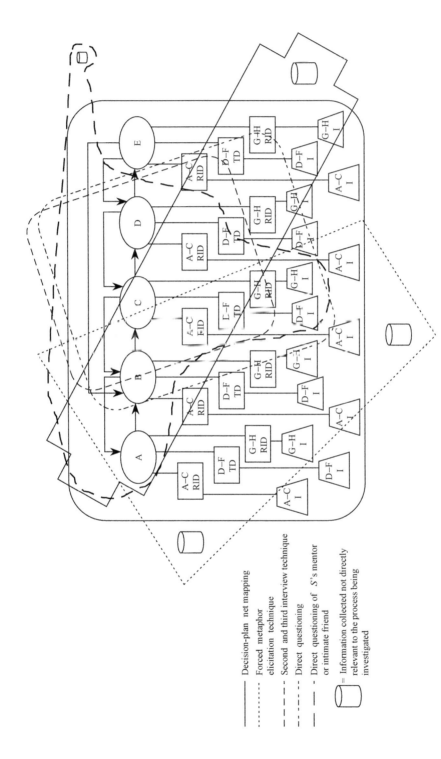

FIGURE 6.6 Research toolkit for surfacing relevant unconscious and conscious thinking–doing processes. RID, rejection-inducing dimension; TD, trade-off dimension; RPD, relative preference dimension.

Decision-plan net mapping

Forced metaphor elicitation technique

Second and third interview technique

Direct questioning

Direct questioning of S's mentor or intimate friend

= Information collected not directly relevant to the process being investigated

IMPLICATIONS FOR THEORY CONSTRUCTION

In some substantial sense, an informant always engages in researcher intro-spection whether she is asking questions implicitly or explicitly to herself, as well as whether she is answering questions to a written survey or put to her verbally. The informant creates an interpretation of the question posed from whatever the source—thus, the informant engages in researcher introspec-tion. Also, metaphorically speaking, the informant has to search the file drawers of her mind to find the drawer somehow labeled by one or more con-cepts interpreted to be in the question. Then the informant has to find the folder in the file drawer, open the folder, read and interpret the folder's con-tents, and select and use words, sentences, and other tools that she feels can be interpreted by her and possibly by others in a manner that she desires. Thus, respondents must make sense of the questions asked of them, and auto-biographical memory in retrospective thinking is involved in all survey research.

The work of Payne (1951), Grice (1975), Hilton (1995), Ericsson and Simon (1993), and Schwarz (1999) supports the view that "question compre-hension involves extensive inferences about the speaker's intentions to deter-mine the pragmatic meaning of the question" (Schwarz, 1999, p. 96). Such inferences apply to whomever asks the question and no matter if the question is asked implicitly or explicitly. Consequently, the informant is always an active participant in framing a question as well as in answering it. From this perspective, Wallendorf and Brucks (1993) note researcher introspection does not lead to the conclusion that the method should be abandoned in consumer research. Rather, the more useful conclusion is that researcher introspection needs to innovate to include carefully executed (rigorous) research procedures and the combined use of multiple data collection instruments. Such data col-lection instruments should include tools designed explicitly to surface uncon-scious thinking processes; especially because substantial scientific knowledge now exists that unconscious thinking processes represent most mental activi-ties by individuals (for a literature review, see Zaltman, 2003).

Researcher introspective case studies aid in "opening up decision mak-ing" (Langley *et al.*, 1995) by demonstrating that different models of deci-sion-making are likely to be relevant for different phases occurring in the process. For example, decision-making as convergence without consciously considering alternatives may best describe the process whereby the RI became committed to attending a university for the purpose of acquiring a degree. After such a convergence has been completed, the phase involving vis-iting alternative universities reflects decision-making following Simon's (1960) three-step sequence: first intelligence (i.e., diagnosing the problem), then, design (i.e., finding alternatives to evaluate), and finally, choice. Langley *et al.* (1995) refer to this view as Model 1, organizational decision-making as sequential.

Regarding the selection and use of criteria to select universities to visit and reach the choice of university to attend appears to represent "insightful man," that is, the RI may listen "to the voices emanating from his [her] own subconscious, or perhaps better expressed, the sights and images that well up in his [her] own imagination" (Langley *et al.* 1995, p. 268). However, the relevancy of these features is questionable because the data from the FMET were collected after, rather than during, the choice process. The FMET data do appear to provide useful clues into the deep meanings of the rejection inducing dimensions in the RI's decision plan net. Thus, decision-making as insightful, identified by Langley *et al.* (1995) as Model 5, appears relevant especially for the selection of dimensions to use for evaluating university alternatives.

Generalizing the results of the RI report to theory suggests that different models of decision-making are at times more or less relevant to the decision process depending on the phase in the process being examined. Thus, asking whether or not the purchase of a major durable good or service is made consciously or unconsciously is less useful than asking where and how both thinking processes contribute to the decision process.

CONCLUSIONS, LIMITATIONS, AND SUGGESTIONS FOR FURTHER RESEARCH

The use of multiple methods in research introspections does appear helpful in confirming the occurrence of specific phases in the decision process and in achieving a deep understanding of primary motivations within the individual that help to explain the presence of attribute dimensions used in her choice of a university. The combined use of decision plan net analysis, the FMET, schedules of survey questions completed by mentors, an inside auditor, and the RI herself represents a blending of emic (conscious and unconscious views of the individual native informant) and etic (interpretation of the researcher after acquiring some distance from the research site) perspectives. Though at first the view that an etic perspective can be acquired in researcher introspection may appear oxymoronic, asking others to confirm the occurrence of specific actions that relate to the behavior of the RI that the RI is examining, as well as seeking views from an inside auditor, serves the RI in viewing herself in the third person. To increase "sensemaking" about what we have done and to deepen understanding of why we did what we have done, Weick (1995) advises that we reflect (e.g., sleep on it) on the meaning of what we do and say, as well as seek the views of mentors about the meaning of what has happened in our lives—steps to achieve distance, an etic view of what happened and why it happened. The use of explicit tools, including survey forms designed and used explicitly by the RI to interview herself and others, as well as the additional tools described in Chapter 6, is more likely to result in achieving a useful etic view than is adopting Holbrook's (2004, p. 13) emic-is-enough assumption (e.g., "I assume that my own introspections resonate so strongly with the photos taken by my grandfather because ATH [Holbrook's grandfather] has, in effect, captured the essence of my own subjective personal introspection-based recollections").

Along with the RI asking herself the same multiple sets of questions on different days (e.g., see Cox (1967) regarding the process being examined in the study), the interviewing of other persons involved directly in the process as well as insider auditors is likely to always improve researcher introspections. The following views by Weick (1995) and Allport (1985) as well as Hirschman's principles for humanistic inquiry are rationales for this suggestion. Those who forget that "sensemaking" is a social process miss a constant substrate that shapes interpretations and interpreting. Conduct is contingent on the conduct of others, whether those others are imagined or physically present (Weick, 1995). Social psychology is "an attempt to understand and explain how the thought, feeling, and behavior of individuals are influenced by the actual, imagined, or implied presence of others" (Allport, 1985, p. 3).

Of course, the intention is not to generalize from one RI case study to many consumers. The specific findings are applicable only to the RI. However, the two core propositions are confirmed by the findings that (CP_1) the decision process examined includes recognizable phases involving several persons participating in one or more phases with conscious and unconscious thoughts/motives affecting their beliefs and actions, and that one or all of the participants are unable to consciously explain the causes of specific milestone sub-decisions occurring in the process (CP_2). Relating to the purchase process such as the selection of a university to attend for a three- or four-year degree, one or more phases of the process likely includes substantial conscious effort and much of the thinking involved, but not all, can be retrieved within a researcher introspective study. Such seemingly intuitive propositions need confirmation and extension by additional research before concluding that they are obviously valid. Heretofore, the fact that whether to buy a major retail service, or whether to attend university, can be a convergence process instead of being *a* decision (Langley *et al.*'s model 4 in organizational decision-making) has received scant attention in the service marketing literature.

PART III

CUSTOMER ASSOCIATE-TO-VENDOR (STORE) RETRIEVAL RESEARCH

7

CUSTOMER AUTOMATIC THINKING AND STORE CHOICE: WHY ASKING CUSTOMERS TO THINK ABOUT A NAMED STORE IS A MISTAKE

Synopsis

This chapter offers a two-step model of how customers select brands and shop at stores that they are familiar with: first, they focus on framing a shopping problem/opportunity. Second, they retrieve a few benefit-to-brand (or benefit-to-store) linkages relevant to the frame in their working memories. Such thinking and problem solving is usually done automatically, without effort. Empirically, the chapter demonstrates models of automatic customer benefit-to-store thoughts that explain store choice and similar models that explain store rejection.

INTRODUCTION: USEFUL MODELS OF CUSTOMER AUTOMATIC THINKING RELATED TO STORE CHOICE

This chapter offers theory, research methods, and findings on models of customer thinking that accurately predict shopping behavior among stores familiar to the customer. While the theory and method apply to brand and store choice, as well as consumer and industrial customers, this chapter focuses on store choice.

Asking what customers think of a given store may be a mistake. For example, the research method of asking a customer to rate competitors' stores for several store features or shopping benefits includes several questionable assumptions: (1) the customer thinks about a given store; (2) the customer thinks about the store features and benefits used in the ratings; (3) the customer selects and rejects stores based on some decision calculus based on the ratings. Because many customers may rarely retrieve the name of a given marketer's store (or brand) when thinking about a shopping problem, and may not focus their attention on reviewing a memory data file of benefits by stores, collection and analysis of such ratings data often lead to incorrect conclusions about the image of each competing store. For many customers, a marketer's store may not have an image in the minds of customers. Some of these customers may be aware of the store name if asked an aided question, but they never retrieve the store name from their memories when thinking about a relevant buying problem. Evidently, marketers of the V-8 brand of vegetable drink recognized such a scenario. Thus, the promotional message, "Oh, I could have had a V-8!" When the V-8 brand name is mentioned, many customers report recalling the brand name, but they do not access the brand name when thinking about beverage selections in different consumption situations. Thus, the "Oh [no]," and the past-tense, "could have had," indicate that the consumer is disappointed in herself for not retrieving V-8 from her long-term memory when thinking about choices for consuming a beverage. Using meta-analyses and literature reviews, researchers of ratings-based models of store and brand choice have concluded that the results from empirical models of customer choice based on attribute/benefit ratings are disappointing (see Lindquist, 1975; Corstjens and Doyle, 1989). In a meta-analysis of 26 studies using multi-attribute/attitude models to predict brand choice, Grunert (1988) found low association between attitude and behavior. Several researchers (Cohen, 1966; Fazio, 1986; Fazio, Powell, and Herr, 1983; Fazio, Powell, and William, 1989; Holden and Lutz, 1992; Woodside and Trappey, 1992a, 1992b; Holden, 1993) have emphasized the need to measure customer memory accessibilities of possible solutions (i.e., stores or brands) when focusing attention on a buying or a consuming frame (e.g., a buying problem, such as daily food shopping). Among customers experienced with buying and using some brands in a product category, their first-order brand access from memory has been postulated and found to be a critical determinant of brand choice (Fazio *et al.*, 1989). Grunert (1988) points out that the vast majority of consumer decisions are in fact not based on conscious thinking, what he identifies as "strategic cognitive processing." He emphasizes that a lot of information processing is unconscious, "retrieval of information from long-term memory into working memory is unconscious," it occurs automatically when a consumer focuses attention on a buying frame and micro-elements in the frame, such as benefits retrieved when thinking about the buying frame. We refer to such unconscious thinking as automatic cognitive processing.

For buying frames consumers have experienced and consequently store, alternative solutions (e.g., store names), and benefits experienced in their memories, asking what associates (e.g., benefits, features, buying frames) evoke which solutions automatically may be useful for modeling both choice and rejection of competing stores. Some associate-to-store retrievals act as cues relevant to the buying or consuming selection frame. That is, we can model store choice as a function of the specific benefit-to-store evocations.

"Consequently, an important priority is to investigate what are the cue con-
stellations that instigate purchase and/or use of a specific brand [store]"
(Holden and Lutz, 1992, p. 106). In modeling customer loyalty to a brand or
store, Dick and Basu (1994, p. 102) define and emphasize the importance of
accessibility by "the ease with which an attitude can be retrieved from memory. The strength of association between an attitude object and its evaluation
influences the accessibility of the attitude. Accessibility may be viewed in
terms of a continuum, ranging from unretrievable to a well-learned attitude
so highly accessible that it will be activated *automatically* upon encountering
the attitude object (italics in original)." Here, we emphasize the importance
of beginning with having the consumer first encounter (focus on) the evaluation (e.g., benefit) to learn which attitude object (e.g., store) is retrieved automatically. Thus, research to learn benefit-to-object retrievals may extend and
deepen the value of research for store and brand names for different categories, for example, supermarkets, department stores, mail order firms, soft
drinks, brands of cereals. This proposal provides an operational step to
achieve customer loyalty as proposed by Jacoby and Chestnut (1978, p. 32),
"If brand loyalty is ever to be managed, not just measured, it will have to be
elaborated in a much more detailed description of cognitive activities"
[micro-understanding of choice versus macro models of behavior]. Learning
benefit-to-store retrievals and their linkages to store choice provides such
detailed description.

A SUMMARY OF PROPOSITIONS FOR MODELING CUSTOMER BENEFIT-TO-STORE RETRIEVALS AND PRIMARY STORE CHOICE

Several propositions follow from benefit-to-store retrieval models of store
choice. The persons and supermarkets depicted in Figure 7-1 are used to
illustrate the propositions. Note that three competing supermarkets are
included in Figure 7-1; each store promotes itself as offering the lowest prices
(a common occurrence) but differs in its constellation of benefits promoted.
For example, Alpha's strategy includes the attempt to position the store in
customers' minds as the most convenient location (MCL); Beta and Gamma
stores do not include MCL as part of their positioning strategies.

P_1: a customer can access a store name automatically from memory,
when asked for the store name that first comes to mind for a specific bit of
information, such as a benefit. For example, in Figure 7-1, when "best quality of meat" (BM) is mentioned, Günther retrieves supermarket Alpha. Note
that BM is part of Alpha's promotional message in positioning this store in
the minds of customers; such a match between a benefit-to-store retrieval and
positioning strategy does not always occur. P_2: for periodic shopping needs
(e.g., daily or stocking-up food shopping) a customer can access a store name
automatically as her or his primary store, that is, the store shopped most

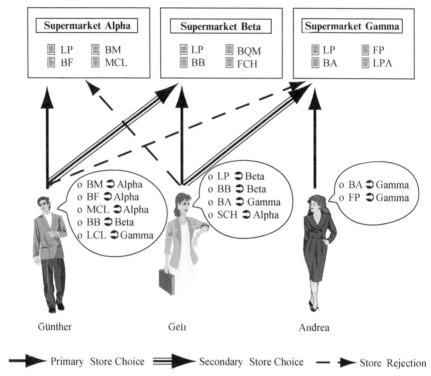

FIGURE 7.1   Model of customer store choice. LP, lowest price; BF, Best quality of fruits; BM, Best quality of meat; BB, Best quality of bakery; BQM, Best quality of merchandise; FP, Friendliest personnel; FCH, Fastest checkout; SCH, Slowest checkout; MCL, Most convenient location; LCL, Least convenient location; LPA, Largest parking area; BA, Biggest assortment.

frequently. For example, the three shoppers in Figure 7-1 are each shown to retrieve different stores as their primary stores. Günther has identified Alpha as his primary store (in later questioning in a telephone survey after first collecting benefit-to-store retrievals for which several stores have been named). In store research in the United States, Fulgoni and Eskin (1983) have reported that most shoppers change their primary supermarket store one or more times each year. To reduce possible bias of benefit-to-store retrievals on customers naming their primary store, momentarily clearing the focus of customers on naming stores is advised when collecting data on primary store choice, additional stores shopped, and information on stores customers would not shop. Asking demographic and open-ended questions on benefits sought might be done between asking questions on benefit-to-store retrievals and store choice and rejection questions.

P_3: some customers' benefit-to-store retrievals are associated with their primary store choice. For example, in Figure 7-1 Geli retrieves her primary store, Beta, for LP and BB. For food shopping, Andrea thinks about biggest assortment and friendliest personnel and she retrieves Gamma store for these benefits; Gamma is her primary store. Tigert (1983) refers to "hot buttons" when he emphasizes these points: a customer views her primary store as superior on at least one benefit she thinks about when shopping; a relatively small number of benefits are likely to drive the store choice process (also, see Alpert, 1971).

P_4: each competing store has a unique configuration of a few dominant, associate-to-store retrievals linked with its selection as primary store. Note in Figure 7-1 that Günther retrieves his primary store for three benefits; Geli retrieves her primary store for two benefits; and Andrea retrieves her primary store for two benefits.

A consumer may be unable to retrieve any store name for the benefits not relevant for her store selections, that is, some attitudes are not well-learned because (1) the consumer focuses attention rarely on these linkages or (2) a supermarket strategy does not include attempts to create such linkages.

P_5: some benefit to store retrievals are not associated to customers' primary store choices. For example, note that best quality of merchandise (BQM) does not result in a store retrieval for any of the three shoppers, even though BQM is used in the positioning strategy by Beta. Customers should be coached to report that, "none comes to mind" is sometimes the most appropriate answer when researching benefit-to-store retrievals. Response latency measures may indicate weak linkage for a benefit-to-store response, for example, an immediate naming of a store for lowest prices (LP) may indicate a stronger LP-store attitude than the same response given after a four-second delay (see Fazio, 1989).

P_6: a customer has associate-to-store retrievals not only for their primary store but also for competing stores; a customer shops sometimes at one or more of these competing stores. For example, in Figure 7-1 for different benefits Günther retrieves all three stores. Notice that he identifies a secondary store where he occasionally shops, Beta. His benefit-to-store retrievals include BB-to-Beta; later in the interview he confirms that Beta is a store he sometimes shops. Additional open-ended questions can be used to confirm that he buys bakery products from Beta.

P_7: for some customers' benefit-to-store retrievals for negatively worded evaluations are linked to store rejection. In Figure 7-1 both Günther and Geli retrieve store names for negative evaluations; these two shoppers identify stores they "would not shop at." Andrea reported, "none come to mind" for not shopping. Learning negative evaluations linked with a store is useful for identifying likely causes of store rejection. David Wing, managing director of Retail Advisors in Seattle, points out, "A business owner has to listen to what the customers aren't saying. The most important person in the store is someone who didn't buy anything...He means that there is crucial information to be gathered from customers who walk by a store or who come in but walk out without making a purchase" (Dauten, 1996; see also Spiggle and Sewall, 1987).

P_8: store retrievals for negative evaluated attributes sometimes contribute to predicting primary store choice of a given store. For example, in Figure 7-1, Günther's LCL-to-Gamma retrieval may be associated with his primary store choice of Alpha. Thus, seemingly unrelated regression analysis of store choice may be useful for learning how customers' negatively worded benefit-to-store retrievals of competing stores help gain primary customers for another store (see Woodside and Trappey, 1992b).

P_9: different benefit-to-store retrievals and primary stores sometimes occur for different problem frames. In Figure 7-2 two problem frames are posed to Günther, Normaleinkauf (German for food shopping for daily needs) and Vorratseinkauf (shopping for stocking up the pantry). Thus, when Günther thinks about Vorratseinkauf he automatically thinks about BA–Beta, LP–Beta, and LPA–Beta, and then driving in his car to Beta. For Normaleinkauf, a different set of benefit-to-store retrievals come to mind for Günther; a few of the retrievals in this second set are associated with Alpha being his primary store for Normaleinkauf.

Note in Figure 7-2 that the store selected for Vorratseinkauf by Günther is the same store he rejects for Normaleinkauf. The most important point related to Figure 7-2 is that whether a store is a customer's primary store choice or a store rejected may depend on the problem framed when questioning the customer.

TESTING SOME OF THE PROPOSITIONS

Correlation analyses and both ordinary least squares (OLS) and logistic regression models may be used to examine the propositions. Given that the dependent variable of primary store choice is constrained to the values of 0 and 1 for a given store being named versus not named, logistic regression analysis is preferred over OLS regression because the predicted values for primary choice is constrained within the range of 0 to 1 and OLS regression is not so constrained. By using logistic regression analysis, other measurement assumptions are not violated (see Menard 1995). However, using either OLS or logistic regression methods results in very similar findings for R^2 and relative importance (betas) of predictors.

In Figure 7-3 summaries are provided for Normaleinkauf of two OLS regression models (betas and R^2 related to primary shopping at Alpha). The data are from a large-scale telephone survey of supermarket shoppers in a metropolitan area located in western Austria (for details of the method of

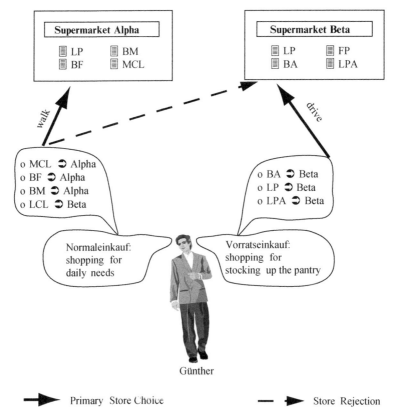

FIGURE 7.2 Two problems for thinking and store choice. LP, Lowest price, BF, Best quality of fruits; BM, Best quality of meat; MCL, Most convenient location; LCL, Least convenient location; FP, Friendliest personnel; BA, Biggest assortment; LPA, Largest parking area.

this study, see Thelen and Woodside, 1997). The names of the stores are disguised for competitive reasons.

The model for primary store choice of Alpha is shown on the left in Figure 7-3; the model includes the responses of the total sample from 401 shoppers: 141 identified Alpha as their primary store and 260 did not. For customers primarily shopping at Alpha (n = 141), the model for Beta being a secondary store is shown on the right: nine of these customers identified Beta as a secondary store. Alpha dominates in being named for benefit-to-store retrievals by over 50 percent of its primary shoppers for four benefits: MCL, BA, LP, and BQM. This finding indicates the store's realized positioning, not necessarily planned positioning, in customers' minds. Some additional benefit-to-store retrievals are associated with Alpha being the primary store:

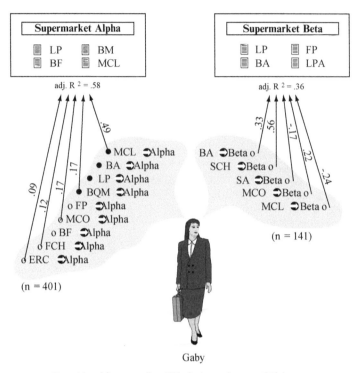

● = retrieved from more than 50% of primary shoppers of Alpha
o = retrieved from less than 50% of primary shoppers of Alpha

FIGURE 7.3 Normaleinkauf (shopping for daily needs) of primary shoppers at primary choice store (Alpha) and secondary choice store (Beta). LP, Lowest price; BF, Best quality of fruits; BM, Best quality of meat; MCL, Most convenient location; BA, Biggest assortment; FP, Friendliest personnel; LPA, Largest parking area; BQM, Best quality of merchandise; FCH, Fastest checkout; ERC, Easiest to reach by car; SCH, Slowest checkout; SA, Smallest assortment; MCO, Most convenient opening hours.

MCO, FCH, and ERC, even though most of Alpha's primary customers do not retrieve Alpha's names for these benefits. Thus, the MCO/Alpha linkage may be viewed as an important contributing factor for gaining primary customers for Alpha.

MODELING STORE REJECTION

In a model with four independent variables, worst-quality merchandise linked to Gamma retrieval was found to influence Gamma's being identified as the store rejected by shoppers. When Gamma was retrieved for lowest prices, rejection was reduced (Beta = −.13). Models of store rejection result in low, but significant, levels of explained variance. The adjusted R^2 was .11 (p < .05) for the model for Gamma. Rationale: customers more often retrieve and strengthen benefit-to-store retrievals because such retrievals help solve buying problems. Although thinking about where not to shop and shortcomings-to-store retrievals is useful, the need for shopping still remains to be solved.

CONCLUSIONS AND STRATEGY IMPLICATIONS

Modeling primary store choice and store rejection based on customer benefit-to-store retrievals offers a useful approach for understanding choice. Such measurements appear to relate closely to how customers go about thinking and making choices for repetitive buying problems. Research on automatic benefit-to-store and benefit-to-brand retrievals builds directly on the pioneering work of Axelrod (1968) and Haley and Case (1979); these researchers demonstrated that product category–to-brand retrievals that first come to mind are accurate predictors of brand choice. Further testing of the associate-to-object retrieval method for additional categories of stores, as well as for brands, is warranted.

8

AUTOMATIC THINKING AND VENDOR CHOICES BY CUSTOMERS OF INDUSTRIAL DISTRIBUTORS: MAPPING CUSTOMERS' VENDOR MIND POSITIONS

Synopsis

This chapter probes the accuracy of the following mental model: "I know what our customers think about us, our products, and our brands. No research on customers' perceptions is necessary. Just ask me if you have a question." The chapter describes the concept of the vendor mind position (VMP) and offers an empirical application of the concept among industrial buyers of maintenance, repairs, and operating (MRO) supplies. The VMP concept relates to the evoked set concept in the consumer information processing literature. An index of a global measure of VMP (a summary empirical measure of an industrial distributor's position in the minds of MRO buyers) is proposed. The results of an exploratory study applying the supplier mind position (SMP) index are reviewed. The findings support the proposition that VMP relates positively with the share of MRO requirements awarded to MRO suppliers. The chapter closes with steps beneficial for marketing executives to check on the accuracy of their views on what customers think about vendors and the products and services being offered by these vendors.

INTRODUCTION: OVERCOMING OUR HIGHLY INACCURATE BELIEFS

Gilovich (1991) begins his book by quoting Artemus Ward: "It ain't so much the things that we don't know that gets us into trouble. It's the things we know that just ain't so." Gilovich's book shows many examples of highly inaccurate views often held tenaciously by executives. "It seems that the process of interpretation is so reflexive and immediate that we often overlook it. This combined with the widespread assumption that there is but one objective reality, is what may lead people to overlook the possibility that others may be responding to a very different situation" (Gilovich, 1991, p. 117). Most of us likely fall prey to believing that our views about what others think are highly accurate. Consequently, Weick (1995) stresses a relevant issue: what can we do to overcome our inherent bias in our own skills in "sensemaking"—for example, in assuming that what we believe about customer thinking must be true?

Possibly a useful first step is to think aloud our views about an issue— what do we take for granted as being true, as well as false, about certain categories of customers for example. Then, we might ask (i.e., probe, verify, confirm, disconfirm) these views by asking others (e.g., a few customers in different categories, for example, loyal customers to nonbuying customers) to tell what they know about the issue. To avoid "sponsor identity bias," this step might best be done by not divulging your own views to the persons who you talk to—for example, having questions asked to customers by a third party without divulging a particular view held by you or the name of the firm sponsoring such a study.

This chapter provides details of an example of such a study comparing an executive's perceptions about customer beliefs with customers' own beliefs. The research setting focuses on industrial distribution and buying of MRO products in the United States. The chapter provides useful tools for improving accuracy in "sensemaking."

Detailed profiles are now available of the marketing activities of industrial distributors (e.g., Narus and Anderson, 1986; Hlavacek and McCuistion, 1983; Keysuk, 2002; Mudambi and Aggarwal, 2003). In 2004 most industrial distributors are small enterprises with sales of less than $30 million, employing fewer than 20 people full-time; at the high sales end, the top ten industrial distributors in the U.S. had total sales of $23 billion (see Mudambi and Aggarwal, 2003). Data from the 1997 *Census of Wholesales Trades* (*http://www.census.gov/epcd/www/97EC42.HTM*) shows that average sales for all industrial distributors were $24 million in 1997. The average number of employees per firm was 18 and the average number of salespersons for all industrial distributors was 5.8.

For MRO supplies, the large-sales-volume customers of industrial distributors have substantially higher sales volume and number of employees than their industrial distributor suppliers. Most MRO supply buyers in large industrial plants (100+ employees and shipments valued at more than $100 million) have more than 100 industrial distributors as current suppliers. MRO supplies typically account for 80 percent of materials normally considered for inventory, but only 20 percent or less of the dollar value of inventory investment. Rarely does any one industrial distributor provide more than 20 percent of the total MRO supply requirements of a large industrial plant.

However, if the 80-20 principle holds, most of an industrial firm's MRO purchase requirements are supplied by a limited number of industrial distributors (e.g., "Are You Purchasing MRO Supplies?," Anonymous, 1986).

Most industrial distributors view their industry as intensely competitive, as many companies attempt to gain a substantial share of the MRO supply requirements of the relatively small number of medium to large manufacturing plants in their geographic markets (Narus and Anderson, 1986).

In nearly all U.S. industrial firms, purchasing responsibilities are divided into two areas: (1) raw materials, component parts, and packaging and (2) MRO items. Usually separate buying departments are assigned to each of these areas of responsibility. When purchasing is centralized in large industrial firms with several industrial plants, at least one raw material/component parts buyer and one MRO supply buyer are usually assigned buying responsibilities at each plant location (Woodside and Samuels, 1980). This chapter describes and applies a summary measure of the effectiveness of industrial distributors' "sensemaking" in marketing MRO supplies.

Prior research findings reported for consumer products indicate that first brand awareness, measured by asking, "What brands first come to mind when you think about buying product category X?" is a sensitive, stable, and accurate predictor of purchase and share-of-purchase among competing brands (e.g., Axelrod, 1968). If true for industrial marketing applications, customer first-brand-, or supplier-, awareness may be a useful predictor of the relative share of requirements awarded to competing suppliers.

The concept "vendor mind position" is used here to indicate the specific awareness position of a supplier in the minds of customers. For example, one group of industrial customers might mention supplier X first using an unaided-awareness question, another group might mention supplier X second, and so on. Some customers are likely to not mention supplier X at all. This last VMP customer segment would be most likely to assign supplier X the lowest share of their MRO requirements, compared to those who do mention the supplier in answering the unaided-awareness question. Most industrial distributors marketing MRO supplies are unaware of the share of a customer's purchasing requirements they have been awarded by specific customers; most customers view this information as confidential (Berkowitz, 1986; Gorman, 1971).

A THEORY OF AUTOMATICALLY MENTALLY CATEGORIZING VENDORS BY B2B CUSTOMERS

"Routinized response behavior (RRB)" (Howard, 1977) likely represents most industrial MRO supply customers' thinking. The decision process and buying behavior for MRO items follow routine patterns—RRB involves no search to find new vendors. MRO buyers are on a first-name basis with a few well-known "inside" (telephone) and "outside" salespersons (Narus and Anderson, 1986). Outside sales reps have pre-determined sales call routes; they call on the same customers once per week or once every other week. Outside sales reps usually have the additional responsibility of making a few (i.e., one to five) cold calls per week.

Exceptions to this general pattern of behavior can be observed; for example, an MRO supply buyer may prefer to buy 30 percent or more of her/his requirements from a distant industrial distributor whose outside sales rep calls once per month.

Given that individual MRO items are often purchased monthly or weekly from the same group of industrial distributors, the buying process tends to become routine. Similar buyer/seller interactions, decision rules, and behaviors (supplier choices) are likely to occur from one week, or one month, to the next.

Thus, Howard's (1963, 1977) concept of evoked set (i.e., alternatives being considered by a decision maker) is likely to apply for MRO suppliers. Here the evoked set refers to the subset of MRO suppliers a buyer considers buying from—out of the set of suppliers the buyer is aware to be available. Campbell (1969) was the first to examine the evoked set concept empirically; he found that the mean evoked set for toothpaste was 3.1 and 5.0 for laundry detergents. Other researchers report that unaided awareness sets, that is, all of the brands that come to mind, are between two to three times larger than buyers' evoked sets (e.g., see Jarvis and Wilcox, 1974; Brisoux, 1980; Lapersonne, Laurent, and Le Goff, 1995; Narayana and Markin, 1976; Thompson and Cooper, 1979; Woodside and Sherrell, 1977).

Several researchers have expanded on Howard's (1963; 1977) original contribution, by suggesting "inert and inept sets" of alternatives (brands or suppliers). The inert set includes those vendors the buyer is aware of, but has insufficient information to evaluate (Narayana and Markin, 1975). The inept set consists of those alternatives the buyer has rejected from purchase consideration, due to either unsatisfactory prior experience, or negative word-of-mouth from other sources (Narayana and Markin, 1975). Brisoux and Laroche (1980, 1981) proposed the "foggy set" as the alternatives not completely processed by buyers; the buyer does not have a clear idea of the alternatives for a number of possible reasons (not enough information is available for the buyer to evaluate the alternatives).

Sherif et al.'s (1965) social judgment theory may be used to explain the evoked set proposition that buyers consider only a limited number of alternatives in their awareness set. Three states of nature are proposed in social judgment theory: the latitudes of acceptance, rejection, and noncommitment. The latitude of acceptance is the position on an issue (or toward a supplier) that is most satisfactory, along with other satisfactory positions on the same issue. The latitude of rejection is the most objectionable position on the issue, plus other objectionable positions. "There remains the possibility that there are positions which the individual neither accepts nor rejects (toward which he prefers to remain noncommittal in his overt reaction)," describes the latitude of noncommitment. This includes those positions not categorized as acceptable or objectionable in some degree (see Sherif *et al.*, 1965).

Myers (1979) proposes a phasing model to explain what heuristics buyers apply in deciding which alternatives (brands or suppliers) are included in their evoked set. He suggests that buyers use one of the noncompensatory rules, for example, conjunctive or disjunctive, to divide alternatives into acceptable and unacceptable categories. The evoked set of acceptable alternatives is then evaluated using a compensatory decision rule to further divide the alternatives into chosen and not chosen alternatives. This phased-rule proposition has been supported empirically in industrial buying behavior research (Crow *et al.*, 1980; Moore, 1969; Vyas and Woodside, 1983).

An industrial buyer is likely to use a limited number of cut-off rules in deciding if a distributor is a viable candidate for inclusion in the buyer's evoked set of MRO suppliers. These cut-off rules are likely to include the following: (1) include only if the industrial distributor carries a substantial number of approved manufacturer product lines, (2) include only if the distributor's delivery performance record is good to excellent, and (3) include only if the distributor's sales rep is known to keep his/her price, product line, and delivery promises. Given that several (five to ten) distributors meet or surpass these cut-off levels, the buyer may use a compensatory decision rule to award shares of the MRO supply requirements to two to four suppliers (the chosen set of vendors for a specific MRO item); most buyers prefer to use two to four suppliers in routine response buying situations (Vyas and Woodside, 1983; Woodside and Möller, 1992).

Thus, conceptualizing several VMPs among MRO supply buyers is useful (see Figure 8-1). The chosen set D_7 in Figure 8-1 is part of the evoked set (D_6) of suppliers that an MRO buyer considers when deciding on suppliers with which to place orders. Based on prior research by Wilson (1981) on consumer behavior and by Corey (1978, 1989), Woodside and Vyas (1983), and Moore (1969) on industrial buying behavior, the chosen mindset of MRO suppliers is limited; usually there are two to three suppliers for most purchases of an MRO item within a given time period (one year or less).

The evoked set is likely to include five, plus or minus two, suppliers for most MRO items. That is, the MRO buyer is likely to consider a limited number of possible suppliers when actively choosing an MRO supplier. Research findings in psychology (Bruner *et al.*, 1959), decision theory (Simon, 1974), and industrial buying behavior (Woodside and Möller, 1986) support the proposition that humans actively consider about five alternatives in choice making. Decision-makers mentally determine the minimum acceptance levels of a few choice criteria (such as product quality and delivery), and ask themselves which four or five suppliers are available that meet or surpass these minimum levels. The "magic number" may be five (Miller, 1956), representing the number of alternatives most decision makers can process easily; the

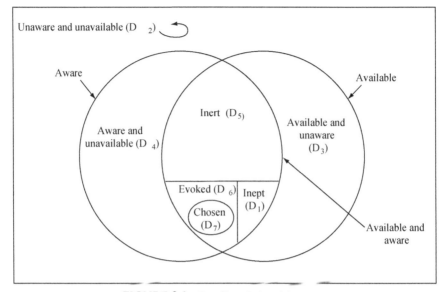

FIGURE 8.1 Supplier mind position map.

number considered may be slightly higher in some situations. Thus, seven suppliers may be considered if the decision maker is instructed to "give maximum attention" to the decision task.

Wilson (1981) hypothesizes that buyers do not divide their purchases equally among the two or three alternatives in their chosen set. The first alternative considered will be purchased or preferred more often than the second or third. Wilson (1981), Axelrod (1968), and Woodside and Wilson (1985) have confirmed this proposition for consumer products and services. If this holds for MRO supply buying behavior, the shares-of-requirements among MRO suppliers in a buyer's chosen set will be unequal and the first supplier considered will most often receive a larger share of the purchase requirements than the second or third supplier considered.

A few suppliers may be considered often, but rarely used. That is, one to three suppliers may be retrieved when a buyer considers a specific MRO item, but they are rarely given a purchase order (D_6 but not D_7).

Industrial MRO supply buyers are usually able to identify several additional suppliers if prompted to recall others in addition to those mentioned when they are asked to name the vendors they would consider when buying MRO supplies. These additional vendors are shown as the inert set of suppliers (D_5) in Figure 8-1. The buyer knows these vendors are available, but is unlikely to consider them in a specific buying situation. Vendors in a buyer's inert mental set may receive a few "emergency" orders, but are unlikely to receive a substantial share of the buyer's MRO supply requirements. The inert set is analogous to the "foggy set" proposed by Brisoux (1980) and Laroche *et al.* (1982). The buyer may be biased toward reducing effort by limiting the alternatives considered to a number that includes one or two satisfactory suppliers. This proposition has been referred to as the "principle of information parsimony" (Haines, 1974). Given a limited amount of time (Wright, 1980) and the need to solve several buying problems daily, an MRO supply buyer is unlikely to actively consider all the suppliers that he/she knows are available.

A limited number of MRO suppliers may be actively rejected from consideration (D_1 in Figure 8-1) based on poor performance, high prices, inappropriate product lines, or negative word of mouth from MRO users in the buyer's plant. Vendors in a buyer's inept set are unlikely to receive a share of a buyer's MRO supply requirements, and face the difficult task of changing the buyer's perceptions.

A buyer may be unaware of certain MRO vendors who consider the buyer's plant to be a potential customer (D_1 in Figure 8-1). Alternatively, the buyer may be aware of a group of vendors that he/she considers to be unavailable (D_4 in Figure 8-1) because of such factors as geographic location or company policies on reciprocity. Finally, vendors may be identified that are unavailable and unfamiliar to the MRO supply buyer—for example, industrial distributors in nearby market areas who are planning on expanding their market coverage, shown as D_2 in Figure 8-1.

Propositions

The following propositions were formulated based upon the insights and literature review presented in the previous discussion.

P_1: The position of an MRO supply vendor in an industrial buyer's mind (or VMP) measured by unaided recall is related positively to the share of requirements awarded to that vendor. The first MRO supplier mentioned by the industrial buyer in unaided recall receives a greater share of the buyer's MRO supply requirements than the second or additional vendors mentioned by the buyer. That is, supplier awareness that first comes to mind is a sensitive predictor of the share of requirements awarded to a supplier.

P_2: Industrial MRO supply buyers can readily identify a set of vendors they are aware of and consider to be available, but who are not actively considered when buying MRO items (an inert set of vendors).

P_3: Industrial MRO supply buyers can readily identify a set of vendors they will include in an inept set of vendors, that is, the buyers definitely will not award a share of their MRO requirements to this vendor. P_4: Industrial MRO supply buyers are likely to use noncompensatory decision rules in deciding which vendors to include in their evoked, inept, and chosen sets. P_5: An MRO vendor's perception of his/her firm's consideration set location in his/her customers' minds is likely to be more positive than the customers' actual perceptions.

Ego-defense may be a relevant rationale for P_5; a general tendency to overestimate the share of customer requirements being received may exist among MRO suppliers. "Since they buy from us, we must be an important supplier for them compared to other vendors," may be part of a supplier's thought process related to current customers.

P_6: An MRO vendor's perception of his/her firm's consideration set location among potential but not current customers is likely to be more positive than these MRO supply buyers' evaluations of the vendor. If P_6 is supported, the rationale proposed for P_5 may be relevant. By believing that customers and potential customers think highly of the vendor's firm, the vendor is able to maintain a positive self-image.

Method

The informants in the study were twenty industrial buyers responsible for MRO supply purchases in twenty manufacturing plants of twenty different enterprises. Each buyer's office was located at a manufacturing site. The following conditions were specified in selecting buyers to be included in the study; the buyer had to be in personal (face-to-face or telephone) contact with two or more MRO suppliers on a daily basis; the buyer had to have the authority of final approval of supplier selection for MRO supplies; the buyer had to be a member of the Purchasing Management Association of the Carolinas and Virginia (PMA-CV), a regional chapter of the National Association of Purchasing Management; and the buyer had to be a current or potential customer of a small industrial distributor located in a southeastern state.

The president of PMA-CV, Erwin Lewis, Wellman Industries, agreed to support the study by serving as a reference if the informants had questions concerning the study. The owner and chief executive officer of an MRO supply distributorship located in the southeastern region of the United States was contacted; he agreed to cooperate in the study by providing the names of manufacturing firms (and MRO supply buyers when possible), which were customers or potential customers located within a 50-mile radius of the CEO's distributorship. The study was described to the participants as a research project to learn how manufacturing plants purchase MRO supplies. The specific concepts and propositions on supplier categorization strategies by MRO supply buyers were not explained to the participants, Mr. Lewis, or the CEO prior to data collection.

The PMA-CV member firms in the geographic area were matched with lists of current customers and identified potential customers of the industrial distributor. The industrial distributors' 12 largest customers who were member firms in PMA-CV were selected for the study. An additional 14 manufacturing firms that were members of PMA-CV and not current customers of the industrial distributor cooperating in the study were also selected. The PMA-CV member selected for the study included electrical utilities, chemical manufacturers, light machinery manufacturers, paper mills, control panel manufacturers, food equipment manufacturers, sealing product manufacturers, and farm equipment manufacturers. Most firms had more than 100 full-time employees and more than $200 million of shipments.

Procedure

Each MRO supply buyer selected to be interviewed was contacted initially by letter. For six manufacturing firms, the MRO buyer was not known initially; telephone calls to the plants were used to identify these MRO supply buyers by name. The initial letter included a brief explanation of the purpose of the study and requested the MRO supply buyer's cooperation. A follow-up telephone call to arrange a personal interview was mentioned in the letter.

Personal face-to-face interviews were arranged with 10 current and 10 potential customers of the industrial distributor participating in the study. The interviews were held in the MRO buyers' offices. Most interviews were completed in 50 to 90 minutes. Participants were assured by letter and at the start of the interview that the names of the buyers and their firms would be identified by letter code only and not by name in the study.

A few preliminary questions were asked concerning how the buying function for MRO items versus raw materials and component parts was organized. Then, the MRO supply buyers were requested to answer a series of questions about their firms' MRO supply requirements, e.g., what major and other categories of MRO items were purchased. To measure awareness that first came to mind of MRO suppliers, the buyers were asked, "Among all the suppliers and vendors you might know of, who first comes to mind when you think about MRO suppliers?" "What other suppliers or vendors also come to mind when you think about MRO suppliers?" was asked after the buyer's response to the first question was recorded. Each respondent was then prompted once to continue to identify "additional MRO suppliers that might come to mind."

The buyers were then asked, "When you think about your current MRO suppliers, what supplier first comes to mind?" "What one, two, three, or other, current MRO suppliers come to mind?" was the next question. These questions were the operational measures used for learning the buyer's evoked set of MRO suppliers. Nearly all of the buyers participating in the study mentioned the location, product lines carried, a sales rep's name, a brief evaluation, or a brief buying experience with one or more of the MRO suppliers identified during this part of the interview. Each participant was then requested to "provide a brief description" about each MRO supplier the participant identified as MRO supply vendors in the previous questions. The buyers were asked if they evaluated the vendors using a numerical rating procedure. Examples of the buyers' formal vendor evaluations were requested; however, none of the MRO buyers reported using a numerical rating system by their suppliers.

Each buyer was then asked, "What MRO suppliers might come to mind that you would be unlikely to buy from?" This question was the operational measure used to learn the MRO suppliers in the buyer's inept set. Among the 20 buyers participating in the study, five refused to name a specific MRO supply vendor by name, but most identified specific vendors. All 20 buyers reported being able to identify one or more MRO suppliers they would be unlikely to buy from. The buyers were then asked what "thoughts first come to mind about each of the MRO vendors you would be unlikely to buy from?"

To gain more information on the buyers' perceptions of the specific industrial distributor cooperating in the study, buyers were asked at the end of the interview if they knew of any MRO suppliers in a nearby city if they had not identified this distributor by name in response to the previous questions. After this question was answered, 19 of the 20 buyers identified the cooperating distributorship by name at some point during the interview.

Information on the annual total-dollar requirements for MRO supplies was then requested from each buyer for the most current completed fiscal year. Each buyer was asked to check written or computer records to confirm estimates of annual MRO purchases. A written record of the total dollar purchases from the buyers' list of MRO suppliers was requested for the same year; if total annual dollar amount by supplier was unavailable, each buyer was requested to estimate the current annual amount of MRO supply purchases (within $5,000 if possible) for each supplier the buyer had mentioned previously.

The buyers were also asked to estimate their current annual dollar requirements for MRO items, and how much they believed the current year requirements would change, if at all, from the previous year. The buyers were further asked whether current monthly records of purchases by MRO suppliers were available, and if they were, to report the dollar purchases for the largest suppliers (purchases greater than $10,000).

Pre-test

Survey questions were pre-tested on a group of five full-time industrial buyers. The buyers were part-time students enrolled in an evening graduate Master of Business Administration (MBA) program. These buyers were requested to respond to the supplier awareness questions and report the intended purpose of each question. Several modifications to the survey procedure were made following this pre-test. The value of prompting, "Do any other MRO suppliers in nearby cities come to mind?" in increasing the number of MRO suppliers in a buyer's awareness set became evident from the pre-test. The five buyers were interviewed individually in the pre-test.

During the pre-test each buyer was given a copy of the VMP map shown in Figure 8-1. The names and definitions of nine SMPs were given to each buyer on index cards. The names of the nine SMPs are listed in Tables 8-1 and 8-2. Each of the five buyers was requested to order the cards, from most preferred to least preferred locations. The buyers were asked to think aloud while they ordered the cards and studied the VMP map.

Kendall's coefficient of concordance (Siegel, 1956) was statistically significant (W = .99. p < .001) among the five buyers and nine SMPs. The buyers' rankings were in complete agreement except for D_2 (unaware and unavailable) and D_1 (inept set location). Of the buyers, two preferred D_1 over D_2. "It's better to be thought of than to start from scratch" was the rationale mentioned by one buyer for this ordering. However, three of them ordered D_2 as more preferred than D_1. "Once the definite decision is made not to use a supplier, he'll never get a part of my business," was an explanation given by one of these three buyers.

Finally, an attempt was made to develop approximate weights reflecting the perceived value of each SMP. The five buyers in the pre-test were asked to assign a value to each location on the SMP map, under the assumption that the value for the supplier mentioned first in the chosen set (D-) was equal to 10. Each buyer was asked to think aloud while assigning a value to the other SMPs. The buyer's value assignments varied only slightly for most SMPs, except that three buyers assigned negative values, −1, −3, and −4; and two buyers assigned +1 to the inept set location. Among the five buyers in the pre-test, at least three of them assigned a value of 8 to the chosen set-second mention location, and seven to the chosen set-third mention location.

Most buyers reported that clear breaks in value assignments should be made between suppliers in the chosen set and those in the evoked set—but not chosen locations; they assigned a weight of 5 to D_6 as shown in the third column of Tables 8-1 and 8-2.

Out of the five buyers, three assigned a value of 3 to the inert set location; two assigned a value of +4 to this location. All of the buyers weighted D_3, available but unaware, less than D_4, aware but unavailable. "A distributor I know could open a branch office nearby and I would be more ready to give him some business than someone local that I didn't already know about," is one rationale provided for this value assignment.

Based on the weights assigned and thought protocols provided by the five buyers in the pre-test, using the arbitrary starting point of assigning a weight of 10 points to the chosen set-first mentioned, values of 0 and −3 were assigned to the unaware unavailable and inept set locations, respectively. While not a true interval scale, the weights assigned for the VMPs may be useful for calculating a rough index of perceptions of different customer segments toward competing suppliers' mind positions. An index of a VMP for a given customer segment would equal the weighted average position assigned by a sample of customers, where VMP equals the weighted average mind position of supplier X in customer segment j.

TABLE 8-1 Supplier Mind Position (SMP) of Supplier X as Perceived by Customers Buying from Firm X and CEO X

D_i	SMP	Weight (W_i)	Customers' Perceptions	CEO X Perceptions
D_7	Chosen Set—First Mention	10	0	2
D_7	Chosen Set—Second Mention	8	0	4
D_7	Chosen Set—Third Mention	7	4	4
D_6	Evoked Set—Not Chosen/ Chosen Infrequently	5	4	0
			1	0
D_5	Inert	3	0	0
D_4	Aware and unavailable	2	0	0
D_3	Available and unaware	1	0	1
D_2	Unaware and unavailable	0	1	0
D_1	Inept	-3	4.8	8.0
	Average weighted response			

t = 3.94; d.f. = 9, p <.01, paired test

Paired sample, statistical significance test results

150

TABLE 8-2 Supplier Mind Position (SMP) of Supplier X as Perceived by Customers Not Buying from Firm X and CEO X

D_i	SMP	Weight (W_i)	Customers' Perceptions	CEO X Perceptions
D_7	Chosen Set—First Mention	10	0	0
D_7	Chosen Set—Second Mention	8	0	0
D_7	Chosen Set—Third Mention	7	0	0
D_6	Evoked Set—Not Chosen/	5	2	5
	Chosen Infrequently		4	3
D_5	Inert	3	0	2
D_4	Aware and unavailable	2	1	0
D_3	Available and unaware	1	0	0
D_2	Unaware and unavailable	0	3	0
D_1	Inept	–3		
	Average Weighted Response		1.4	3.8
	Paired sample, statistical significance test results			$t = 3.42$; d.f. $= 9$, $p < .01$, paired test

The VMP index was used to estimate the weighted average SMP among current customers and noncustomers of the industrial distributor participating in the study. The perceptions of the distributor's CEO on how samples of these two customer segments would locate his distributorship in their minds, versus the locations customers actually placed his distributorship in were compared using the VMP index.

FINDINGS

All 20 of the buyers surveyed reported that they expected little change in their total-dollar requirements for MRO supply items for the current year compared to the most recently completed fiscal year. The only changes expected were minor price increases in specific industries. All buyers were able to estimate the dollar amount of MRO supply purchases by major suppliers after consulting annual company records, or from memory. These purchases varied substantially by industry and value of shipments of buyers' manufacturing plants. To permit comparisons across the 20 participating manufacturing plants, the share of requirements was computed for each MRO supplier for each buyer. The reported annual dollar amount of MRO supply purchases from the supplier was divided by the total annual dollar requirements of the plant. This normalizing procedure is analogous to computing sales as a percent of all commodity volume (ACV); share of ACV is often used as a dependent measure in retailing experiments on the effects of price and advertising changes on sales (e.g., Eskin, 1975).

Findings for P$_1$

To test the first proposition, the average shares of requirements (SORs) awarded to the first three MRO vendors mentioned in the initial unaided recall questions were calculated. The average SORs were 20, 15, and 9 percent for first, second, and third VMPs, respectively. Using a treatment-by-informants design (Winer, 1971), the differences between average shares for the three SMPs were found to be statistically significant. An omega-squared estimate (Hays, 1972) indicates a substantial degree (Sawyer and Peter, 1983) of association between VMP and SOR awarded ($\omega^2 = .46$). An orthogonal components test for trend indicates a significant positive linear trend (F linear = 38.79, < .001) in SOR due to VMP. Detailed results are provided in Table 8-3.

Wilson (1981) reports that consumers purchased more than 90 percent of their groceries at the first three supermarkets they mentioned. However, the results of this study indicate a substantially lower share of requirements awarded by MRO buyers to the three industrial distributors they mentioned first. Because of the specialized applications of many buyers' MRO supply

TABLE 8-3 Average Share of Requirements (SOR) Awarded to Suppliers in First, Second, and Third Mind Positions and Analysis of Variance Results

Supplier Mind Position	Average SOR	Standard Deviation
First	20%	8.7
Second	15	5.8
Third	9	3.9

$F = 19.40$; d.f. = 2 for treatments, 19 for subjects, and 38 for error; $p < .01$ for treatments; $\omega_2 = .46$

requirements their current use of suppliers included more than 35 distributors for each buyer included in the study.

The order of mention of MRO supply vendors in response to the initial questions of what suppliers and vendors "you might know of who first come to mind" was associated somewhat more with SOR awarded than with buyers' responses to the questions, "When you think about your current MRO suppliers, what supplier first comes to mind?" and "What one, two, three, or other current MRO suppliers come to mind?" Using the evoked set question, the first three suppliers mentioned accounted for an average of 34 percent of the buyers' MRO supply requirements. Prompting the buyers to identify "additional MRO suppliers that might come to mind" before asking the evoked set questions likely influenced the buyers to focus their thoughts on vendors providing specialized MRO supply items. However, substantial overlap did occur among vendors identified in the initial first-come-to-mind questions and the evoked set question.

Findings for P$_2$

The findings partially support the second proposition. After prompting, the MRO buyers identified an average of 11.7 suppliers. No supplier identified following a second prompting received more than a 5% share of MRO requirements; however, 96 percent of the vendors identified had been issued purchase orders during the most recent fiscal year. Vendors mentioned but not actively considered were usually those recalled fondly by three buyers when these buyers were employed in other firms in other geographic areas.

Findings for P$_3$

The findings support P$_3$. All of the MRO buyers in the study were able to identify one to four vendors that came to mind that the buyers would be unlikely to buy from. Not keeping commitments agreed to by the specific suppliers named was the most frequently cited reason for *not* awarding purchase orders to an MRO distributor. "A big difference between an outstanding supplier and a poor one is that the outstanding one will tell me if he can't supply an item by the time needed; the poor one will lie just to get the order," was a typical response made by an MRO supply buyer. Failure to carry the product lines specified was the second most frequently mentioned reason for not awarding purchase orders to an industrial distributor. Evaluating the distributor's sales rep as incompetent, and the distributor as too small were additional reasons mentioned by several MRO supply buyers for not awarding shares-of-requirements to vendors.

Findings for P_4

As proposed originally by Myers (1979), phased decision rules appeared to be used by the buyers. All the MRO suppliers first mentioned in response to the initial set of questions on what suppliers and vendors first came to mind met minimum levels of performance on four criteria:

- Earned many of the product lines required by the buyer.
- Had a history of keeping delivery promises.
- Inside/outside sales reps were knowledgeable.
- Prices were stable and reasonable.

First-mentioned distributors were also judged by the buyers to excel on one or more of these criteria: anecdotal evidence of outstanding performance in locating and delivering required items was provided by buyers for the first, second, and third vendors that came to mind. None of the twenty buyers reported using a standard form for evaluating MRO supply vendors. Thus, the use of a combination of two decision rules—conjunctive followed by lexicographic—may best describe MRO supply buyers' heuristics associated with the suppliers that first come to mind. An industrial distributor may need to develop a history of outstanding performance meeting at least one criterion, while meeting minimum levels of performance on several others in order to receive a substantial share (> 5%) of a buyer's total available MRO supply requirements, and to gain a first, second, or third mind position among MRO supply buyers.

Findings for P_5 and P_6

The findings support the fifth and sixth propositions. The industrial distributor participating in the study believed his firm's customers representing large shares of sales would identify his firm without a second prompt as one that easily came to mind. The CEO identified two of the firm's current customers that would mention his firm first in answering the first supplier/vendor awareness question, and four customers who would identify his firm second. In reality, none of the industrial distributor's major customers mentioned his firm first or second. Most (eight) of the major suppliers did mention this supplier by name without a second prompt, but four of them stated that the distributor was one of their small suppliers, or one they rarely used. The VMP index averaged 4.8 for the distributor for the firm's 10 customers, versus a perceived index of the distributor's CEO of 8.0. The difference between the two average index scores was significant using a t-test for related measures. Details appear in Table 8-1.

One of the distributor's major customers named the supplier only after additional prompting; the supplier was classified in the inert set for this customer. One customer reported that he would not buy from the distributor:

"Not much, anyway. The firm is too small. If I did give him some real business, the company would depend too much on me. He doesn't have a real sales rep anyway. The guy who calls on me is really their office manager."

Because this buyer reported that he would not buy from the industrial distributor, the supplier was assigned to this buyer's inept set, even though the supplier did actually provide a small share of the buyer's MRO supply requirements.

Among potential but not current customers, three MRO supply buyers identified the distributor as a vendor they would not buy from. Specific reasons for including the distributor in the buyers' inept sets follow: "They don't have the better product lines." "Too small." "They don't even have a brochure—just a three-page duplicated price list. You could barely read it." "The sales rep did call on me but he seemed confused."

One potential customer reported being unaware of the distributor. Another four mentioned the distributor only after additional prompting to name other distributors located nearby; the distributor was classified in these buyers' inert sets. Also, two buyers mentioned the distributor when asked "what other suppliers or vendors come to mind when you think about MRO suppliers?" These buyers mentioned that they had been called on by the distributor's sales rep, but they had no immediate plans to buy MRO supply items from the firm.

The VMP index for the distributor among the ten potential customers was 1.4. The estimated VMP index of the distributor's CEO was 3.8 for the same ten potential customers. The difference in the two index scores was significant statistically using a t-test for related measures. Details appear in Table 8-2.

LIMITATIONS

The reported results are intended only as an initial, small-scale test of sensitivity of the "first-brand [supplier] awareness" measure proposed by Axelrod (1968, 1985) and Wilson (1981) applied to an industrial marketing situation. A very limited sample size was used in the present study. The study was focused only on MRO supply items. The proposed VMP index was applied to only one distributor.

Only unaided awareness measures were examined in the present study. Axelrod (1968) examined ten measures and found three to be sensitive predictors of purchase: first brand awareness, the constant sum scale, and first brand advertising awareness. A critical test examining several intermediate criteria measures to predict purchase in large-scale industrial marketing settings is needed.

There is also the question of the unknown error from multiplying, adding, and summing scores assigned arbitrarily to the different VMPs. While appealing intuitively to the five buyers in the pretest, the VMP index does include unknown errors, and additional research is needed on its usefulness.

DISCUSSION AND STRATEGY IMPLICATIONS

The findings this chapter describes support the use of first-supplier-awareness and the proposed VMP index as sensitive indicators of whether or not a given supplier is receiving a major, minor, or no share of a buyer's MRO supply requirements. As suggested by Howard (1963, 1977), the concept of an evoked set of suppliers in a buyer's mind appears to apply to both consumer and industrial buyers. While estimates of the evoked set from consumer research studies range from four to seven brands, depending on the product categories studied, larger evoked set ranges may be expected among professional, industrial MRO supply buyers. MRO supply buyers interact with inside and outside sales reps daily; unlike ultimate consumers, MRO supply buyers often refer daily to supplier and manufacturer's brochures.

Additional industrial marketing research is recommended incorporating the use of first-supplier-awareness and also first-supplier-advertising awareness (the supplier advertising that first comes to mind in one product category among industrial buyers) as measures of the effectiveness of marketing variables, e.g., advertising and sales rep performance. *Advertising Age* and the SRI Research Center report first-brand advertising-awareness shares for brands in several product categories as a measure of consumer advertising effectiveness. The reports appear in the "Ad Watch" column each month in *Advertising Age*. Tests of the validity of first brand advertising awareness for predicting first brand awareness and brand preference (measured by a constant sum scale) support the hypothesized positive relationships (Woodside and Wilson, 1985). Since 1986 the SRI Research Center has reported the use of first-supplier advertising awareness as a measure of industrial advertising effectiveness (Nielsen, 1986).

Specific industrial marketers may benefit from learning their VMPs among segments of current and potential customers. Industrial marketers may be surprised at the level of customer awareness of their firms. If the validity of the VMP index is supported by additional research, tracking changes in the VMP indexes among competing suppliers annually may be useful in measuring marketing effectiveness, and as a lead indicator of growth or decline in the share of requirements among key accounts. Learning the thoughts that first come to buyers' minds about specific vendors is likely to provide information on these buyers' perceptions of the strengths and weaknesses among competing vendors. Specific buyer awareness goals and changes in an industrial marketer's strategy might be recommended based on research on buyers' awareness and thoughts associated with specific vendors.

For example, while specific awareness levels and thoughts of buyers were not provided to the industrial distributor participating in the study, the distributor's CEO decided to make several changes in the firm's marketing strategy, based on a summary of the findings. For the first time, a written annual marketing plan for gaining and increasing the distributor's share of business among new customers and key accounts was prepared. The CEO began to make sales calls himself and review the marketing plan with MRO supply buyers in order to convince them that his firm had a plan for growth, and would not be dependent on any one customer. A search was conducted for a full-time, experienced sales rep to hire. A brochure describing the distributor's product lines was designed, printed, and distributed to MRO supply buyers. The CEO formed a product planning committee to review the firm's product lines and make recommendations for additions and deletions. O'Shaughnessy (1984) identifies four competitive tasks to be achieved by a marketing strategy. These four include:

- Converting customers from rivals.
- Increasing the level of individual product usage.
- Attracting new customers.
- Retaining existing customers.

Which strategic objective should be dominant in competitive marketing strategies may depend upon the marketing organization's location in the minds of targeted customers. A summary of strategic objectives and tactical examples for different MRO VMPs is provided in Table 8-4. If an MRO supply vendor has a dominant share of the MRO supply requirements among a substantial number of large MRO supply customers, the vendor's first strategic objective should be to maintain existing customer loyalty. Linking the vendor's computer-based inventory system with the buyers' computer-based MRO supply information and inventory system to increase marketing–buying effectiveness is one tactic for maintaining existing customer loyalty (Hakansson, 1982).

Corey, Cespedes, and Rangan (1989) include case histories of suppliers who receive smaller SORs attempting to change the balance in their favor by increasing the level of services provided to key customer accounts, compared

TABLE 8-4 Strategic Implications of Supplier Mind Positions (SMPs) for Maintenance, Repairs, and Operating (MRO) Supply Marketers

SMP	First Strategic Objective	Tactical Example
D_7	Chosen set, first mention	Gain direct access with customer's information system
D_7	Chosen set, second/third mention	Demonstrate higher service delivery compared to larger competitor
D_6	Evoked set, not chosen/chosen infrequently	Gain trial of new products
D_5	Inert set	Find a mentor in the customer's firm
D_4	Change customer's distribution perceptions	Offer 48-hour delivery; open new branch
D_3	Gain awareness in D_6	Sales calls; brochures; publicity
D_2	New market entry	Create new market entry team
D_1	Shift customer's attitude about vendor	Introduce new product lines, sales team, and improved service levels

to the service levels provided by larger rivals. Woodside and Sherrell (1980) describe the marketing and buying process of small MRO supply vendors attempting to gain trial among buyers in the paper mill industry, when buyers often consider but rarely actually buy from these vendors.

Vendors located in most MRO buyers' inert set may need to establish credibility as viable contenders for the buyers' MRO supply business. Finding mentors among MRO supply users, e.g., machine operators, maintenance personnel, plant engineers, to promote favorable word-of-mouth advertising with buyers may be one tactic useful for such vendors.

Vendors located in buyers' inept sets may face the most difficult marketing challenge of all. If such buyers are too important to bypass, then a combination of several new marketing actions is likely to be necessary to influence a major shift in attitude favorable to the vendors.

PART IV

CASE-BASED RESEARCH FOR LEARNING GESTALT THINKING/DOING PROCESSES

9

APPLYING THE LONG INTERVIEW METHOD FOR COMPARING EXECUTIVE AND CUSTOMER THINKING

Synopsis

This chapter illustrates the use of the long interview method and degrees of freedom analysis (DFA) to case study data. The results include reports of competing "mental models" of senior executives in a national retail firm. The core propositions in these mental models are compared with customer beliefs and reported behaviors. Limitations in applying DFA are discussed with suggestions made for overcoming them. An epilogue reports how the firm used the results of the field study.

INTRODUCTION: BUILDING DEGREES OF FREEDOM INTO CASE STUDY DATA TO PROBE COMPETING MENTAL MODELS

This chapter builds on the work of Campbell (1975) in applying DFA analysis to case study data. The application permits testing alternative "mental models" (Senge, 1990) of senior executives within a national U.S. retail firm.

This application examines the belief systems of two senior executives regarding a number of strategic issues facing the organization. Their opposing views include stark differences concerning customer preferences and behaviors. The views of the two executives are compared and contrasted with customers' own views. This chapter demonstrates Campbell's (1975) unique and valuable proposals empirically for increasing the theoretical and practical importance of case study research. Consequently, the reported study probes consumer behavior and executive strategy phenomena from the perspectives of

---

This chapter was co-authored by Elizabeth J. Wilson (Suffolk University, Boston) and Arch G. Woodside.

two scientific styles: analytical science and particular humanism (see Hirschman, 1985; Mitroff and Kilmann, 1978).

DFA is a pattern-matching theory formulation and testing approach that Campbell (1975; see also Cook and Campbell, 1979) advocated in his revised view that case study research can be useful, replacing his earlier view that such research reports are nonscientific and useless (for the earlier view, see Campbell and Stanley, 1966). While DFA has been mentioned in passing by other case research methodologists (e.g., Miles and Huberman, 1994; Yin, 1994), few published applications of the testing method are available (Dean, 1968; Wilson and Wilson, 1988; Wilson and Woodside, 1999, are three organization science applications of DFA). In essence, the social scientist builds in degrees of freedom (i.e., usually competing sets of ten or more propositions) in a case study based on the belief systems of two or more participants about the phenomenon of interest (see Eisenhardt, 1989; Mintzberg, 1979; Pettigrew, 1992). To examine the nomological validity (i.e., the relative accuracy of predictions in the alternative belief systems, see Peter, 1981) additional data are collected independently from other sources (e.g., from direct observations or from third parties, such as other executives or customer perceptions, preferences, and behaviors) to permit comparisons to the theoretical propositions in the competing belief systems. The degrees of match are examined between the independently collected data and the belief systems of the participants in the case under study.

A "mental model" is the set of assumptions that forms a system of beliefs. For example, a mental model may consist of the views of an executive about "how things get done here" or the executive's perceptions about how and why particular customer segments will respond to alternative retailing strategies. An individual is unlikely to be fully aware of core propositions in his or her own belief system that influence his or her own decisions and actions. Weick (1995) captures this point well by noting that individuals partially learn what they think by hearing what they have to say. Bargh (1989) demonstrates that an individual's observed behavior may be influenced by a belief system held implicitly while the same individual explicitly expresses an opposing (more socially acceptable) belief system.

Thus, rather than based on deeply thought out and formally tested paradigms, mental models are based mainly on episodic memory of personal experiences and biases of an individual or group. An individual is likely to retrieve and report bits and pieces of his or her mental model automatically (see Bargh, 1989) when asked to describe details on the focus of the case study. Such automatic retrievals may be followed by more strategic (i.e., controlled) thoughts to support and deepen preliminary expressed views; the individual reporting his or her views of reality may also engage consciously and unconsciously in self-editing while "thinking aloud" while answering questions during interviews. Consequently, asking a respondent to provide responses that first come to mind and to think aloud in how he or she would make specific decisions during face-to-face interviews only partially captures the details of his or her mental model. A deepened perspective of a respondent's mental model may be learned from conducting multiple interviews across several different days, weeks, or months, and by observing the respondent's behavior directly in different contexts (e.g., alone, or in meetings with other executives, supplier representatives, or customers). Reports of such research are available in organization science (e.g., Mintzberg, 1973; Pettigrew, 1979) and consumer research (Arnould and Price, 1993; Bettman and Park, 1980).

While not formally stated as global paradigms for explaining behavior, one category of mental models is the alternative view held by senior executives about customer preferences and behaviors regarding the company's product and retailing efforts. Case study research data, in the form of long interviews (McCracken, 1988) with executives and customers, aid in assessing the relative merits of the alternative views of managers. As well as illustrating an application of DFA, we present follow-up information on what happened within the company as a result of the analysis and ultimate strategic path that was taken.

DFA of case study data represents reconciliation and synthesis of two of the four scientific styles of inquiry as described by Mitroff and Kilmann (1978): the analytical scientific (i.e., sensing-thinking perspective) and particular humanist (sensing/feeling) research approaches. "The analytical scientist's basic drive is toward certainty and the corresponding desire to avoid uncertainty. It is a basic tenet of the analytical scientist's approach that precision, accuracy, and reliability necessarily serve the ultimate aim of scientific knowledge, which is unambiguous theoretical or empirical knowledge" (Mitroff and Kilmann, 1978, p. 33). Statistical hypothesis testing is the preferred method of data analysis by the analytical scientist. While valuable streams of research are available in the literature using alternative styles of theory and research (e.g., conceptual theorist, conceptual humanist, and particular humanist), the analytical scientific style is the dominant logic in training consumer researchers and organization scientists.

The particular humanist style of research centers on the Jungian traits of sensing and feeling. The particular humanist desires to conduct science by means of personal involvement with other humans—to seek insights into their lives, motives, and values, and to understand them as individuals holistically. The typical methodologies employed by the particular humanist are the case study, in-depth interview, participant observation, and/or some other related qualitative technique. "Instead of reducing the individuals who have served as the objects of inquiry to a set of data points or conceptual generalities, the particular humanist will try to recreate them in as holistic a way as possible" (Hirschman, 1985, p. 235). The body of work by Levy and his colleagues (e.g., see Levy, 1981; Sherry, McGrath, and Levy, 1995) exemplifies the particular humanist style. The work by Bettman and his colleagues (e.g., Bettman, 1974; Bettman and Park, 1980) is representative of the analytical scientist style of inquiry (for elaboration, see Hirschman, 1985).

THE CONTEXT FOR EXAMINING ALTERNATIVE MENTAL MODELS

The research study includes an application of the "long interview technique" (McCracken, 1988) in the context of conducting customer research for a direct marketer of gardening seeds, plants, bulbs, and related products. Characteristics of the long interview technique include the following:

* Face-to-face interviews individually with five to ten members representative of unique population segments (e.g., new buyers, prospects not converting into buyers, long-term loyal buyers).
* Setting in contexts and environments that are natural for the respondent.
* Inclusion of both open- and closed-ended questions.
* Frequent use of think-aloud method and "auto-driving" tools (whereby the respondent is invited to both formulate and answer questions regarding photographs of self, known catalogs, physical products, and/or problem scenarios, see Heisley and Levy, 1991; Wallendorf and Arnould, 1991).
* Extended time period (i.e., one to three hours) and possible multiple meetings (e.g., Cox (1967) interviewed the same two housewives individually once per week in 15 hourly sessions on topics related to buying and consuming groceries).

The direct marketer, Rosemont, Inc. (a fictitious name used for competitive reasons), was seeking information from members of several customer segments in order to make short- and long-range strategic marketing decisions. The long interview study was part of Rosemont's ongoing marketing research program for addressing specific issues as well as more general environmental scanning purposes (Kotler, 2000). In many instances, different senior and middle managers in the same direct marketing firm may propose conflicting strategies based on unique mental models regarding the preferences and buying behaviors of a targeted customer segment. The context of the study included conflicting strategic views held by two senior managers; the differences in views motivated a full explication of the mental models of senior executives in the firm as well as a field study on customer behavior using the long interview technique.

Rosemont, Inc. is one of the top five direct marketers of gardening products in the United States. Most (99%) of their sales are via mail or telephone with customers ordering from a catalog. Rosemont was faced with making decisions on a number of strategic issues including new product development, new target markets, environmental concerns, customer satisfaction, and catalog production/execution. Rosemont, Inc. has been in business for over 100 years and started conducting formal, independent (sponsored not identified) surveys of customers and prospects in the mid-1970s.

In annual marketing strategy planning sessions, different senior and middle managers in this same direct marketing firm propose very different mental models regarding the major consumer trends in consuming gardening-related products. Initiating the study were the conflicting mental models (described below) held by Rosemont's CEO and Senior VP of Marketing regarding major trends in customer preferences and behaviors.

Based on data from prior studies by Rosemont, the firm divided customers into five groups, as follows:

- Heavy-loyals—customers who buy every year with annual purchases in the top quartile of all buying customers.
- Light-loyals—customers who buy every year with annual purchases in the mid-to-lower quartile of all buying customers.
- Once-only customers—those who buy one time but do not buy in following years.
- Catalog requestors—customers requesting a catalog but do not buy.
- Divorced customers—those who have bought in previous years but have stopped buying in recent years.

Other groups of interest to Rosemont include non-customers who buy similar products from retail stores, non-customers with demographics and lifestyles similar to loyal customers but not buying gardening products from any source.

CREATING DEGREES OF FREEDOM ANALYSIS PREDICTION MATRICES

In the course of their work, senior executives at Rosemont developed their own hypotheses and mental models about framing and solving the strategic issues facing the firm, as well as behavioral explanations regarding the various customer/non-customer groups. Based on a total of six one- to two-hour interviews, each interview conducted separately with each of two senior managers, twenty sets of opposing intuitive propositions were derived from the mental models of the CEO and VP of Marketing for Rosemont. These two sets of propositions form distinctive patterns in views held by the two executives.

Four additional interviews were held individually with other executives (the senior seed buyer, the advertising manager, the head of catalog design, and the executive VP) in the firm who were mentioned by the two senior executives as being knowledgeable in particular about marketing strategy and customer behavior. To extents somewhat lower in zeal, two of these executives supported the mental model of the CEO and two supported the mental model expressed by the marketing VP.

Making explicit core propositions in two or more alternative mental models enhances the value of applying DFA in case study research. A "critical test" (Carlsmith, Ellsworth, and Aronson, 1976) is made possible when empirical findings are compared to competing predictions of multiple theories. The result may go beyond concluding that one model is more useful than the other; a synthesis may be reached by combining the confirmed strengths of each theory while replacing their weaknesses.

Children and Gardening

Who is the next generation of Rosemont customers? This question motivated one senior manager to propose that young children (6–15 years old) should be a group for which Rosemont has an active marketing program. The rationale was that such products would allow gardening to be a family activity. The executive advocating this view collected news clippings of stories describing parents gardening with their young children. The other senior manager's opposing proposition was that in general, given the relatively short attention span of a young child, marketing efforts to this group would not be particularly worthwhile. Thus, the two opposing propositions are as follows.

P_{1a}: Customers with young children participate with one or more of their children in buying gardening products and in related gardening activities.

P_{1b}: Customers do not include any of their young children in buying gardening products and in related gardening activities.

Special Seed Packs for Children

Related to this issue of children and gardening, the senior manager's group in favor of the position that children are involved in gardening (P_{1a}) also felt that special seed packets should be designed for young children. These special designs would include seed- and plant-related drawings and artwork that would appeal to children (e.g., use cartoon-type figures in bold primary colors, large print planting and growing information, etc.). The parents would find these products attractive in that it would create interest on the part of the child. The opposing viewpoint is that such products are not necessary since young children are not very involved in gardening with their parents.

P_{2a}: Customers with young children will find seed packs for kids highly attractive compared to the regular seed packs.

P_{2b}: Customers with young children will not find seed packs designed for kids any more attractive than the regular seed packs.

Age of New Gardeners

Again, the group of managers that find young children to be a viable new target market, maintain that the average age when people start gardening is decreasing. They expect more parents to get their young children involved at a relatively early age. It is thought that these children gardeners will then continue to be involved, as they become adults. The opposing viewpoint is that the average age people begin gardening is stable, beginning at about 30 years of age. The rationale for this viewpoint is that by 30 years of age, a consumer likely is a homeowner and will need to garden around his/her property.

P_{3a}: The average age of consumers beginning to garden and use mail order for buying gardening products is decreasing.

P_{3b}: The average age of consumers beginning to garden and use mail order for buying gardening products is stable.

Preferences of Heavy-Loyal Customers

Heavy-loyal customers that regularly buy from direct marketers have similar attitudes about the major (top five) suppliers, according to the results of a prior national survey conducted for Rosemont (for details, see Woodside and Moore, 1983). Given the age of the previous study, Rosemont managers wanted updated information on this issue. Should Rosemont be positioned as the direct merchant most preferred by its repeat customers for long periods of time (from parent to adult child to adult grandchild)? This question motivated the following opposing propositions:

P_{4a}: Rosemont heavy-loyal customers strongly prefer our firm over our leading competitor.

P_{4b}: Rosemont heavy-loyal customers do not have a strong preference for our firm over our leading competitor.

Behavior of Divorced (i.e., Former) Customers

Why do customers stop buying? Rosemont managers disagreed about whether customers were being lost because of aggressive actions by competitors or because of some other reason. How much marketing effort should be expended to win back the former customers? If many customers are being lost to competitors, then a very aggressive response to new competitor actions is warranted. However, if loss of customers has little to do with new competitor actions, it probably is not worthwhile to spend much time and money on trying to win back these lost customers (Woodside and Wilson, 1995, p. 44). Thus, the third set of opposing propositions is as follows.

P_{5a}: Former customers stopped buying mainly because competitors have made attractive product and promotional offers that they prefer over our offers.

P_{5b}: Former customers have stopped buying mainly because they have stopped gardening.

Regional Influence on Customer Purchasing Behavior

Rosemont managers were in disagreement over the issue of offering region-ally oriented inserts in its national "Big Book" catalog; the largest catalog mailed to customers annually.

P_{6a}: Substantial differences in purchase and consumption behavior occur across all regions of the United States: north, south, east, and west.

P_{6b}: Regional effects on purchase and consumption behavior are only sig-nificant in a few regions.

Catalog Shopping Behavior

Rosemont managers had questions about customers' catalog shopping behavior in terms of planned versus unplanned (impulse) purchases. How much impulse buying is occurring? Rosemont managers were interested in this question because the catalog routinely contains "reason why" copy and four-color photographs to affect such unplanned buying behavior.

P_{7a}: Many, if not most, customers buy products they did not plan to pur-chase when shopping from gardening catalogs.

P_{7b}: Many, if not most, customers follow planned buying strategies when shopping from gardening catalogs

Use of Four-Color Photographs

How important are four-color photographs in the Rosemont catalog? This question was motivated by the high catalog production cost that Rosemont incurred. Rosemont managers were interested to know customer preferences for color photographs versus black and white pictures for at least some (1/4 to 1/2) of the pages in the annual Big Book.

P_{8a}: Customers do not expect, nor prefer, to see four-color photographs of all products on all pages of the catalog.

P_{8b}: Most customers prefer seeing four-color photographs for all flower and vegetable products on all pages of the catalog.

Photograph Size

Some of Rosemont's competitors were using larger, sharper photographs. In particular, a competitor specializing in flowers, Mason and Thomas, had achieved some growth in market share over the past two years after implementing this change in their catalog. Thus, an issue for Rosemont was whether photographs should be larger and of higher resolution. Such a move would increase the cost of producing the catalog significantly but may generate more sales, especially among the heavy-loyal flower customers.

P_{9a}: Many customers prefer seeing large versus small photographs for flower products in the catalog and such preference helps increase customers' buying intentions.

P_{9b}: Use of large photographs for flower products will probably not result in a significant increase in intention to buy from Rosemont.

Catalog Content

A tradition at Rosemont is to include photographs of people and families enjoying gardening activities in the Big Book catalog. Does this matter to customers? There is some expense and time involved in getting the models and gardening scenes together. If this expenditure were reduced (or eliminated), would demand be significantly affected?

P_{10a}: Customers enjoy seeing pictures of people/families in the catalog; if these pictures were omitted, purchase behavior would be significantly negatively affected.

P_{10b}: Customers have no strong preference for seeing pictures of people/families in the catalog; if these pictures were omitted, purchase behavior would not change significantly.

Catalog Style

A small, but growing competitor, Harrison's, had a unique catalog with strong appeal to a relatively small but affluent target market. Members of this target market would be described as upscale, well educated, with an appreciation of the arts. The overall style of Harrison's catalog reflected the tastes of its target market by having copy written in a somewhat "flowery" style. The copy was supplemented with pen-and-ink drawings of plants and other gardening products rather than photographs. The paper stock used for the catalog was unbleached and flat (not glossy) that was of a slightly heavier weight than most competitors' catalogs. The result was a catalog with a "Victorian" image, more or less. The emergence of Harrison as a competitor generated the following sets of opposing propositions.

P_{11a}: Most Rosemont customers prefer more entertaining copy about Rosemont products compared to the copy currently being used.

P_{11b}: Most Rosemont customers do not care to have more entertaining copy; the current content in terms of information about the products is satisfactory.

P_{12a}: Many Rosemont customers prefer product photographs to be supplemented with some pen-and-ink drawings in the catalog.

P_{12b}: Most Rosemont customers do not care to have photographs supplemented with pen-and-ink drawings in the catalog.

Special Varieties

Similar to the previous discussion, some direct merchants were beginning to offer special varieties of flowers and vegetables. Some of these were to bring back "old-fashioned" varieties, called heirloom varieties, while others had been specially developed for various regions of the U.S. Regional varieties were available that withstand extremely hot areas (e.g., parts of Texas), wet areas (the Gulf Coast region), colder areas (the northern U.S.), etc. These issues motivated two more sets of opposing propositions:

P_{13a}: Customers prefer and will likely purchase heirloom varieties of flowers and vegetables.

P_{13b}: Customers are satisfied with the current product offerings; heirloom varieties are not likely to significantly affect preference or intention to buy.

P_{14a}: Customers prefer and will likely purchase products especially suited for their own region.

P_{14b}: Customers are satisfied with current offerings; regional varieties are not likely to significantly affect preference or intention to buy.

Planned Gardens

Based on competitor offerings of "planned gardens" (i.e., a kit with landscape plan, seeds, and plants all included), Rosemont managers were interested in customer preferences for such products. If planned gardens were offered, how much space in the catalog should be devoted to this product?

P_{15a}: Some customers like the idea of buying a planned garden.

P_{15b}: Few, if any, customers like the idea of buying planned gardens.

Environmental Concerns

Do customers care whether direct merchants have an "environmentally friendly" orientation in their operations? Rosemont management wanted to investigate this question as it applied to the seed packages, the catalog, and organically raised seed and plant products. Seed packets were of a foil material that does not biodegrade easily. Would this be a hindrance to inducing purchase? How important is it to produce the catalog on recycled paper? Finally, the growing popularity of organically grown seeds and plants (not exposed to herbicide and pesticide chemicals) might lead some customers to look for these products in Rosemont's catalog.

P_{16a}: Some important customer segments are concerned about buying from direct merchants who are environmentally friendly in using recycled paper in their catalogs and biodegradable packaging materials.

P_{16b}: When buying seeds and plants from direct merchants, few, if any, customers are concerned about whether the direct merchants are environmentally friendly.

Service Guarantees

The guarantee of superior product quality and high customer service was a source of pride for several senior managers at Rosemont. Should this part of Rosemont's operation be actively promoted in their Big Book catalog and in other advertising? Empirical support for one of the following opposing propositions would provide an answer.

P_{17a}: A substantial number of customers perceive differences among direct merchants in the product/service guarantees offered and how well direct merchants live up to their guarantees.

P_{17b}: Few, if any, customers perceive differences among direct merchants in the guarantees offered, or how they live up to their guarantees.

Rosemont History

Rosemont, Inc. has been a direct merchant supplier of seeds and plants to customers for 100+ years. A long successful history conveys a sense of stability and reliability. Should this history be actively promoted in the catalog as a way of building trust among customers?

P_{18a}: New customers want to learn about the history and development of Rosemont; this information will help to build the customer's trust and confidence in buying gardening products from Rosemont.

P_{18b}: New customers do not particularly care about the history and development of Rosemont; this information will have no effect on the customer's trust and confidence in buying gardening products from Rosemont.

Non-Response Catalog Requestors

There is a substantial number of "non-response catalog requestors," that is, people who request a catalog but never respond (buy) afterwards. The reasons for such behavior are explained by two opposing viewpoints. One group of senior managers believes that requestors don't respond because of the actions of competitors. Other managers believe that requestors don't respond because they just enjoy receiving and looking at the catalog for its own sake. Given the cost of producing and mailing the catalog, this issue has substantial implications for marketing expenditures.

P_{19a}: Consumers who request a direct merchant's catalog, but who do not purchase from the catalog, are buying from competitors' catalogs.

P_{19b}: Consumers who request a direct merchant's catalog, but who do not purchase from the catalog, are not buying from any competitors' catalogs.

Demographic Effects on Customers

Some Rosemont managers were of the opinion that changes in their customer purchase segments were mirrored in overall demographic patterns. For example, more buyers were thought to be "single" person households as opposed to married couples.

P_{20a}: Changes in customer purchase segments are following changes in demographic patterns.

P_{20b}: Changes in customer purchase segments are not following changes in demographic patterns.

Of all the issues included in the study, these 20 were the most salient to Rosemont management for purposes of strategy formulation for the next three to five years. As mental models we can group the propositions into two categories: "Stay the Course" and "New Wave." Propositions associated with the Stay the Course theory advocate minimal changes to current operations and strategies; the New Wave propositions are associated with more radical change compared to Rosemont's prior organizational behavior.

Figure 9-1 summarizes a large portion of the New Wave model. The display of a few double-headed arrows in Figure 9-1 illustrates closely associated assumptions expressed by advocates of this mental model. For example, P_{2a} and P_{3a} were mentioned closely together during the first interview with the VP of Marketing. P_{3a} was described, in part, as a rationale for the predicted success for the new product line for young children. Two propositions shown to be distantly linked represent one proposition associated by the respondent with something she/he said earlier in the interview or in a prior interview, for example, P_{6a} was mentioned again by the marketing VP when discussing P_{14a} later in the interview.

One limitation of DFA in case study research is applying the method to a set of highly associated propositions (lots of double-arrow relationships). Such a situation actually results in establishing few degrees of freedom: by answering one proposition associated highly with many others, the answers to the other propositions are known. Because a response bias may occur to appear logical and consistent even when such traits do not reflect deeply held beliefs, the researcher should be encouraged to cover lots of seemingly unrelated topics and to interview the respondent in more than one time period. Degrees of freedom concerning unrelated, or distantly related, propositions may be increased by asking for descriptions and beliefs about seemingly unrelated topics, such as customer preferences for alternative product packaging materials, reasons why customers are lost, and the demographic profiles of new customers.

Covering many topics in multiple interviews with the same respondent may result in uncovering substantial inconsistencies and negatively associated propositions in the mental model of the respondent. For example, P_{9a} and P_{10a} are associated negatively: more large photographs of flowers in catalogs

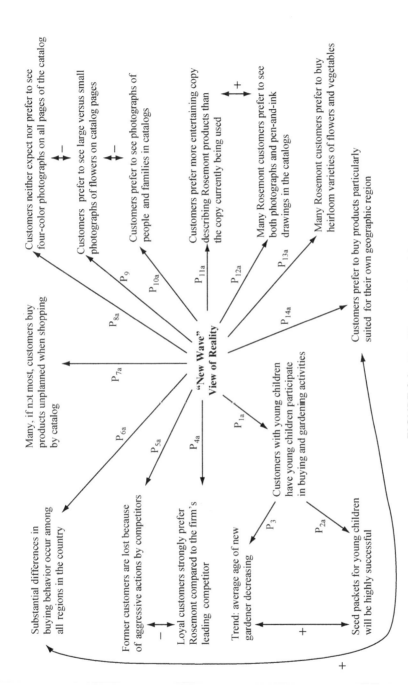

Customers neither expect nor prefer to see four-color photographs on all pages of the catalog

Customers prefer to see large versus small photographs of flowers on catalog pages

Customers prefer to see photographs of people and families in catalogs

Customers prefer more entertaining copy describing Rosemont products than the copy currently being used

Many Rosemont customers prefer to see both photographs and pen-and-ink drawings in the catalogs

Many Rosemont customers prefer to buy heirloom varieties of flowers and vegetables

Customers prefer to buy products particularly suited for their own geographic region

Many, if not most, customers buy products unplanned when shopping by catalog

"New Wave" View of Reality

Substantial differences in buying behavior occur among all regions in the country

Former customers are lost because of aggressive actions by competitors

Loyal customers strongly prefer Rosemont compared to the firm's leading competitor

Trend: average age of new gardener decreasing

Customers with young children have young children participate in buying and gardening activities

Seed packets for young children will be highly successful

P_{8a} P_9 P_{10a} P_{11a} P_{12a} P_{13a} P_{14a} P_{7a} P_{6a} P_{5a} P_{4a} P_{1a} P_3 P_{2a}

− − + + − + +

FIGURE 9.1 New Wave mental model.

175

reduces the space available for photographs of people unless the number of pages in the catalog is increased. One aim of case study research is to uncover paradoxes in closely held beliefs, as well as between expressed beliefs and actions, and to resolve such paradoxes by asking additional questions and directly observing interactions among respondents as well as their behaviors. In some instances the respondent may be unaware of inconsistencies in his or her mental models; care may need to be exercised in asking the respondent to resolve such issues. Because the aim of the study was not to engage in organizational development or action research (Whyte, 1965; Wells, 1995), except for purposes of clarification, attempts to resolve inconsistencies in the mental models expressed by executives were not attempted.

The Stay the Course model is not displayed in a figure because it is, for the most part, the mirror opposite of the New Wave model. However, advocates of the Stay the Course model expressed more thoughts and spent more time discussing maintaining close ties with existing customers and less time on the issue of launching new products compared to advocates of the New Wave model.

Table 9-1 summarizes the propositions and predictions for the Stay the Course and New Wave models. In the same way that academic theories have been investigated, so can such managerially oriented mental models.

FIELDWORK

Research Method and Data Collection

A "long interview" technique (McCracken, 1988) was used to obtain data. Respondents were chosen based on several heuristics as recommended by McCracken (1988).

> Respondents should be perfect strangers (i.e., unknown to the interviewer and other respondents) and few in number (i.e., no more than eight). They should not have a special knowledge (or ignorance) of the topic under study. Most important, the selection of respondents is an opportunity to manufacture distance. This is done by deliberately creating a contrast in the respondent pool. These contrasts can be of age, gender, status, education, or occupation. (p. 37)

To investigate the strategic issues associated with the Stay the Course and New Wave theories, we modified these heuristics to contrast five customer groups identified by Rosemont managers. A central objective was to contrast the thinking and feeling processes of customers likely to have some knowledge and experience with gardening-related direct marketing firms.

Gardening/Direct Marketing Industry Background

Mail order buying of gardening products is an interesting area for an application of the long interview technique. Direct marketing of plants and seeds is one of the oldest mail-order industries in the U.S. Before World War I, most

TABLE 9-1 A Prediction Matrix For Two Mental Models

Managerial/Strategic Issue	Model A: New Wave	Model B: Stay the Course
Customers with young children involve children in buying gardening products.	Yes	No
Customers with young children will find special seed packs for kids highly attractive compared to the regular seed packs.	Yes	No
The average age of consumers beginning to garden and use mail order for buying gardening products is decreasing.	Yes	No
Rosemont heavy-loyal customers prefer Rosemont products over competitors' products.	Yes	No
Former customers have stopped buying mainly because competitors have made attractive product and promotional offers that are preferred.	Yes	No
Substantial regional differences in customer purchasing exist.	Yes	No
Most customers follow planned buying strategies when using catalogs.	No	Yes
Rosemont customers prefer four-color photographs for all products shown in the catalog.	No	Yes
Customers prefer seeing larger, sharper photographs for flower products in the catalog.	Yes	No
Seeing pictures of people/families in the catalog is important to customers and will likely affect buying behavior.	Yes	No
Customers prefer more entertaining copy about Rosemont products.	Yes	No
Customers prefer product photographs to be supplemented with pen-and-ink drawings.	Yes	No
Customers prefer and will likely purchase heirloom varieties of flowers and vegetables.	Yes	No
Customers prefer and will likely purchase products especially suited for their own region.	Yes	No
Customers prefer and will likely purchase a planned garden kit.	Yes	No
Customers are concerned about buying from direct merchants who are environmentally friendly in using recycled paper in their catalogs and biodegradable packaging materials.	Yes	No
Customers perceive differences among direct merchants in the guarantees offered.	Yes	No
Customers want to know the company history of Rosemont in order to have more trust and confidence about buying and using Rosemont products.	Yes	No
Non-response requestors of a Rosemont catalog are buying from competitors' catalogs.	Yes	No
Changes in customer purchase segments are following changes in demographic patterns.	Yes	No

Source: Woodside and Wilson, 1995.

177

plants and seeds for home gardening were purchased using mail order. Mail order buying of plants and seeds now (i.e., 2004) represents less than 10 percent of total purchases in the U.S. Total industry sales are less than $1 billion. One or two firms do not dominate the mail-order gardening industry; however, the top 10 firms in sales represent about 40 percent of total mail-order industry sales. In the past 20 years, the industry has stabilized its share of total gardening sales. However, the market shares and profits of individual firms fluctuate, sometimes substantially, from year to year. Competitors in the industry need to be concerned with two marketing objectives: a) maintaining close relationships with their core customers, and b) attracting/retaining new customers.

Rosemont Managerial Input

The senior executives at Rosemont worked with us to design the study. During three planning meetings a market research project team was formed and 23 customer groups were identified for possible study. As mentioned earlier, five core groups were identified (e.g., heavy loyals, light loyals). The project team's 23 groups represent finer gradations of customer groups. In consultation with the project team and Rosemont's CEO, five customer categories were designated for study.

1. Core customers: persons buying a higher than average dollar amount in three or more years during the most recent five years from Rosemont's main annual catalog (the Big Book).
2. New customers: first time buyers in 1993, spending a higher than average dollar amount, using the major annual catalog, which they got from Rosemont's direct response advertising offer.
3. Non-response requestors: persons requesting the annual catalog from direct response advertisements but not buying.
4. Once-only customers: persons buying more than the average dollar amount in one of the two years prior to 1993 but not in 1993.
5. Divorced customers: persons buying more than the average dollar amount in two or more years, but not since 1990.

These groups represent some departure but also some overlap with the five basic groups mentioned earlier. For example core customers and new customers can be heavy loyals or light loyals. Customer groups three to five correspond to the same groups identified earlier. The senior managers developed the twenty opposing propositions as well as other managerial/strategic issues with input from the researchers. Given that large-scale, national surveys had been conducted on the five customer groups (see Woodside and Moore, 1983), the planned comparisons were exploratory attempts to offer richer insights and nuance into the details of known differences among the groups.

Respondents

Respondents were selected from three urban areas of the U.S. that represent important geographic markets for Rosemont: Rochester, NY, Raleigh, NC, and Dallas, TX. For each of the five customer groups, 10 names and addresses of customers were selected from Rosemont's database. Again, to emphasize McCracken's (1988) advice on respondent selection, traditional sampling rules do not apply to this type of research. Respondents were sought from each customer group based on past sales and catalog requests in Rosemont's marketing database.

Initial Contact

Three weeks before visiting each of the selected markets, subjects for each customer group were sent a letter on university stationary introducing the research project and investigators. Rosemont was not identified as a sponsor of the study in order to avoid bias. Subjects were informed that they had been selected for the study from the names of households that had either requested and/or purchased products using mail order. The letter included an offer of $30 for participating in an in-home, personal interview.

Telephone Contact

Four to five days after the letter was sent, each subject was telephoned and asked to participate in the study. With the exception of the divorced customers, over 70 percent of the subjects agreed to be interviewed. Those refusing to participate were replaced; letters and phone calls were made to new subjects in an attempt to interview one or more persons in each of the five groups in each of the three cities. Close to 60 percent of the divorced customers reported by telephone that they did not wish to participate; most of those subjects reported not gardening in 1993.

Confirmation Letter and Interview Schedule

Following the telephone contact, a confirmation letter for the personal in-home appointment was mailed to each subject who had agreed to be interviewed. The interviews were scheduled during Friday, Saturday, and Sunday in March (Dallas), May (Raleigh), and June (Rochester). Two to five interviews were completed each day over the three-day period per city. The planned and completed interviews scheduled per city are summarized in Table 9-2.

In-Home Interviews

Both authors participated in all of the 26 completed personal interviews. Audiotape recordings were made for 24 of 26 interviews (electrical outlets were not available for two interviews). Two to four photographs were taken

TABLE 9-2   Research Design for 1993 Plant and Seed Customer Study: Planned/Completed In-Depth Interviews

Customer Group	City			
	Dallas	**Raleigh**	**Rochester**	**Total**
Current Core: combination vegetable and flower buyer	2/1*	2/3	1/2	5/6
New Customer: 20+ multi-product buyer	1/2	2/4	2/2	5/7
Non-Response Requestor	2/2	1/0	2/2	5/4
Once-Only Customer	2/2	2/3	1/1	5/6
Divorced Customer	1/0	2/2	2/1	5/3
Total	8/7	9/11	8/8	25/26

*Two interviews were scheduled but only one was completed due to a cancellation. Since cancellations must be expected, some "back-up" interviews were scheduled to maximize the researchers' data collection time. For example, in Raleigh, two interviews were scheduled with Current Core customers but a third interview was done with one of the back-up respondents since time permitted.

for all respondents; 25 were photographed in their gardens. The average time to complete the interview was 90 minutes. Three interviews were completed in less than 45 minutes; all of these brief interviews were with once-only and divorced customers.

Part of the interview was geared toward data collection through a technique called "autodriving" (Heisley and Levy, 1991). "Autodriving" means asking a respondent to comment on photographs, a video, or some other directly relevant stimulus. He/she is then asked to provide an account of what is seen in these visuals, and whether or not the depiction relates to him/her (and if so, how). In our context, we use the long interview to show a respondent competing gardening catalogs and products (seed packs) and ask him/her to comment on and compare the catalogs and products. Numerous other questions pertaining to competing company, alternative retail sources (e.g., stores versus mail order), and product issues were asked in order to address the 20 sets of opposing strategic propositions, as well as others.

FINDINGS

Findings about the twenty sets of opposing propositions are presented here to record the prediction confirmations for the matrix in Table 9-1. A separate report includes thick descriptions with photographs of example case studies for each of the five customer segments (see Woodside and Wilson, 1995).

P_1: Children and Gardening

Nine of the 26 households interviewed included young children or teenagers. Joint gardening activities by parents and children were reported by none of these nine households; P_{1b}, not P_{1a}, is supported. An interesting nuance that emerged from the data was that respondents with young children reported being influenced by **their** parents in buying from gardening direct merchants and their choice of specific direct merchant firms. Thus, family influence was found to occur, but not as expected by the New Wave proposition of parent/young child influence. For Rosemont, the advantage of being a very well-established mail order gardening firm with positive word-of-mouth recommendations between parent and adult child was an unexpected finding of the study.

P_2: Special Seed Packs for Kids

Following on the findings of P_1, respondents did not report a high likelihood of buying special seed packets with child-oriented designs. Since none of the nine households with small children reported gardening with their children, there was little need for special seed packets. Among households without children, three respondents thought that the special seed packs for children were cute, but they would not purchase them. Five respondents had grandchildren; when asked if they would buy these products as gifts for grandchildren, the majority indicated a low likelihood. The reason given was because the grandchildren do not find gardening of long-term interest during visits with the grandparents. Thus, P_{2b} is supported over P_{2a}.

P_3: Age for Beginning Gardeners

The New Wave theory-in-use asserts that young children are becoming active in gardening and this is associated with a decrease in the average age of beginning gardeners. Based on the interview findings, however, the pattern for beginning gardeners is when adult children become homeowners and look to their parents for advice on what to buy and which merchants to buy from. This finding was discussed regarding P_1. Based on the small sample of in-depth interviews, the youngest respondents were in their late 20s with the average age being 50 years of age, approximately. Indeed, Rosemont's own company records indicate that among their customer base, the average age of first-time buyers is increasing slightly. Thus, P_{3b} is supported.

P_1–P_3 all address related issues of gardener demographics. For all three propositions, the Stay the Course theory was supported. Based on the interview findings and information from other sources (Rosemont records and industry-level data), the strategic decision was made not to invest substantial funds in promoting gardening as a parent/young child activity.

P_4: Preferences of Heavy-Loyal Customers

All of the heavy-loyal customers interviewed reported preferring two or more direct gardening merchants to others; thus, P_{4b} is supported over P_{4a}. We found it interesting that heavy-loyal customers consistently reported negative feelings toward only one direct merchant (out of many we asked about). In other words, heavy loyals to Rosemont did not have negative feelings about other direct merchants (with the one exception), they just exhibit a high degree of behavioral loyalty in their buying from Rosemont.

This finding has interesting implications for market research and strategy for Rosemont. For example, rating scales would not likely capture heavy-loyal customer preferences toward a particular direct merchant because preferences were based on experience. From the interview transcripts, the following summary statement can best describe preferences of heavy loyals: "I always buy from Rosemont; that's the reason I prefer them."

The strategy implication for direct marketers is that an extensive trial period of different suppliers is unlikely to occur among heavy loyals. In other words, a direct merchant's catalog must be readily available during the strategic window of opportunity when the heavy loyals start to garden.

P_5: Behavior of Former Customers

Former customers reported a decrease in gardening activities during the most recent years and some had stopped gardening entirely because of advancing age and/or deteriorating health. Some former customers also reported more buying directly from retailers. Again, the Stay the Course proposition, P_{5b}, is supported. The strategic implication for this issue is that efforts to win back such lost customers are likely to fail.

P_6: Regional Influence on Purchase

Respondents in the Dallas, TX area were most affected by regional conditions compared to respondents in the other areas (Rochester, NY and Raleigh, NC). Four of the seven respondents in Dallas reported a high incidence of buying from a regional company, Pendleton Brothers, because of special growing conditions in the Southwestern U.S. Thus, P_{6b} is supported. No comparable regional supplier emerged for respondents in New York and North Carolina.

This finding has significant strategic implications for Rosemont; given the size of the Texas market and the possibility of substantial regional bias of customers, the development and advertising of products uniquely suited for dry, hot climates may be a viable strategy. Managers at Rosemont discussed the possibility of a special catalog insert for customers in the Texas market and the possibility of purchasing the Pendleton Brothers business outright.

P_7: Shopping Behavior

All respondents who did buy gardening products from direct merchants in 1993 reported some unplanned purchases. Thus, P_{7a} (New Wave theory) is supported. Respondents that did buy from direct merchants were similar in their shopping behavior in terms of examining the catalogs they requested and received from direct merchants. Heavy-loyal customers reported buying some favorites each year, plus buying some unplanned items each year. The strategic implication of this finding for Rosemont is that providing "reason-why" copy and four-color photographs in the catalog should be continued.

P_8: Four-Color Photographs

Respondents (across all customer groups) consistently indicated a desire to see very frequent use of four-color photographs of plants in the catalog. Thus, P_{8b} is supported. Data on this particular research question were collected using "autodriving" techniques. Respondents were asked to examine two catalogs in-depth during the interview, one of which was always the sponsoring firms catalog. Based on the interviews, customers tend to perceive that Rosemont has a competitive advantage in that their catalog is the most complete in providing four-color photographs of products. The strategy implication for this issue is not to try and cut costs by moving away from color in the catalog. For Rosemont, the savings from switching to using black and white photographs on some pages may weaken brand equity in the minds of customers.

P_9: Larger Photographs for Flowers

For respondents who did buy flowers from direct merchants, some were asked to compare the Rosemont catalog to a competitor's book that has larger four-color photographs of flowers; in fact, this direct merchant specializes in flowers only. The general reaction was that the competitor's catalog was very nice to look at, but larger photographs would probably not cause them to buy more from this merchant compared to Rosemont. Thus, P_{9b} was supported over P_{9a}.

P_{10}: Photographs of People

Rosemont customers reported that reading the catalog is an enjoyable activity. Photographs of people are somewhat interesting but have little effect on either planned or unplanned buying. A general response was that customers buy "favorite" plants or seeds each year that have done well in their gardens in the past. For unplanned purchases, the photograph and description of the plant is important. Seeing people in the photographs provides momentary enjoyment but is not likely to influence behavior to buy. Thus, P_{10b} is supported. Typical responses include the following comments:

- "I really don't pay much attention to photographs or stories about people in seed and plant catalogs."
- "I don't pick up such catalogs to look at or read about people."

P_{11} and P_{12}: Catalog Writing Style and Drawings

To examine the issue of writing style and use of pen-and-ink drawings, three customers in each market were asked to examine the Harrison catalog along with Rosemont's catalog in the "autodriving" section of the interview. The nine respondents were upscale, relatively young, and approximated the target market addressed by Harrison. All nine respondents noted the unique style of Harrison's book, but seven of the nine said they would not change their general buying habits. Of these seven, four said that they might place a small order with Harrison to experiment. The general conclusion after examining the two catalogs was that while the Harrison book has a nice appearance and was enjoyable to read, the Rosemont catalog is familiar, products are easy to find, and Rosemont is a trusted source of gardening material. Only two respondents said they would substantially change their buying habits to order from Harrison instead of Rosemont.

Thus, P_{11b} and P_{12b} are supported. Making drastic changes to the Rosemont catalog would likely not result in an increase in the customer base and would probably alienate many of the current customers.

P_{13} and P_{14}: Special Varieties and Regional Products

When asked about the "heirloom" varieties of some plants (e.g., herbs, roses, and vegetables), the more experienced respondents, in particular, were interested to learn of their availability and would buy some items to try them. If the types tried were a success, respondents indicated that they would buy more of these products. In general, approximately half of the active gardeners (n = 10) could be considered "highly knowledgeable/experienced" and their intention to buy these products was high. Thus, P_{13a} is supported.

Related to P_6, P_{14} addresses the "regional" effect on buying. The Texas respondents were particularly likely to try products suited for their region compared to respondents in North Carolina and New York. Based on this finding, P_{14a} is supported. The implication for Rosemont management is that some regional varieties should be included in the catalog. Cost permitting, special catalogs for the Southwest market or a special insert in the "Big Book" may be a viable way to address this customer need.

P_{15}: Planned Garden Kits

None of the respondents bought planned gardens and none reported a willingness to buy such products. Thus, P_{15b} is supported. The strategic implication for Rosemont is that devoting substantial catalog space to planned gardens is unlikely to be profitable. They are unlikely to gain widespread customer acceptance. "The whole idea for me is to come up with my own garden arrangements," was a typical response to the idea of planned gardens. Several respondents reported that they could see why someone would like the idea of planned gardens, but such plans were not "for them, personally."

P_{16}: Environmental Concerns

With the exception of one respondent in the Rochester, NY, area, all reported that helping the environment was not something they consider when looking at gardening catalogs. No company was mentioned as being particularly environmentally friendly. Thus, P_{16b} is supported.

During the "autodriving" portion of the interview, respondents were shown several seed packets from different direct merchants. While they did recognize some of the packets as being made from natural materials while others contained metal and plastic in the packaging, none reported that they would be influenced to buy or not buy based on this factor. The strategic implication for Rosemont is that being perceived as "uniquely environmentally friendly" is not likely to increase sales significantly.

P_{17}: Perceptions of Guarantees

All respondents who purchased gardening products by mail in 1993 reported that the merchants offered money-back guarantees. "All the companies do a good job in guaranteeing their products," was the usual response when asked about this issue. Thus, 17_b is supported. For Rosemont, attempting to focus customer attention on a guarantee is unlikely to be effective in increasing customer loyalty.

When asked about past complaints, most of the respondents indicated some past communication with direct merchants regarding mistakes on orders. In all instances, though, the merchant involved usually offered a prompt response and the customer was satisfied with how the situation was handled. One merchant, however, was mentioned as consistently sending poor quality products; this company was specifically criticized by four respondents in two different regions and was mentioned in a negative light by other respondents.

P_{18}: Company History Information

Rosemont, Inc. recently celebrated its 100th year in business and managers wanted to make this event a focal point of that year's catalog. An "old-fashioned" cover was chosen and some debate ensued among the managers about devoting two pages in the Big Book to the history of the founders. This issue is salient to new customers, in particular who might be new to gardening, Rosemont, and other direct merchants of gardening products. When asked about the importance of the company's history, all five of the "new customer" respondents indicated that their own experience with the company was more important in maintaining trust. In other words, satisfaction with orders and resolution of complaints is more important than company history in determining whether future orders will be placed. Thus, P_{18b} is supported.

P_{19}: Non-Response Requestors

Four non-response requestors of catalogs were interviewed. All reported that they were buying gardening materials from local retailers rather than from direct merchants. P_{19b} is supported. Contrary to the proposition of the New Wave theory, these customers are not being lost to other direct merchants. All four non-response requestors were familiar with the Rosemont catalog and those of other direct merchants. None of the respondents had bought from any of the direct merchants, though. "I like to just look at the catalogs, especially the ones in color," is a general statement that summarizes the relationship of respondents in this customer group.

The strategic implication for Rosemont is that these non-response requestors are not likely to convert into buying customers. Thus, identifying and purging the names of non-response requestors would be a way to maintain/manage the resources devoted to mailing costs.

P_{20}: Demographic Effects

Based on the respondents interviewed for this study, P_{20b} is supported. Only one respondent was a single individual; all others were members of a household with some combination of other relatives (e.g., spouse, partner, and small children, grown children). Since our respondent group was small, Rosemont managers examined their own sales database information to note whether the number of single-person households was increasing. No evidence of this trend was found at the time of the study.

CRITICAL TEST OF COMPETING MENTAL MODELS

The Stay the Course mental model is supported for 17 of 20 propositions. The New Wave mental model is supported only for Propositions 7 (unplanned buying strategy), 13 (heirloom varieties), and 14 (regional varieties). This 17 to 20 "hit ratio" for the Stay the Course theory is statistically significant ($p < .002$) by a two-tailed sign test (Siegel, 1956). Although most of the propositions of the Stay the Course model are supported by the interview data, three of the New Wave propositions are accurate and should not be ignored by Rosemont.

THEORETICAL AND STRATEGIC IMPLICATIONS

Building on the work of Campbell (1975), Holbrook (1984), Hirschman (1985), and Mitroff and Kilmann (1978), DFA of case study data represents one method of reconciling the principal tenants of the scientific styles of the analytical scientist and the particular humanist. Such reconciliation may enable the behavioral scientist to envision a symbiotic style of inquiry, rather than taking an antagonistic stance toward logical positivism or qualitative research. Thus, DFA of case study data is one approach for achieving Hirschman's (1985, p. 238) wish, "Imagine how much one could learn about a phenomenon by personally examining it from [two to] four different points of view!" Certainly other approaches are possible for achieving reconciliation of scientific styles of inquiry. For examples of other approaches used in marketing-related field studies that synthesize the styles of the analytical scientist and particular humanist, see Ellis and Pecotich (2001), Hall (1976), Hall and Menzies (1983), Howard and Morgenroth (1968), Montgomery (1975), and Pettigrew (1975).

Figure 9-2 expands on Holbrook's (1984, p. 2) views on reconciling departures from initial theoretical structure: this figure displays the main tenants of both the analytical scientist and the particular humanist as well as DFA as one tool for achieving synergy by taking steps to reconcile the two styles. The steps include a triangulation approach to data collection, such as applying long interviews for explicating the implied assumptions behind the mental models of executives and comparing these assumptions with observed and reported behaviors of customers.

Using multiple methods to collect data helps achieve several useful outcomes that go beyond pattern matching (i.e., confirming evidence or viewpoints of two or more participants). Triangulation serves to increase the likelihood of uncovering useful knowledge about diverse mental models as well as helping to uncover nuances in thinking and action to resolve such diversities (Wells, 1995, p. 450). In the study reported, DFA serves as an etic interpretation (i.e., the interpretations of the data by the researcher as a third party) by comparing and conjoining the mental models of executives (one form of emic, participant interpretations) about how customers will respond to marketing strategies with data collected from long interviews with customers (a second form of emic data).

In this application, the long interview method of collecting case data proved very useful to management at Rosemont for gaining in-depth insight into the behavior of five customer groups. Managers often make the mistake of assuming they know their customers and that a particular view (i.e., mental model by the dominant group of executives) is valid, without being able to refer to any supporting evidence. Use of the long interview and DFA allows a researcher and/or executive to test competing views to find out about customers' thoughts, feelings, preferences, and actions. In reality, at Rosemont one group of managers

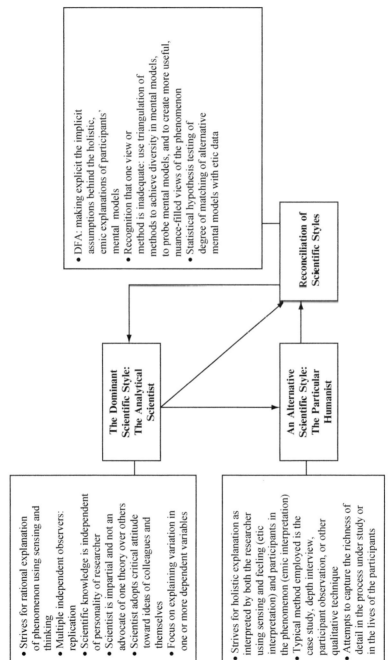

FIGURE 9.2 Reconciling alternative scientific styles in research related to marketing and consumer behavior.

(New Wave modelers) was *certain* they knew what customers want; while a second group (Stay the Course modelers) was equally sure customers want something else. In a separate follow-up study, Rosemont conducted a large-scale mail survey to re-examine the 20 issues included here plus many others. The survey form was eight pages long and required a respondent approximately 20 minutes to complete. Even so, the research firm conducting the study for Rosemont obtained a 60 percent response rate after two mailings. Members of the same five customer groups plus others were included in the 1995 survey.

The core findings from the long interview were corroborated in the survey findings. For example, using rating scales, respondents indicated that they did not involve young children in gardening, nor would they be interested in buying gardening products (seed packs) for children. Similarly, mean preference scores and intention to buy scores were low for planned gardens. Respondents did indicate a need for regional varieties of plants and seeds and heirloom varieties were highly preferred by respondents in the core customer group, in particular.

EPILOGUE

In closing, competing mental models may seem equally viable to different executives within the same company. Furthermore, there may be even more riding on strategic decisions than the simple choice of one model over another—organizational politics may enter the picture and pit managers against each other in a "win-lose" situation (e.g., see Pettigrew, 1975). Such a political conflict happened at Rosemont when the results of the long interview study were presented to the senior executives. The VP of Marketing was the primary proponent of the New Wave theory-in-use. When most of his theory's propositions were not supported, he grew quite angry with us (the researchers) and even left the meeting for a time. He remained at Rosemont for several more months before moving to another job. Most likely (because most assumptions within the CEO's mental model were represented by the Stay the Course model) the findings and conclusions of the study were used to help justify the decision not to launch the product line for parents and children. The general strategic implication may be that executives should not assume they know the answers about customer behavior without making explicit the core assumptions behind their mental models, as well as examining these mental models with independently collected data.

Yogi Berra's prescription to take both forks when they appear in the road is useful advice for embracing multiple scientific styles for research on consumer and executive behavior. Campbell's insights about building degrees of freedom in case study research may be helpful for taking both forks. By using such tools Hirschman's (1985, p.238) image of examining phenomena from two or more scientific styles can become the new dominant logic in behavioral research.

10

HOLISTIC CASE-BASED MODELING OF CUSTOMERS' THINKING/DOING BRAND EXPERIENCES

Synopsis

This chapter reviews grounded theory studies available in the literature that deepen understanding of holistic case-based modeling of customers' thinking/doing brand experiences. The chapter includes an empirical study to illustrate the method. The reported study includes applying the *long interview method* and *theoretical sampling* in completing personal, face-to-face interviews of travel parties at the moment when they have just ended their visits to a Canadian province. The empirical analysis focuses on acquiring process data held in the minds of customers—that is, the analysis illustrates emic-based storytelling of what was planned and what actually happened leading to specific outcomes. Achieving such holistic, case-based views of customer decisions and behavior provides a rich, deep, and nuance-filled understanding of the causes and consequences of such behaviors.

INTRODUCTION: EMIC VERSUS ETIC INTERPRETATIONS OF THINKING AND DOING

Grounded theory development often includes "thick descriptions" (Geertz, 1973; Glazer and Strauss, 1967) of behavioral processes from the perspectives of informants participating in these processes (i.e., emic interpretations) rather than only from the researcher's own perspective (i.e., etic interpretations). This chapter reviews grounded theory studies available in the literature that deepen understanding of leisure travel decisions and tourism behaviors. The chapter includes a set of core propositions that are examined empirically.

The reported empirical study includes applying the long interview method (McCracken, 1988) and theoretical sampling (Ragin, 1987) in completing personal, face-to-face interviews of travel parties at the moment of just completing their visits to a Canadian province. The study's findings support the core proposition in building grounded theory: a few (more than two but less than 40) major process paradigms arise inductively from the data that conjunctively (i.e., holistically) link: (a) antecedent-to-trip conditions to (b) trip planning strategies to (c) destination activities to (d) participants' evaluations of outcomes. One aim of such grounded theory development is to provide a gestalt understanding of the unconscious and conscious thoughts and behaviors of specific travelers who are representative of each visitor segment of all the segments relevant for a given destination.

This chapter illustrates gestalt profiling for Canadian domestic and foreign tourists visiting Prince Edward Island (PEI), a Canadian province. The data are from long interviews (McCracken, 1988; Woodside and Wilson, 1995) of PEI visitors; the data were collected for most cases on the final day of the visitors' stays in PEI. The findings provide nuances on "what makes the difference" for each of the travel parties in their selection of PEI and whether they perceive themselves returning to PEI to be likely or not. Unlike etic reporting via participant observations and interviews collected by the researcher (e.g., see Arnould and Price, 1993; Belk and Costa, 1998) the aim here is to capture complexity in reporting the nuances and process details of complete purchase consumption systems for leisure-related trips—from the seemingly mundane to the extraordinary thoughts, actions, and outcomes that reflect the emic views of processes planned and experienced.

REASONS FOR HOLISTIC CASE STUDIES IN LEISURE RESEARCH

Reports of holistic case studies may be valuable for several reasons. First, episodic memory dominates much of the conscious reporting and unconscious thinking of individuals—the metaphor of file drawers of stories in a human's memory is apt (see Shank, 1999). Frequently, humans catalog and retrieve episodes (i.e., stories) that represent their lives. While useful for developing and testing theory, the dominating logic in travel research of variable-based empirical positivism (e.g., Woodside and Dubelaar, 2002) needs to be complemented by additional theory-research paradigms—such as holistic case-based empirical relativism—that focus on thick descriptions of an individual's thoughts and actions constituting the stories in her lived experiences.

Second, humans have limited cognitive access to most of the details of the stories stored in their memory file drawers (see Zaltman, 2003); most thinking occurs unconsciously (Wegner, 2002; Zaltman, 2003). Consequently, many details of the thoughts and behaviors that occur during an overnight destination visit are available only unconsciously to the tourist—especially as days turn into months and years after visiting a destination. The stories that individuals report weeks or months after visiting a destination are summaries of the minutia of events and thoughts that occurred while experiencing the visit. The old saying, "God is in the details," applies here: theory and research to capture as much detail as possible of holistic stories may help increase understanding of the unconscious thinking that supports individuals' summary conscious thoughts and evaluations about their destination visits.

Third, consumers prefer narrative forms of events related to a destination visit rather than simply listings of features and benefits (Adaval and Wyer, 1998): using different travel brochures, the attractiveness of vacation trips was greater in the Adaval and Wyer study when a story described visits rather than listing of features and benefits of visits. Given that consumers store and retrieve stories, and may prefer stories for processing communications, storytelling research may help tourism marketing strategists (TMSs) design destination experiences and communications that partially shape fondly held–retrieved memories, as well as design experiences and communications that lead to a "bad trip" summary evaluation. Thus, learning emic, holistic stories of visits may have practical importance for offering products and services customers prefer—by providing deeper and broader information than found in variable-based (e.g., waiting time and customer satisfaction) reporting systems.

THEORETICAL SAMPLING IN HOLISTIC CASE STUDIES

Note that if a destination identifies 20 distinct visitor segments by origins (e.g., 10 domestic and 10 foreign) and breaks visitors into two distinct length-of-stay groups (e.g., short versus long-term); and into repeat versus first-time visitors, then a total of 80 potential profiles may occur (i.e., $20 \times 2 \times 2 = 80$ theoretical segments). About 10 to 20 of these segments are likely to be important strategically for the quality of life (e.g., economic and social well-being) of the destination (or hotel, car rental firm, or airline company), assuming that tourism is a major industry for the destination. For the study that this chapter reports, the quality of life for many PEI residents depends substantially on the success of its tourism industry—the province's largest employer.

Empirical evidence from several studies often supports propositions that appear to be "just common sense," such as, domestic visitors to a destination usually stay longer and manage to spend less than foreign visitors; domestic visitors are more often repeat visitors to a destination compared to foreign visitors. However, the conjunction of the seemingly unexpected combinations of levels of different attributes among some visitors do occur frequently and the examination of such unusual cases increases our knowledge substantially of causes, consequences, and trends in the behaviors of visitors. As such, comparative analysis (see Ragin, 1987) advocates abandoning the concept of "statistical outlier" and rejects the practice of discarding outlier cases. Thus, the 23-year-old domestic visitor who stays two nights and spends over $1,000 during her visit becomes as intriguing in comparative analysis as the possibly more often appearing 23-year-old domestic visitor who stays twenty nights and spends $400 during her visit.

Theoretical sampling in comparative analysis does not attempt to plan for a representative sample of respondents from a population but rather considers the theoretical possibilities of all unique combinations of case profiles typically across four to seven attributes. For example, theoretical sampling might include recognizing the existence of domestic/foreign, short/long time, first/repeat, small/big expenditure visitors. After providing operational measures to the constructs, a quota sampling plan (assuming visitors can be found for all possible factor combinations) is implemented to attempt to interview enough visitors representing each of the combinations (i.e., 16 combinations for the four constructs just listed). McCracken (1988) recommends five to eight interviews per cell.

The objective of such research is to build and generalize to theory rather than to test and generalize theory to a population (see Langley, 1999; Yin, 1994). Comparative analysis and process data from cases fits well with the wisdom that marketing strategists need to design product/service use experiences that satisfy the individual customer. The contents and levels of customer satisfaction and dissatisfaction may be learned from the stories that they tell when describing their travel experiences and the "good and bad memories" that surface when describing these experiences.

The aim for comparative process case-based reports is to examine all theoretically identified customer samples that occur in real life and provide thick descriptions for each multiple-attribute-based conjunctive segment. Such reporting embraces an alternative paradigm from the positivistic view that some data cases should be discarded from analysis (and assigned the label, "statistical outliers") because they include extreme point values for one or more variables (i.e., unusually high expenditures spent in the destination area). The comparative analysis adopts an alternative paradigm that we should search for "the tipping point" (Gladwell, 1996) of the seemingly unusual combination of events or levels (or the seemingly rare occurrence) of some antecedent attributes that results in the observed seemingly extreme behavior.

Grounded Theory Construction of Tourism Behavior

The concept of purchase consumption systems (Woodside and King, 2001; and Woodside and Dubelaar, 2002) is useful for grounded theory construction of tourism behavior. A purchase consumption system (PCS) is the sequence of mental and observable steps a consumer undertakes to buy and use several products for which some of the products purchased lead to a purchase sequence involving other products. Becker (1998) and others (e.g., Ragin, 1987) recommend the use of qualitative comparative analysis (i.e., the use of Boolean algebra) to create possible typologies and then to compare these typologies to empirical realities. Possible types of streams of trip decisions from combinations of five destination options with six travel mode options and four accommodation categories, three accommodation brands, five within-area route options, and four in-destination area visit options result in 7,200 possible decision paths.

The central PCS proposition is that several decisions within a customer's PCS are dependent on prior purchases of products that trigger these later purchases. While appearing to be intuitively obvious, empirical research for grounded theory construction is needed to verify how well emic views match etic mental models of how and what streams of tourism behavior are implemented—and the causes and consequences of these streams.

Woodside and King (2001) describe category level data relevant for grounded theory construction among visitors to the "Big Island" of Hawaii, for example, the decision processes for selecting and the doing-behaviors while visiting the "Big Island" of Hawaii. Their research report is useful for answering several strategic policy issues, such as whether the Big Island can be positioned as a brand standing alone from the State of Hawaii (the answer: not according to Woodside and King's report). However, their study does not include in-depth reporting at the individual visit party level. The suggestion here is that grounded-theory construction needs to capture the emic holistic view of individual-level causes and consequences of processes in tourism behavior. Thus, the stress of such theory construction is on applying Weick's (1995) wisdom to deeply learn by staying complex and providing thick descriptions of complete destination-related behaviors. Generalization to customer segments may then follow from building a collection of individual case studies of tourism behavior processes.

While Woodside and Dubelaar's (2002) report is useful for describing how specific nuances in destination-area behaviors affect other behaviors, their empirical analysis does not actually include analysis of complete PCSs. The empirical report provides a variable-level-only analysis—two variables at a time—and not a deep understanding of complete decisions and flows at the individual level.

Figure 10-1 displays nine issues relevant for grounded theory construction of the flows of decisions and behaviors that focus particularly on destination choices—including antecedents and consequences of implementing these choices. Other tourism foci for grounded theory construction (not shown in Figure 10-1) includes mode/route to and while visiting decisions; accommodations decisions; dining-out choices; decisions and actual behaviors regarding search and use of information and advice of where to visit and what to do; gift-buying decisions. For all these foci, decision topics that might be included focus on learning the alternatives that came to mind but were rejected in favor of what was done—and what made the difference in the choices made.

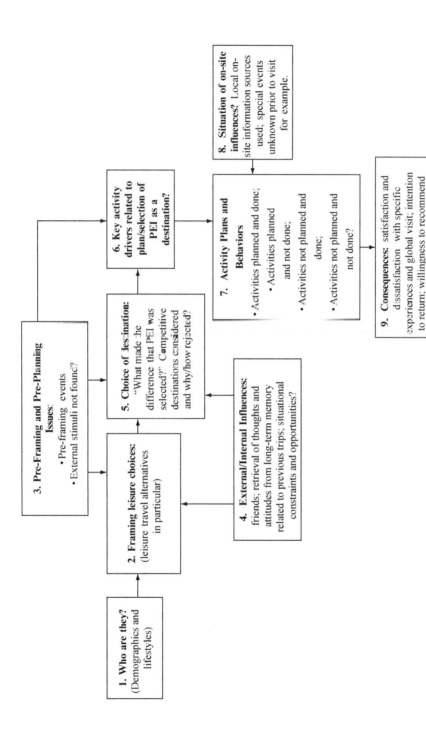

FIGURE 10.1 Theoretical and empirical issues.

3. **Pre-Framing and Pre-Planning Issues**:
• Pre-framing events
• External stimuli not found?

6. **Key activity drivers related to plan/selection of PEI as a destination?**

8. **Situation of on-site influences?** Local on-site information sources used; special events unknown prior to visit for example.

5. **Choice of destination:** "What made the difference that PEI was selected?" Competitive destinations considered and why/how rejected?

7. **Activity Plans and Behaviors**
• Activities planned and done;
• Activities planned and not done;
• Activities not planned and done;
• Activities not planned and not done?

9. **Consequences:** satisfaction and dissatisfaction with specific experiences and global visit; intention to return; willingness to recommend similar trip and PEI as a destination?

4. **External/Internal Influences:** friends; retrieval of thoughts and attitudes from long-term memory related to previous trips; situational constraints and opportunities?

2. **Framing leisure choices:** (leisure travel alternatives in particular)

1. **Who are they?** (Demographics and lifestyles)

GROUNDED THEORY PROPOSITIONS

The arrows in Figure 10-1 represent propositions relevant for grounded theory development and for guiding questions for thick descriptions of visitors' behaviors. While the propositions may imply a variable-based analysis, the research objective of Figure 10-1 is to provide a template of topics to ensure coverage during long interviews in case studies—not to test statistically for generalizing to a population of visitors. The following discussion summarizes each proposition.

P_1 (box 1 to 2 in Figure 10-1): demographics and lifestyles of visitors influence how they frame leisure choices. For example, households with two teenage children will often consider only leisure trips that include "things to do" for teenagers but the same things to do are not found among visiting households traveling without teenagers.

P_2 (box 3 to 2): unexpected or unplanned events occur (or might be available, but are not used) that influence (or do not affect) the framing of leisure choices. For example, a household may receive an unsolicited brochure about a destination that triggers initial thoughts of planning a visit. If such brochures trigger such thoughts, the brochures may represent a necessary but not sufficient condition resulting in a visit to the given destination.

P_3 (box 4 to 2): external and internal personal influences affect the framing of leisure choices. For example, a comment made by a friend about the joyful experiences visiting a destination might be retrieved and mentioned during the framing of leisure choices.

P_4 (box 2 to 5): the features and benefits included in framing leisure alternatives affects the destination choices selected and rejected. For example, a specific activity benefit resulting from visiting Destination X may tip the balance in favor of X versus alternative destinations considered by the visiting travel party.

P_5 (box 3 to 5): information collected for framing and trip planning affects the process of selecting and rejecting destination alternatives.

P_6 (box 4 to 5): friends' opinions and thoughts retrieved from memory influence the selection and rejection of destination alternatives.

P_7 (box 5 to 6): "key activity" drivers solidify the decision to visit the destination selected—such drivers are concrete plans and pre-trip actions (e.g., bookings) regarding a specific visit to the destination selected.

P_8 (box 6 to 7): key activity drivers affect what is planned and done in the destination area. Note in box 7 that activities can be categorized into four quadrants: planned–done, planned–undone, unplanned–done, and unplanned–undone.

Activities planned and done are often key activity drivers related to deciding to visit a specific destination. Acquiring data on planned-done actions may provide information particularly helpful for designing destination attractions and positioning messages that match with activities important for some visitors.

Unplanned and done activities may represent destination features and benefits worthy of more attention by destination marketing strategists. Some unplanned and done actions may represent the largest share of leisure time pursuits done by many visitors—given that in-depth prior trip planning does not occur for many travelers (see Fodness and Murray, 1999).

Planned and undone activities may be the result of loss of interest, some unexpected situational contingency preventing the activity from being realized, or some on-the-scene trade-off/replacement of a planned action with some other action judged more desirable. Collecting data on planned and undone activities may prove particularly valuable for destination attractions receiving many customer inquiries but few customer visits.

Unplanned-undone activities are tourism-related activities that are possible to do but the visitor does not plan on doing and does not do. For example, from time to time a deep-sea fishing service operation starts-up in PEI but soon fails because unplanned-undone deep-sea fishing behavior occurs among PEI visitors during the one to three years such services operate. The visitor may be aware that deep-sea fishing sometimes exists on some ocean islands but the activity never "comes to mind" during her visit. Identifying such unplanned-undone activities relevant for specific destinations may be useful for designing experiences that visitors may find rewarding and serve as an early warning system of what activities may not get implemented by visitors.

P_9 (box 8 to 7): information and events learned by the visitors while visiting affects their plans and behaviors. To apply Weick's (1995) "sensemaking" wisdom, visitors sometimes only think about doing something after they see it being done.

P_{10} (box 7 to 9): the activities done (and not done) affect much of the attitude and intention consequences resulting from, and associating with, visiting a destination. Thus, "what we saw" and "what we did" that results in specific outcomes are the antecedents to a "good" or "bad" trip (see Frazer, 1991).

A DECISION-STAGES-BY-TRIP-COMPONENTS TEMPLATE

A decision-stages-by-trip-components (DSTC) template was designed before data were collected to ensure that at least some information collected covered multiple components of visitors' purchase consumption systems. The template includes four decision stages by seven trip components. The decision stages include (1) consideration set and choice made; (2) motives and situational conditions affecting the choice; (3) search and use of information in making the choice; (4) a summary of the outcome of the experiences related to the choice—each of these four stages are considered across the seven trip components.

The seven trip components include data on: (1) destinations; (2) route/mode to and in the principal destination; (3) accommodations during the stay in the destination; (4) activities done in the destination; (5) regions visited in the destination; (6) attractions visited including restaurants; and (7) gifts and other purchases made in the destination area for taking away. Figure 10-2 displays the template and provides summary data from one case study for the four decision stages across the seven trip components.

One objective of the DSTC template is to briefly summarize key thoughts and actions across multiple components of a visitor's purchase consumption system. A second objective is to use such a template to help to easily place each case into one category among 20 to 80 theoretically possible categories of visitors (e.g., domestic/foreign; regional area; short/long stay; new/repeat) and to consider the nuances in the decisions and behaviors within each of the real-life cases available per category. Thus, by examining several (n > 5) cases among repeat visitors to PEI from New England who stayed 7+ nights in PEI, the key drivers (in actions and thoughts) relevant particularly to such visitors more than visitors in other categories are identified.

Method

A field study was designed to examine the propositions and to explore the usefulness of writing reports of the holistic purchase consumption systems of visitors at a time very close to completing their visits to a given destination. The field study was designed to allow for 90- to 120- minute, in-situ interviews using a 22-page questionnaire that permitted probes and follow-up questions (e.g., "What makes you say that?") to issues raised by the respondent that were not thought about by the researchers in planning the study.

Informants and Procedure

The informants for the study were Canadian, American, and overseas overnight visitors to PEI. All the data were collected two to four hours before the informants departed PEI. The data collection locations included ferry terminals, Charlottetown (PEI's capital city) Airport, and hotels and motels. The data were collected in 1993—before the "fixed link" (i.e., the bridge linking PEI to New Brunswick) was constructed. At the time of the study nearly all overnight visitors to PEI entered and left the province via the ferry terminals and the Charlottetown Airport. The specific findings relevant for PEI visitors in the following report may differ from data collected after the opening of the fixed link connection; however, such influence is unlikely to alter the findings related to the propositions in developing a grounded theory of leisure travel. Most often, to qualify for the study, a visiting party had to have completed two-thirds or more of his/her total time for their current visit in PEI.

Many interviews were conducted at the island's two ferry terminals. The occupants of personal vehicles with non-PEI license plates were approached and asked to participate in a PEI Visitor Survey. A University of PEI T-shirt was offered as a gift for cooperating in answering the questions. The questions were asked by an interviewer who wrote down the answers to the questions. Three interviewer training sessions and two rounds of pre-tests of the questionnaires were completed before the authors reached agreement that the questionnaire was ready for use.

Decision Stages 2.2.C03	Destinations	Route/Mode to and in PEI	Accommodations During PEI Stay	Activities in PEI	PEI Regions Visited	Attractions Visited, Including Restaurants	Gifts and Purchases Made
Consideration Set and Choices	PEI versus other Maritime tourist areas	Moncton – Borden Ferry – Charlottetown Private vehicle	MacLaughlan's Motel – Charlottetown, could not get first choice Rodd's Cottages, Montague	Rainbow Valley (1st day) Wax Museum, Woodleigh Replicas, Ripley's – planned. Very pleased with RV	Cavendish area was the only region they planned to visit	Cavendish area; Rainbow Valley (planned). Museum, Woodleigh Replicas, Ripley's eating at McDonald's and Pizza Delight	No gifts or other purchases and no intention to buy gifts or other purchases
Motives	Getaway leisure trip. Rest and relaxation	Shortest and fastest way to PEI	Love to swim in pool (children & parents), so looked only at places with pools	Children, particularly the son, wanted to visit Rainbow Valley and some other theme parks	To take the children to attractions and theme parks in that area	Fun and enjoyment, particularly for children, relaxing for parents	No desire to purchase gifts on this trip

Information Search and Use	Read *This Week in PEI* to learn about attractions (mainly Cavendish area)	No assistance required *en route*	*This Week in PEI* helpful	Hear about RV from friends, found other attractions in *This Week in PEI*	Found their way on their own as had been to PEI before. Used small map in publication.	*This Week in PEI* received prior to visit	None
Outcomes	As expected, for both attractions and destination. Pleased with accommodation particularly	Route and experiences as expected	As expected	Loved Rainbow Valley	Pleased with Rainbow Valley; very pleased with pool.	As expected	None

FIGURE 10.2 The visit to Prince Edward Island (PEI) of a family with two children (Case 21). From Moncton, New Brunswick. Stayed 3 nights at Charlottetown. Income range: not given. Expenditures: $655. Repeat visitors. Both parents in their forties, boy aged 10, girl aged 5 years of age. Work status: father full-time. Visitor segment: near-distant, domestic, short get-away leisure, young family market. Primary destination: PEI. This family lives close to PEI and made a decision to go to PEI after a *This Week in PEI* newsletter was put in their mailbox. They had not been to the island for "many, many years." The son was the primary decision-maker for the locatior. They had some trouble finding accommodations on short notice. They ended up in a motel with a pool that suited the children. Other activities were centered on the children. They were looking for a short family vacation, to relax and escape daily concerns. They enjoyed their stay and said they would be very likely to return. Key words: younger family, three-day stay, local repeat visitors, mostly unplanned activities, drive, moderate involvement once on island, very short planning time frame.

To reduce unknown self-selection biases, at the ferry terminals the fourth and twelfth vehicles in line were selected for the study. Similarly, at the airport, the fourth person arriving at the departure gate was selected for participation in the study.

The questionnaire used included requests for:

- A complete demographic description of the members of the travel party.
- Total nights away from home as well as total nights spent on PEI for this trip.
- Details of the trip itinerary actually completed for the trip.
- Amount and details of the planning done before the trip.
- Use of travel professional help, if any.
- Request and use information (PEI Visitors' Guide) from government travel offices, if any.
- Who was involved (and how) in deciding to visit PEI?
- Use of the province's official visitor's guide after arriving in PEI.
- Destinations visited in PEI for this trip.
- Overnight accommodations used in PEI and how/why selected.
- Prime motives in visiting PEI.
- Prior visit history to PEI.
- Activities done and attractions/places visited in PEI for the current trip.
- Whether the informant considered different modes of travel to PEI.
- Whether the informant considered different routes of travel to PEI.
- Visiting friends and/or relatives in PEI.
- Evaluation of specific activities done, attractions experienced, accommodations used, and PEI as a leisure destination and reasons for these evaluations.
- Gift buying behavior: what was bought if anything; what was considered and not purchased; principal reasons for buying and not buying; where purchased; "what 'clinched the deal' for you" for buying the highest-priced item purchased?
- Expenditures related to travel to/from PEI and while in PEI including specific breakouts for accommodations, recreation/entertainment, food, gifts, within PEI travel.
- Likelihood of returning to PEI within the next two years.
- Detailed demographics: age, martial status, education, employment, and income.

Analysis

A total of 34 interviews were completed: 27 at the two ferry terminals and seven at the airport. For each informant travel party, thick, written descriptions were completed and the interviewer filled in the DSTC template. Each case study report was read and revised following questions asked of the interviewer by the research team.

Findings

The origins, prior PEI visit experiences, and lengths of stay of the informants reflect the core PEI total visitor data:

- The majority of visitors are from two domestic origin markets: other Maritime provinces and the province of Ontario.
- The majority of foreign visitors are Americans.
- Nearly all maritime visitors to PEI are repeat visitors.
- Most Ontario visitors to PEI are repeat visitors.
- Most American visitors to PEI are first-time visitors.

Economically, three visitor segments are vital for tourism as a PEI export industry: repeat visitors from other Maritime provinces; repeat and new visitors from Ontario; and new visitors from the U.S. The following discussion provides holistic case-study summaries of a travel party planning and visiting PEI for each of these three critical visitor segments as well as two additional case studies from non-critical origin markets: western Canada and Europe.

A YOUNG FAMILY FROM NEW BRUNSWICK VISITS PRINCE EDWARD ISLAND: INTERVIEW SYNOPSIS

This case study includes responses by a young family visiting PEI for pleasure, for three nights, in late July 1993. The family includes a husband, wife, and two children, a 10-year-old boy and a 5-year-old girl. A fun trip, primarily for the children, was the motive. No particular destination was considered until a copy of *This Week in PEI* appeared in the family's mailbox (not sent for), approximately two weeks before departure. The son was the primary decision-maker in deciding where to spend this leisure time. Total expenditures for this trip were estimated to be $655.00. This total did not include any purchased gifts or other items to take home, nor was there any plan to make such purchases before returning home. The family primarily used the publication *This Week in PEI* while they were visiting. They were unfamiliar with the *PEI Visitors Guide* and had never heard of this publication. The family reports being very likely to return to PEI in 1994.

The data in Figure 10-2 apply to this family's trip. Note Figure 10-2 indicates high impact of the publication, *This Week in PEI*, for triggering the visit, booking accommodations, and selecting activities to engage in. The publication was a necessary but not sufficient condition for the decision to visit PEI. Figure 10-3 includes external influences that influenced the decision to visit PEI, including the son's friends highly recommending going to PEI's Rainbow Valley theme park. Voicing this recommendation and desire by the son was a necessary but not sufficient condition for completing the decision to visit PEI.

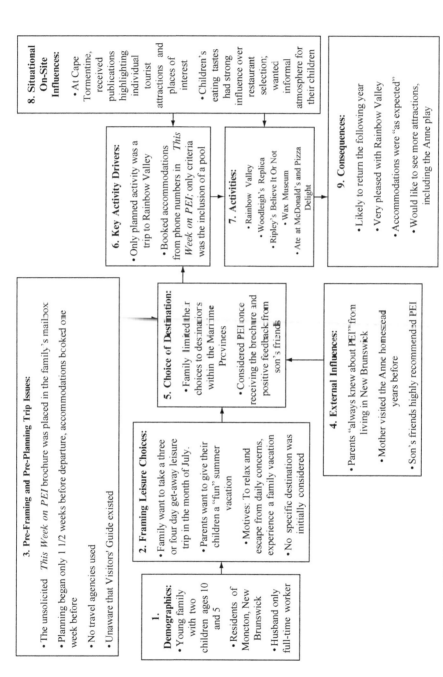

3. Pre-Framing and Pre-Planning Trip Issues:
- The unsolicited *This Week on PEI* brochure was placed in the family's mailbox
- Planning began only 1 1/2 weeks before departure, accommodations booked one week before
- No travel agencies used
- Unaware that Visitors' Guide existed

8. Situational On-Site Influences:
- At Cape Tormentine, received publications highlighting individual tourist attractions and places of interest
- Children's eating tastes had strong influence over restaurant selection; wanted informal atmosphere for their children

6. Key Activity Drivers:
- Only planned activity was a trip to Rainbow Valley
- Booked accommodations from phone numbers in *This Week on PEI*; only criteria was the inclusion of a pool

5. Choice of Destination:
- Family limited their choices to destinations within the Maritime Provinces
- Considered PEI once receiving the brochure and positive feedback from son's friends

2. Framing Leisure Choices:
- Family want to take a three or four day get-away leisure trip in the month of July.
- Parents want to give their children a "fun" summer vacation
- Motives: To relax and escape from daily concerns, experience a family vacation
- No specific destination was initially considered

7. Activities:
- Rainbow Valley
- Woodleigh's Replica
- Ripley's Believe It Or Not
- Wax Museum
- Ate at McDonald's and Pizza Delight

4. External Influences:
- Parents "always knew about PEI" from living in New Brunswick
- Mother visited the Anne homestead years before
- Son's friends highly recommended PEI

1. Demographics:
- Young family with two children ages 10 and 5
- Residents of Moncton, New Brunswick
- Husband only full-time worker

9. Consequences:
- Likely to return the following year
- Very pleased with Rainbow Valley
- Accommodations were "as expected"
- Would like to see more attractions, including the Anne play

FIGURE 10.3 Visit to Prince Edward Island (PEI) of a young family from the Maritime provinces.

Description of the Family Visiting PEI and Interview Site/Day

The travel party included Larry McKnight (LM), his wife Charlene (CM), and their two children, a girl and boy, ages five and ten respectively. CM answered all the questions. CM and her husband are both in their forties. CM has some college/university education while her husband has a high school diploma. CM does not work outside the home; her husband is employed full-time. LM did not reveal his occupation. The interviewer was unable to determine the level of family income, as CM declined to answer this question. They reside in Moncton, New Brunswick.

Interview Site/Day

The interview was conducted in the poolroom at McLaughlin's Motel in Charlottetown. CM's two children were enjoying swimming in the pool while CM was watching them. The interviewer and CM sat at a poolside table in the poolroom so that CM could have a good view of the children. LM was in the family's motel room resting. It was a beautiful evening outside (19 degrees Celsius). The poolroom was very hot. The family had just returned from a day trip to Rainbow Valley.

Trip Decisions for the Total Trip

This trip to PEI for CM and her family was planned about 1.5 weeks prior to their departure for PEI. They planned a three- or four-day getaway leisure trip. Using the publication *This Week in PEI*, plans for accommodations were also made about one week before departure. At the same time, tentative plans were made to visit some attractions while on PEI. The only concrete plan was a one-day visit to Rainbow Valley. No other destinations were named in the planned trip, only "somewhere in the Maritime Provinces." Marketing management implication (MMI): if such customers represent an important target market for maritime visitors to PEI, their planning time is very brief, thus advertising media schedules should include in-season advertising placements and messages to reach such customers.

Planning Horizon

CM noted "very little" planning time prior to making the trip to PEI. No other destinations outside the Maritimes were considered. MMI: Once on PEI, the family saw and read about many attractions of interest to them, through their travels about the island and from publications passed out to them in the compound at Cape Tormentine prior to driving onto the ferry. Note also that the arrival of the publication in their mailbox at their home in Moncton was the critical deciding factor or "clinched the deal" (a publication at no cost to the consumer and one which they had not requested). As soon as the publication was looked at, the decision was made to come to PEI as the son had heard his friends talk a lot about PEI, primarily Rainbow Valley as a fun place to visit.

Assistance by Travel Professionals

No assistance was considered or sought from travel professionals prior to the trip. Such assistance would likely have benefited the McKnights as they had to make several phone calls prior to the trip to book accommodations.

Requesting Information from Travel Offices Before Visiting

No information was requested prior to the visit, nor was any sought once the family arrived on PEI. They were, however, given handouts at the ferry terminal at Cape Tormentine. Other than a planned visit to Rainbow Valley, the rest of the visit was unplanned as they went along.

PEI Planning Issues

The family "always knew about PEI" but had not visited for "many, many years." CM stated that she had once visited the homestead at *Anne of Green Gables* in Cavendish, but that her husband and children had not seen it. No one in the family had read the *Anne of Green Gables* book collection nor had they seen the play. [The play is presented in Charlottetown six days per week during the summer months.] They did state, however, that on a return visit they would like to see many more attractions including the play.

The Publication Used: *This Week in PEI*

From this guide the family was able to make telephone calls to obtain reservations, as well as to decide on a number of other attractions that they might like to see besides Rainbow Valley during their visit: Woodleigh Replicas, Wax Museum, and Ripley's Believe It Or Not.

Decision-Making Process for the Trip

Although all family members took part in the decision-making process in terms of where to go on this trip, no one person was really adamant as to where they should go. The son finally became very excited about a visit to PEI, but only after the publication *This Week in PEI* appeared in the mail and he then remembered comments made to him by his friends about the wonderful time they had had at Rainbow Valley. This conversation was the turning point in their decision on where to go on their leisure trip. The rest of the family also agreed that PEI would be a "fun place to visit."

PEI Visit Issues

Decision-Making Process for Accommodations

The family made reservations for accommodations on PEI only one week prior to leaving home. The publication *This Week in PEI* listed several possible accommodations that this travel party considered. Although they could not remember the names of the places that they called, they did express an interest in staying in the eastern part of the island, around the Montague area and possibly at Rodd's Brudenel Resort. Friends had recommended the area because of its beautiful scenery. However, they were unable to obtain a reservation in that area from those listed in the publication. They called three other places before they finally obtained a reservation at MacLaughlan's Motel. Once they found an opening there they stopped looking. They planned to stay a total of three nights at MacLaughlan's Motel before heading back home. A pool in which the children could enjoy themselves was of major importance in the selection of an accommodation. Those accommodations without an indoor pool were not considered.

Assessment of Accommodations

The assessment of the accommodation was "about as expected." The motel was found to be "reasonably priced" and there were no negative comments on the accommodations. The pool "clinched the deal." The McKnight's also enjoyed the layout of the rooms in that there was a separate room in which the children could sleep, apart from the main bedroom. Total dollars spent on accommodations was $320.00.

Mode of Transportation and Route Taken

This travel party traveled to PEI by car directly from Moncton (a one-hour drive to Cape Tormentine). No other route was considered, as the family wanted to travel the most direct route possible. They were pleasantly surprised to be able to drive onto the ferry very shortly after coming into the ferry terminal, as they had expected to have to wait in a line at the compound. During the interview their plans were to return home by the same route.

Purchases of Gifts and Other Items

Prior to visiting PEI, there were no plans to buy gifts or other items to take home. When interviewed, CM stated that they indeed had not purchased any gifts and had no plans to do so. MMI: This market segment tends to stay for shorter periods of time and spend less money on gifts/souvenirs.

Activities and Attractions Visited

Rainbow Valley was the only planned attraction. Rainbow Valley turned out to be as expected and CM commented that it was "reasonably priced." However, others that were considered were the Wax Museum, Woodleigh Replicas, and Ripley's Believe It Or Not. The plan was to "play it by ear and see what develops," while driving around the Cavendish area the next day. The beach area at Cavendish was also under consideration but plans were very flexible. MMI: This travel party completed little formal planning prior to the visit.

Eating Places

The children in this travel party were the primary decision-makers in where to eat while on the trip to PEI. On the trip they preferred to eat in places such as Pizza Delight and McDonald's. The parents preferred these places for the children, as they were not admitted into formal dining rooms with children of these ages. Total food expenditures were around $200.00.

Motives for the Trip

The motives for this trip were evenly distributed between a chance to experience a family vacation and a chance to relax and escape from daily concerns. MMI: This travel party appears to reflect a more relaxed, slower-paced experience in which recuperation may be more important than stimulation.

Summary

CM and her family plan to return to PEI in one year. MMI: A significant number of near-home travelers predict that they will actually return to the site in the near future. Also, near-home travelers have a higher potential of being repeat customers if they are satisfied. These conclusions suggest important marketing implications for design of an offering and the way it should be promoted for the near-home traveler. The near-home market segment may spend only a brief time planning their trip, so advertising and media are important in reaching this market. Product positioning is an important prerequisite to designing market strategies for this group as well as for the distance traveler.

HOW THE PROPOSITIONS APPLY TO REPEAT MARITIME PROVINCE VISITS TO PEI

This first case study provides strong support for P_1, demographics and lifestyles of visitors influence how they frame leisure choices. Ensuring fun experiences for the children was the key motivation behind the visit.

P_2 is strongly supported. An unexpected event occurred that influenced the framing of leisure choices: the arrival of *This Week in PEI*. While not a controlled experiment demonstrating influence (see Woodside, 1990), this case study provides strong investigative evidence the this publication is a necessary if not a sufficient condition for causing some share of repeat PEI visits from travel parties residing in other Maritime Provinces.

P_3 receives strong support. Both external and internal personal influences affect the framing of the trip to PEI by this family.

P_4 receives modest support. Visiting a particular theme park, Rainbow Valley, is the specific PEI attribute that was mentioned by the son that became a key motivation in deciding to visit PEI. However, this case report does not include thinking processes that reflect destination rejection or comparing PEI with alternative destinations. A key motivation was also identified that influenced their choice of accommodations: the presence of a swimming pool.

P_5 receives strong support: information collected for framing and trip planning affected the process of selecting and rejecting destination alternatives. However, the principal information used was not sought—it just arrived in the mailbox.

P_6 receives strong support: friends' opinions and thoughts retrieved from memory influenced the selection and rejection of destination alternatives. P_7 receives strong support: "key activity" motivations solidified the decision to visit the destination selected—in this case the key motivation was one theme park. P_8 receives strong support: one activity driver (the theme park visit) affected what was planned and done in the destination area.

P_9 receives support: information and events learned by the visitors while visiting affected their plans and behaviors. For example, where they ate meals was very much affected by their frequently passing fast-food restaurants. P_{10} receives support: visiting Rainbow Valley was a successful experience—the activities done (and not done) affect much of the attitude and intention consequences resulting from, and associating with, visiting a destination. Not-done activities include visiting more attractions and seeing the *Anne of Green Gables* production in Charlottetown.

HIGH-INCOME COUPLE FROM ONTARIO VISITS PRINCE EDWARD ISLAND

This section provides a descriptive analysis of a middle-aged couple's recent pleasure trip to PEI for a total of three nights during the first week of August. The couple had originally planned a week's stay on the island, but left because of unsuitable accommodations and their inability to find appropriate ones. The couple described their visit to PEI as a "complete disaster," as they spent the entire three days driving around the island in search of accommodations. The primary and sole motive of the married couple's visit to the island was to relax and escape in a "quaint cottage close to the ocean." There were no competing destinations for this trip to PEI, as the trip had been planned for four years in advance of the visit. Expenditures for the couple's three-day stay amounted to $925.

The couple received the Visitors' Guide before arriving on PEI, and used it heavily to assist in locating accommodations and attractions. The couple was very unsatisfied with the trip to PEI, as they spent the entire three days searching for accommodations, and finally became frustrated and cut their trip short to return to Ontario. Both the husband and the wife said they would most definitely not return to PEI in the next year or any year after. Figures 10-4 and 10-5 summarize details of the planning, visit activities, and trip evaluations by this couple.

Decision Stages 2,0,S07	Destinations	Route/Mode to and in PEI	Accommodations During PEI Stay	Activities in PEI	PEI Regions Visited	Attractions Visited, Including Restaurants	Gifts and Purchases Made
Consideration Set and Choices	PEI only	Flight to PEI, Toronto to Halifax to Charlottetown	Shaw's Hotel. Rodd Royalty Inn, Rodd Charlottetown Hotel	Wanted to visit beaches. Lobster suppers / museums / Anne of Green Gables House	None	No attractions visited	No gifts bought; accommodations, meals, car rental, gas.
Motives	Relax, escape daily concerns, tap into island offerings	Flew as time was a primary consideration	Wanted a cottage by the sea (booked Steadman's Cottages but not acceptable)	Could not do any, as all time was spent looking for alternative accommodations	Looking for accommodations	Looking for accommodations	Only necessities

Information Search and Use	Visitors' Guide, from having lived on island for 4 months	Visitors' Guide, from previous visit	Charlottetown VIC	Visitors' Centre	None	Visitors' Centre	On the way
Outcomes	Negative impression of PEI	Negative impression of PEI	Grading system of Visitors' Guide was only fair. Star system misleading, less than expected	Negative impression of PEI	Negative impression of PEI	Negative impression of PEI	Negative impression of PEI

FIGURE 10.4 Summary of visit by couple to Prince Edward Island (PEI) (Case 26). From Ontario. Stayed 3 days (of planned 7 days) at Brackley and Charlottetown. Income range: $75,000–$100,000. Expenditures: $925. One repeat visitor (husband had worked on the island). Both aged in their late 40s. Work status: full-time with post-graduate training. Both responded. Visitor segment: medium–distant, domestic, touring, market. PEI was the primary destination. This middle-aged couple cut short their planned week-long trip because of problems with the accommodations. The planning horizon for the trip was four years, ever since the husband had spent four months working on the island. They aimed to relax in a cottage by the sea. They had used the Visitors' Guide to locate the cottages they thought fit their criteria. On arrival they found the cottages were substandard and had no view of water. This they considered to be false advertising. They then spent the rest of their time trying to find suitable accommodations. They stated that they would never consider returning to PEI. Key words: middle-aged couple, medium to high income, three-day stay, one first-timer, one repeat, planned activities but did none—disaster, fly/drive, involvement only in finding alternative accommodation, planning, long planning time frame

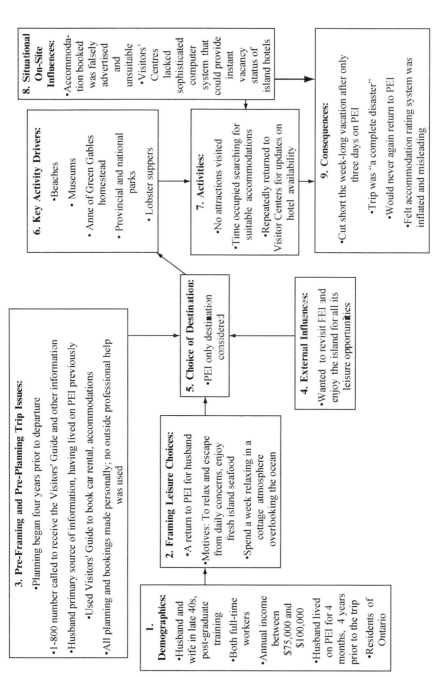

3. Pre-Framing and Pre-Planning Trip Issues:

•Planning began four years prior to departure

•1-800 number called to receive the Visitors' Guide and other information

•Husband primary source of information, having lived on PEI previously

•Used Visitors' Guide to book car rental, accommodations

•All planning and bookings made personally; no outside professional help was used

6. Key Activity Drivers:

•Beaches
• Museums
• Anne of Green Gables homestead
• Provincial and national parks
• Lobster suppers

8. Situational On-Site Influences:

•Accommodation booked was falsely advertised and unsuitable
•Visitors' Centres lacked sophisticated computer system that could provide instant vacancy status of island hotels

7. Activities:

•No attractions visited
•Time occupied searching for suitable accommodations
•Repeatedly returned to Visitor Centers for updates on hotel availability

9. Consequences:

•Cut short the week-long vacation after only three days on PEI
•Trip was "a complete disaster"
•Would never again return to PEI
•Felt accommodation rating system was inflated and misleading

5. Choice of Destination:

•PEI only destination considered

2. Framing Leisure Choices:

•A return to PEI for husband
•Motives: To relax and escape from daily concerns, enjoy fresh island seafood
•Spend a week relaxing in a cottage atmosphere overlooking the ocean

4. External Influences:

•Wanted to revisit PEI and enjoy the island for all its leisure opportunities

1. Demographics:

•Husband and wife in late 40s, post-graduate training
•Both full-time workers
•Annual income between $75,000 and $100,000
•Husband lived on PEI for 4 months, 4 years prior to the trip
•Residents of Ontario

FIGURE 10-5   High-income couple from Ontario.

212

Demographics of the Family Visiting PEI and Interview Site/Day

The travel party that was interviewed consisted of Edward Ausborne (EA) and Anita Ausborne (AA). Both actively participated in the interview and answered all directed questions. EA and AA were in their late forties, both with post-graduate training and working outside the home full-time. EA works in an accounting firm, while AA works with the Province of Ontario. The couple's annual income before taxes ranges between $75,000 and $100,000. The Ausbornes currently reside in Ontario.

The interview was conducted in the Charlottetown Airport waiting area as the Ausbornes awaited their departing flight to Toronto. The time of the interview was 12:30 p.m. and lasted until 1:15 p.m. At first the interviewer was reluctant to do the survey with them, as their flight departure impeded the amount of time required to talk with them. The Ausbornes said they would really like to talk about their trip because it had been such a horrible experience. The interviewer sat alongside the Ausbornes in the waiting area to conduct the interview. The day was sunny, warm, and humid, with a temperature of 22 degrees Celsius.

The Decision for the Trip

The total trip included a one-week stay on Prince Edward Island, with no secondary destinations planned. The Ausbornes started planning this visit to PEI in 1989, as EA lived on PEI for a period of four months and had made plans to return for leisure purposes. The primary reason to return to PEI was the opportunity to escape and relax in a cottage atmosphere overlooking the ocean, and to enjoy fresh island seafood delicacies.

The couple had planned to stay on the island for a week in the St. Peters area, but because of the quality of the accommodations and their endless search to find respectable accommodations, they decided to return to Ontario four days earlier than planned.

When asked about the extent of planning involved in their trip to PEI, EA responded that the trip had been "four years in the making," and as a result no other destinations were included in their destination choice set. Prior to arriving on PEI, EA made accommodation arrangements, car rental arrangements, and telephoned the toll-free number for information on PEI and to receive a visitors' guide. PEI was the sole province contacted for travel information, but upon calling PEI, he was also sent visitor guides from the 3 other Atlantic provinces. EA responded that this was useless information and was discarded because they had no intention to visit the other provinces. The Ausbornes indicated that if they had the time available they might venture to Nova Scotia for a day. But this was uncertain, and would have been decided on during their stay on PEI.

Planning Decisions

Both of the Ausbornes were involved actively in the decision to visit PEI, but EA was the person who initiated the trip to PEI. He was more involved because he had lived there for a short period, and EA believes that he knows all of what PEI had to offer, specifically, fine beaches, a relaxing atmosphere, and great seafood. He became aware of PEI when he had to move there to work for a short period, and had no recollection of anyone actually recommending a visit to the island.

Prince Edward Island Visit Questions

The primary motive to visit PEI was to escape and relax. When asked to assign votes in a constant-sum question of 10 votes with 9 alternative motives for visiting PEI, the Ausbornes both assigned "relax and escape" all 10 votes. The fine beaches and seafood were also motives, but they were adjunct to the idea of relaxation and escape.

   The Ausbornes chose to fly to PEI, as it was easier and occupied less leisure time. This would enable them to spend more time on PEI enjoying the attractions and relaxing. They flew Air Canada out of Toronto into Halifax and then on to Charlottetown. This was the only route debated, as the Ausbornes wanted to get there as quickly as possible. An automobile, as a means of travel, was not even discussed or considered.

Assistance by Travel Professionals

The Ausbornes took care of all their travel arrangements on their own prior to leaving Ontario. They made reservations for their flight, accommodations, and car rental without professional assistance.

   After arriving on PEI and discovering that their accommodations had been falsely advertised, they visited the Charlottetown Visitor Centre to have the Centre assist in finding accommodations. Because PEI was highly booked at the time, they had to keep returning to the Visitor Information Centre to see if anything better had turned up—preferably an oceanside cottage.

   The Ausbornes were relatively pleased with the travel counselors at the Centre and reported them to be very friendly and helpful. They did not hold them responsible for the lack of vacancies. The only criticism was the inability to get immediate responses. Because of this, the Ausbornes were required to constantly check in with the Centre. MMI: PEI might consider upgrading the reservation system to be more technologically advanced, thus providing visitors with quicker responses through the use of computerized reservations. A system such as that in place in Nova Scotia, "CHECK INS," is sophisticated and provides callers with an immediate response to accommodation inquiries. The system in place on PEI is not as modern as the one in use by Nova Scotia.

Requesting Information from Travel Offices Before Visiting

Prince Edward Island was the only destination contacted for information. The Ausbornes indicated that they called a toll-free number for the information and specified that they only required information on PEI. When the information was received the Ausbornes found information on all the Atlantic provinces. The Ausbornes did not appreciate this and quickly discarded the information they had not requested.

Whether and How the Visitors' Guide Was Used During the PEI Visit

Since the guide was received prior to arriving on PEI, the Ausbornes had the opportunity to go through it and see what attractions they wished to visit. Their reservations had already been made at this point, but they referred to the guide to see the grading of the property.

The Ausbornes took the guide on their trip, and used it heavily to find replacement accommodations. They did not use it for anything else because they spent the entire trip traveling around the island in search of accommodations. They evaluated the guide as very helpful, but thought the grading system to be only fair. They did not feel that standards were set very high and the star system was very misleading. MMI: PEI might consider enforcing stricter standards on the accommodations grading system so that visitors know exactly what to expect and are not upset after arrival.

Accommodation Decisions and Experiences

Initially, the Ausbornes had planned to spend their entire vacation at Steadman's Cottages in St. Peters. They read about this property in the *Toronto Star* and it seemed to meet their expectations: a quiet oceanfront cottage with some amenities. Upon arriving at the cottages the first day, they were outraged at what they saw. Their description of the cottages included being in the middle of nowhere, poorly furnished, pre-1950 decor, no curtains, no amenities, and no view of the water. This situation was unacceptable, and they refused to stay, thus losing their $100 deposit.

The Visitors' Centre was contacted, and accommodations were found at Shaw's Hotel in Brackley. This night did not turn out very well, as there were bugs throughout the room that kept them awake all night. The operators were very apologetic and did not charge them for the night.

The next two nights were spent at the Rodd Royalty Inn and the Rodd Charlottetown Hotel. The Ausbornes had to settle for something they did not want. These two facilities were rated as fair, as the couple had their mind set on a cottage atmosphere that was relaxing and secluded. Thus, their experience at these downtown hotels was less than expected.

When asked what they would like to see changed in their accommodations Mr. Ausborne replied, "updated facilities, amenities, cleanliness, and proper advertisement of facilities." MMI: these findings reinforce the need for a stricter grading system, as well as a greater need of supporting infrastructure. The summer demand for updated and better-quality accommodation facilities suggests that PEI may be discouraging visitors by not being able to accommodate this need.

Attraction Decisions and Experiences

Some of the attractions that the Ausbornes were interested in visiting included the beaches, lobster suppers, museums, *Anne of Green Gables* House, and provincial and national parks across the island. Because they had to spend all their time searching for accommodations, they were unable to visit any attractions. Their first day included driving from the airport to St. Peters, looking for new accommodations, and driving to Brackley for accommodations. Day two involved a search for new accommodations again. Day three also involved looking for accommodations and running to and from visitors' information centers, a half-hour visit to the Charlottetown Mall, and finally a decision to return home.

Evidently, the low-quality accommodations caused the Ausbornes to be unable to enjoy their vacation. They did say that the Visitors' Guide was very helpful in planning what attractions they would visit each day. MMI: ensure that visitors receive the Visitors' Guide prior to or after arriving on the island so they can learn about attractions and regions they would otherwise be unaware of and make plans in advance to visit them. This objective can be achieved by distributing the Visitors' Guide to all incoming visitors at the airport and both ferry terminals.

Expenditures

Again the accommodation dilemma was so discomforting that the Ausbornes did not have the opportunity to shop for gifts for friends and relatives or themselves. They had intended to purchase some gifts to return home with.

Total expenditures came to $925: accommodations $300, meals in restaurants $200, car rental $350, and gas $75. From this, it is easy to say that the Ausbornes spent money only on necessities, but had been willing to spend much more on attractions and gifts. Because of the accommodations, PEI lost money on shopping, attractions, food, accommodations, and gas for the remaining three nights.

Conclusions and Implications

This experience of the Ausbornes gives an example of how one sub decision within a vacation can ruin an entire vacation. Because of the poor quality of accommodations the Ausbornes spent less money, returned home four days early, and will most likely tell people about their horrible PEI vacation.

Instead of influencing the Ausbornes to return, their PEI experience created a negative impression that will produce bad word of mouth, which could affect other potential visitors' intention to visit. PEI may have lost additional travel parties, as a result of this one bad experience.

The Ausbornes report focuses theoretical attention mostly on P9 (box 8 to 7 in Figure 10-5), that is, information and events learned by the visitors while visiting affects their plans and behaviors. Note that high occupancy rates in alternative sought-after accommodations were a contributing condition to the couple's reports of misery in searching for suitable accommodations. Note in Figure 10-5 that an additional association (thick arrow) is included to indicate the direct influence of situational conditions affecting this couple's overall evaluation of visiting PEI.

FIRST-TIME VISITORS FROM A FAR-DISTANT DOMESTIC ORIGIN

This case study focuses on the responses by Shelley and Dave Ozinko, who visited PEI on a pleasure trip for seven days and six nights during the first week of August. Figures 10-6 and 10-7 summarize the couple's decision process and purchase consumption system.

This young couple resides in Calgary, Alberta. Their main motivation for coming to PEI was to learn about another "culture," including PEI's art, history, and cultural events. Accordingly, they chose bed and breakfasts as their main accommodations while on PEI. Other destinations considered and rejected (for reasons of driving time and distance between attractions) included the New England states. Their primary travel destinations, PEI and Nova Scotia, provided them with enough things to do in a three-week period with little driving time—in comparison to travel to the New England region of the U.S.

This trip was their first visit to PEI. Total expenditures while on PEI will amount to approximately $1,200. They have no criticisms of PEI and suggest that it has exceeded their expectations. Information was sought out in April and accommodations/attractions booked upon receipt of the Visitors' Guide. They are very unlikely to return to PEI over the next two years but may do so in 10 years' time.

Background Data

The Ozinkos have never previously visited the island. They have no friends or family on the Island and as a result their primary intention in visiting eastern Canada was to see PEI and all that it has to offer. They learned of PEI from friends, who assured them, "You'll love it." Upon attending the 1992 Calgary

Decision Stages 2,0,S04	Destinations	Route/Mode to and in PEI	Accommodations During PEI Stay	Activities in PEI	PEI Regions Visited	Attractions Visited, Including Restaurants	Gifts and Purchases Made
Consideration Set and Choices	PEI, Nova Scotia, and New England. Choice was PEI and Nova Scotia	Air from Calgary to Halifax, rental car to PEI	See whole island starting at Cornwall, then go west, north, and east.	*Anne of Green Gables* play, Olde Dublin movie, Charlottetown walking tour, St. Ann's Lobster Supper, Victory-by-the-Sea, Potato Museum, Woodleigh replicas, Anne House, Beaches	Charlottetown, South Shore, West Prince, North Shore–Cavendish, East Kings	Olde Dublin Confederate Centre, City Hall, Chocolate Factory, Woodleigh, Anne House, Anchor & Oar Dunes House	Anne doll and poster
Motives	Places of interest close. Experience "culture"	See Nova Scotia for 1 week then go to PEI by shortest route possible	Have one week to see all of PEI. read Visitors' Guide, planned and booked the things of interest.	Crafts shopping; wanted to experience whole culture of PEI and learn all about PEI	Reach attractions throughout PEI	Experience island way of life and attractions representative of it.	Read Anne books, likes unique crafts

Information Search and Use	Recommended by friends, Calgary Stampede information booth. 1-800 number. Direct calls to PEI operators.	Follow map totally and stop at places according to Visitors' Guide	Extensive use of Visitors' Guide and to choose B&Bs and country inns. Clean, homey atmosphere	Read about attractions in Visitors' Guide and brochures from VIC	Read about accessing places by certain routes & used map.	Visitors' Guide and brochures	Visitors' Guide for New London to purchase Anne doll.
Outcomes	Enjoying PEI far more than expected. Accommodation B&B and *Anne of Gen Gables* play good.	PEI map makes PEI bigger than it really is. It takes no time to go from one area to another on PEI	Very pleased thus far. Not one complaint. Much better than Nova Scotia	Enjoyed play and Irish pub immensely	Very beautiful, more than expected	Great portions (food). Great prices and atmosphere	Pleased

FIGURE 10.6 Summary of a far-distant domestic Canadian couple's visit to Prince Edward Island (PEI) (Case 15). From Calgary, Alberta. Stayed 6 nights at various B&Bs. Income range: $75,000–$100,000. Expenditures: $1,195. First-time visitors. Both in their early thirties. Work status: both full-time and had post-secondary education. Visitor segment: far-distant, domestic, touring "experience" market. Both Nova Scotia and PEI were primary destinations for this young couple from Calgary, Alberta. The planned three-week vacation included six nights spent on PEI. The strongest influences on their choice were friends and knowledge of *Anne of Green Gables*. They stayed in bed and breakfast accommodations. Booking of accommodations, travel, and the various attractions was done without the assistance of a travel agent. They visited a lot of the tourist attractions and areas, covering most of the areas on the island. Key words: younger married couple, medium–high income, seven-day stay, first-timers, fly/drive, high involvement, "experience," knew of *Anne of Green Gables*, long planning time frame.

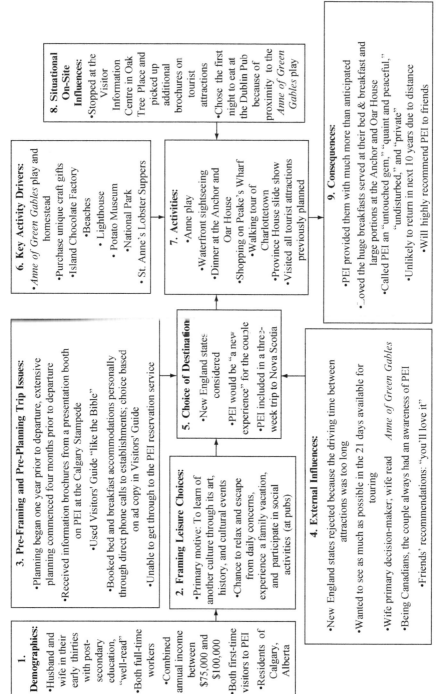

1. Demographics:
- Husband and wife in their early thirties with post-secondary education, "well-read"
- Both full-time workers
- Combined annual income between $75,000 and $100,000
- Both first-time visitors to PEI
- Residents of Calgary, Alberta

2. Framing Leisure Choices:
- Primary motive: To learn of another culture through its art, history, and cultural events
- Chance to relax and escape from daily concerns, experience a family vacation, and participate in social activities (at pubs)

3. Pre-Framing and Pre-Planning Trip Issues:
- Planning began one year prior to departure, extensive planning commenced four months prior to departure
- Received information brochures from a presentation booth on PEI at the Calgary Stampede
  - Used Visitors' Guide "like the Bible"
- Booked bed and breakfast accommodations personally through direct phone calls to establishments; choice based on ad copy in Visitors' Guide
- Unable to get through to the PEI reservation service

4. External Influences:
- New England states rejected because the driving time between attractions was too long
- Wanted to see as much as possible in the 21 days available for touring
- Wife primary decision-maker; wife read *Anne of Green Gables*
- Being Canadians, the couple always had an awareness of PEI
- Friends' recommendations: "you'll love it"

5. Choice of Destination:
- New England states considered
- PEI would be "a new experience" for the couple
- PEI included in a three-week trip to Nova Scotia

6. Key Activity Drivers:
- *Anne of Green Gables* play and homestead
- Purchase unique craft gifts
- Island Chocolate Factory
  - Beaches
  - Lighthouse
  - Potato Museum
  - National Park
- St. Anne's Lobster Suppers

7. Activities:
- Anne play
- Waterfront sightseeing
- Dinner at the Anchor and Oar House
- Shopping on Peake's Wharf
- Walking tour of Charlottetown
- Province House slide show
- Visited all tourist attractions previously planned

8. Situational On-Site Influences:
- Stopped at the Visitor Information Centre in Oak Tree Place and picked up additional brochures on tourist attractions
- Chose the first night to eat at the Dublin Pub because of proximity to the *Anne of Green Gables* play

9. Consequences:
- PEI provided them with much more than anticipated
- Loved the huge breakfasts served at their bed & breakfast and large portions at the Anchor and Oar House
- Called PEI an "untouched gem," "quaint and peaceful," "undisturbed," and "private"
- Unlikely to return in next 10 years due to distance
- Will highly recommend PEI to friends

FIGURE 10.7 Couple in early 30s from Alberta, PEI, Prince Edward Island.

Stampede (the theme was "Provinces in Canada") they visited the PEI booth with literature displays and agents from the Island promoting the area as a vacation destination. Information was available for their perusal and plans were made. As their flight arrived in the Halifax airport, they chose to tour Nova Scotia first. This provided close approximation to PEI if they were well planned in their itinerary. Shelley was the organizer of the whole expedition, and as a result, plans have proceeded smoothly after completing just over half of their vacation. Their trip will conclude in Halifax when they depart back to Calgary to continue the savings plan that will take them on another voyage in the forthcoming year.

Demographic and Psychographic Information

The Ozinkos are in their early thirties. They have no children. They both have post-secondary educations. Dave is a college graduate; Shelley has graduated from university. They both hold full-time jobs. As a result of their double income, they are categorized in the upper income bracket (earnings of $75,001–$100,000 per year). This couple seeks out new cultures with a focus on the historical aspect of a travel destination. PEI provided them with much more enjoyable experiences than they had anticipated.

Interview Site and Day

The interview was completed at Chez-Nous Bed & Breakfast, located in Cornwall. An appointment was set up with the owner (Sandi Gallant) of the establishment and the interview took place at 9:30 a.m., August 4. The interview took one full hour to complete with discussion and suggestions as to where to visit while on PEI. It was a very hot, sunny day with no interruptions during the course of the interview.

Planning Decisions for the Total Trip

The planning process for this trip began, technically, during the previous year at the Calgary Stampede. The actual "extensive" planning of when they were coming and requesting the information began in early April. Upon receipt of all requested information, Shelley proceeded to circle the accommodations and attractions that appealed to her taste. (Note that her main focus was on B&Bs and country inns as they provided her with more of a personal touch in allowing them to experience the culture to a greater degree during their short visit.) The descriptions in the ad copy "clinched the deal" on booking the chosen accommodations. Upon review of the circled portions of the guide, she proceeded to call the reservation service on PEI. She was unable to get through to the reservation service, so direct calls were made to the local establishments for bookings. Shelley mentioned that she did not mind dealing directly with the local operators as this was a chance to briefly establish a "feeble relationship" and obtain a feel for the place through conversing with the owners. Brochures were then sent to her, but by this time her mind was made up that she and her husband would stay at the sites that were sending her the literature.

For attractions such as organized tours and theatre (*Anne of Green Gables*), reservations were also made so the whole itinerary was planned four months in advance of departure. At no time was a travel agent consulted. MMI: if this couple is representative of the typical younger couple, any advertising or booth displays at major events throughout the country might be targeted toward females in early April. The reservation system should also be more accessible for convenience purposes.

Travel Route

The modes of travel included air and rented vehicle. The Ozinkos flew out of Calgary on July 25, heading for Halifax, Nova Scotia. Upon arrival they proceeded to rent a car (that they took over to PEI). Over the next seven days, they toured the southwestern portion of Nova Scotia before proceeding to PEI via the Caribou Ferry Terminal. Their wait was expected and lasted two hours. They have accommodations booked for six nights and seven days of entertainment on PEI. The conclusion of their trip will entail seven more nights in Nova Scotia before flying out of Halifax back to Calgary.

Planning Issues: PEI vs. Nova Scotia

Shelley was the main decision-maker and planner of this trip, as was previously mentioned, although it was a joint decision between she and Dave to actually come to PEI and Nova Scotia.

Being Canadians, they had an awareness of PEI, although it might not have been in their consideration set of possible destinations to visit if it had not been for the *Anne of Green Gables* book that Shelley had previously read or the recommendations from friends to visit the Island. As a result of the prompting from friends and prior readings and promotional displays (Calgary Stampede), all things were pointing to a visit to PEI.

Other destinations under consideration included the New England region. This idea was ruled out due to the distance to travel from state to state. The Ozinkos wanted to see as much as possible in the 21 days available for touring. Since PEI was their main destination considered, they chose this area along with Nova Scotia. Prince Edward Island was allocated six nights while Nova Scotia garnered 15 nights. Nova Scotia was allocated more time due to its larger size and the appeal of Cape Breton for its scenery and culture. MMI: to persuade tourists to visit PEI over Cape Breton, management might focus on PEI's competitive advantage over Cape Breton through the promoting of more things to do and experience while on PEI (e.g., festivals, amusement parks, beaches). While both destinations have beautiful scenery, Cape Breton does not have as much to see or do for the younger market outside of viewing the landscape. PEI may be "a little bit above and beyond Cape Breton" in this respect, as mentioned by Shelley.

Motivational Drivers

Being young and well read, this couple came to learn about another culture, PEI's art, history, and cultural events. This objective was their primary motive for including PEI on their vacation. This trip was also their first visit to PEI so all that there was to experience would be new to them. This view may account for the heavy weight that was placed on cultural experiences motivating their visit.

Secondary motives were numerous including: a chance to relax and escape from daily concerns, experience a family vacation, participation in social activities (pubs), and a chance to see nature on PEI.

Daily Itinerary

Day 1

Upon arrival on Prince Edward Island, they visited Point Prim's Chowder House and Art Gallery for dinner. They were very impressed by the food and service provided. Next, they departed for Charlottetown to the Visitor Information Centre located in Oak Tree Place. While conversing with one of the tourism officers, they picked up additional brochures on local attractions and advice on particular sites to visit. Next, they proceeded to Chez-Nous to check in and get ready for an eventful evening in Charlottetown. Dinner was enjoyed at the Olde Dublin Pub. Their choice of this location was for its casual atmosphere and reasonably offered prices. The proximity of this location also allowed them to spend more time over a relaxed meal before a short walk to the *Anne of Green Gables* main stage production at the Confederation Centre of the Arts. The play was a highlight for Shelley as she had read the book and cried at the conclusion of the performance! "I bawled" were her words. Finally, they retired back to Chez-Nous to recuperate from their exhausting day.

Day 2

They enjoyed a huge breakfast at Chez-Nous, which Dave remarked was uncharacteristic of B&Bs in Nova Scotia where they would serve themselves a meager continental breakfast. MMI: management should educate the local operators on servicing the customer more effectively in small details. These are the things that are remembered during recall when conversing with friends. As these small operators do not have the budgets for advertising, they rely heavily on word-of-mouth advertising. The Ozinkos then departed for Charlottetown for participation in an educational walking tour of the capital city.

While on the tour, Dave had an uninvited guest attend. A mosquito lodged in his inner ear and was buzzing. It was driving him to the point of annoyance, so, upon completion of the walking tour, they made a detour to the Queen Elizabeth Hospital for flushing of the intruder (after a two-hour wait).

After the mishap, they ventured to Province House for participation in the slide presentation and guided tour throughout the building. They found the actor portraying the keeper of the house during that time period to be quite amusing. As they were close to the waterfront, they proceeded to view the crafts available at Peake's Wharf. (Shelley's intentions on PEI are to purchase unique crafts that were typical of the culture and reflective of the heritage of islanders.) Next, they visited Cow's for a $2.54 single ice-cream cone. The waterfront was, yet again, frequented later that afternoon for dinner at the Anchor and Oar House located just behind the CP Prince Edward Hotel. There they enjoyed an Italian meal at a reasonable price in the outdoor seating area. Dave remarked that the "portions were huge" at a reasonable price. Shelley had not made any purchases on Peake's Wharf that day other than a picture of PEI so they left Charlottetown for the Stoneware Pottery Shop in Winsloe. While there she made a purchase of spice holders. Their uniqueness appealed to her taste and for $20 she could not refuse. To end the day, they proceeded to the Charlottetown Cinemas to view "The Firm." Upon its completion, they departed for Chez-Nous to end the day in conversation with Sandi Gallant (owner).

Day 3

As the interview was conducted at the beginning of the third day, they proceeded to tell me their plans, which included visits to Island Chocolate Factory, Victoria-by-the-Sea (beach), Summerside/Spinnaker's Landing (waterfront), West Point Lighthouse (beach and B&B), and PEI Potato Museum (possibly).

Days 4 and 5

These days will be spent touring the Cavendish area including planned visits to: New London (purchase of *Anne of Green Gables* doll); *Anne of Green Gables* House; Shining Water's Country Inn & Cottages; St. Ann's Lobster Suppers; National Park beaches.

Days 6 and 7

These days will be spent touring the eastern portion of PEI in the Kings County region. They plan to visit Beasin Head, which is just north of Souris. This beach area supplies relaxation for mainly locals. They will spend one night in a B&B in Murray Harbour before departing via the Wood Islands Ferry Terminal.

Expenditures

Some costs are based on projections while others are based on receipts thus far in the tour. Below is the breakdown of expenditures:

Accommodations	$ 400
Recreation/Entertainment	100
Meals in Restaurants	180
Food Purchased in Stores	15
Handcraft Purchases	500
	$ 1,195

Conclusions

This couple represents ideal tourists that spend seven days on PEI and see and do all there is to experience. They used the Visitors' Guide as a bible on the trip and referred to it along with the map when approaching different craft shops or attractions. MMI: ensure that this type of traveler leaves with a positive affection for PEI so they will translate into repeat visitors even if it is a few years later. As destinations are sought out largely through recommendations from friends, there is no better way of advertising than through the provision of excellent service while visiting the island. (The Visitors' Guide is a closure on the sale to visit the local establishments. It plays a major role in the short-listing decision process.)

For the majority of the attractions that the Ozinkos visited, they read about them in the Visitors' Guide. When queried from their current experience of PEI and what adjectives came to mind to describe the Island, the following statements were mentioned by one or both of them: "Undisturbed;" "So quaint and peaceful;" "Untouched gem;" "Privacy / Seclusion;" "Natural beauty;" and "Friendliness."

Note that Figure 10-6 includes important details affecting the Ozinko's trip to PEI. These details include the wife reading the *Anne of Green Gables* book in her youth, attending and receiving literature at the PEI booth while at the Calgary Stampede, friends' recommendations to visit PEI, and the availability to make travel plans that combined visits to both Nova Scotia and PEI. Each of the four factors appears to represent necessary but not sufficient conditions leading to the decision for leisure travel to PEI.

The main conclusions for theory are that: (1) each of the ten propositions receives strong support in this case study; and (2) conjunctive occurrences of unplanned and planned events and thoughts are antecedents leading to first-time leisure visits. Consider how encouraging the reading of *Anne of Green Gables* at least among Canadian school children likely influences leisure travel some ten to twenty years later in their lives—given that the reading is enriched by additional information collected at such events as the Calgary Stampede. Such case studies evidence the marketing value of participating in distant special attraction events.

FIRST-TIME VISIT BY AN OLDER AMERICAN COUPLE

This interview report includes responses by an American couple visiting PEI for pleasure for seven nights in August 1993. The traveling party is a senior American couple—first-time visitors to PEI. A chance to relax and escape from daily concerns was the principal motive of the trip, with additional motives being a chance to learn about another culture, and to observe and experience nature. PEI was the primary destination, with the secondary destination being Iles-de-la-Madeleine. Figures 10-8 and 10-9 summarize this couple's decision process and purchase consumption system with respect to visiting PEI.

The couple spent their nine days touring PEI from west to east exploring beaches and hitting every lobster dinner they could find. "We love lobster," they were reported as saying. Total expenditures at the time of the interview were $955. Their PEI criticism: "We were *Anne*d to death." They also did not like the National Park's $5.00 entrance fee just for driving through, and therefore did not make the drive. They found the Cavendish area overcrowded and overcommercialized.

They used the PEI Visitors' Guide to plan their itinerary and found it very useful. When asked what first comes to mind when thinking of PEI, Mr. Dougherty said, "The gorgeous coastline and lush growth on the island." Mr. Dougherty reported an unlikelihood of returning to PEI in 1994 or 1995 due to his age, although since he is a frequent traveler, there are many other places he may visit while he is still able.

Interview Procedure

The questionnaire was completed over a one- to two-hour period, in a face-to-face and a telephone interview. The final portion of the interview was conducted over the telephone, following the day of departure, due to the Doughertys' schedule. Data on the visiting party's intentions and actual actions were gathered. A one-hour interview was conducted in a tense environment in a limited time frame, where the visiting party communicated their decisions and activities related to their visit to PEI.

Description of the Party Visiting PEI and Interview Site/Day

Demographics

The travel party interviewed consisted of a wife, Mary Dougherty (MD), and her husband Donald (DD). MD answered all the questions at the airport and DD answered the questions asked over the telephone. MD and her husband are both over sixty. Both have post-graduate training and work full-time. The couple's annual income before taxes is between $35,000 and

$50,000 (U.S. funds). They live in Cedar Grove, New Jersey, just outside of Newark.

Interview Site and Day

The interview took place at the Charlottetown Airport at noon on August 3, 1993, one hour prior to their flight departure. MD completed the interview while her husband was trying to retrieve a lost credit card. The temperature outside was in the high 20s Celsius, and the air conditioning was working on overtime.

Decisions for the Total Trip

PEI was the main destination of this visit, with a two-night, three-day excursion to Iles-de-la-Madeleine. They had planned their visit to PEI within the past year. The party flew from Newark, NJ to Halifax, where they caught a connecting flight to PEI.

Planning Horizon

MD reported extensive planning for this trip due to the fact that they had to contact the majority of the bed and breakfasts in advance to make reservations. Very few of the reservations could be made through a toll-free number. MMI: bed and breakfasts enterprises may want to use the toll-free number service to ease bookings from distant clients and possibly increase their revenues.

Assistance by Travel Professionals

MD used a travel agent (Cedar Grove Travel) to book their flight and arrange their rental car (a Ford Escort) through Budget Rental. Bed and breakfast information was given to MD by the travel agent and they in turn booked their own accommodations as they wanted to travel across PEI and would be staying in different places for each night.

Requesting Information from Travel Offices Before Visiting

No information was requested from any Canadian Provincial travel office. They received the Visitors' Guide before beginning their visit and with this continued making bookings and doing further research and planning for their visit. They did find the Visitors' Guide very helpful.

PEI Planning Questions

First Learning About PEI

MD did not recall how she had learned of PEI and reported always knowing about it, "Through geography I guess." MD had read the book

Decision Stages 2,0,S05	Destinations	Route / Mode to and in PEI	Accommodations during PEI stay	Activities in PEI	PEI Regions Visited	Attractions Visited, Including Restaurants	Gifts and Purchases Made
Consideration Set and Choices	PEI with added excursion to Iles-de-la-Madeleine	Driving too far and time consuming. Flew Newark-Halifax-Charlottetown Rental car.	B&Bs; a different one each night	Beaches, museums, boat tour, lobster suppers, pubs, restaurants, and crafts store.	Queens County Kings County Prince County. Followed the shore west to east.	Dublin Pub, St. Anne's, St. Margaret's, Northumberland lobster suppers, Miscouche Acadian museum, Orwell Museum Seal watching, Lighthouses	*Anne of Green Gables* books and tape, earrings, multiple small gifts
Motives	Explore a new area, escape daily concerns, relax. Learn about another culture. Economical	Car "more freedom." Ferry for off-island trip.	Wanted to explore the whole island with a limited time span.	Nature interest. Educational learning experience.	Nature lovers. Wanted to stay away from "commercialized areas."	They "love lobster". Wanted to observe nature. Educational experience for museums. Irish music.	Books requested. Earrings (native work) wanted for wife. Gifts of local work.

228

	Read Visitors' Guide prior to coming to PEI. Arranged B&B	Based their routes on Visitors' Guide	Used B&B brochures provided by travel agent and Visitors' Guide 1-800 number for bookings	Promotional literature, Visitors' Guide word of mouth	Visitors' Guide included the routes that went through each region.	Used Visitors' Guide, some word of mouth, some discovered on their own.	None other than Anne of Green Gables paraphernalia found by chance
Information Search and Use							
Outcomes	Very pleased. Incredible coast line, the Visitors' Guide is "worn out;" Felt "Anned to death"	Route and mode gorgeous and as expected, "lush growth"	Very pleased, no complaints	Did not like Cavendish! Museums "were great." "We love lobster!" Avoided most craft shops.	Enjoyed the coastline. Felt some areas were ruined.	Lobster dinners great.	Loved local (native) work—very unique.

FIGURE 10.8 Summary of senior American couple's visit to Prince Edward Island (PEI) (Case 16). From Cedar Grove, NJ. Stayed 7 nights at various B&Bs. Income range: $35,000–50,000 (US). Expenditure: $955. First-time visitors. Both over 60 years of age. Work status: both work full-time and have post-graduate training. Respondent: Elizabeth. Visitor segment: medium–distant, foreign, touring (fly/drive), senior market. PEI was primary destination. This couple travels frequently, and this is their first trip to PEI. They had been planning for a year. They used an agent for their travel arrangements. Their bed and breakfast accommodation, during their seven-night stay, they booked themselves. They made extensive use of the Visitors' Guide both prior to their visit and once they were on the island. They felt the Cavendish area was ruined and that "Anne" had been overdone. Key words: older couple, medium income, seven-day stay, first-timers, fly/drive, high involvement once or island, lobster, extensive arrangements (accommodation), travel agent, long planning time frame.

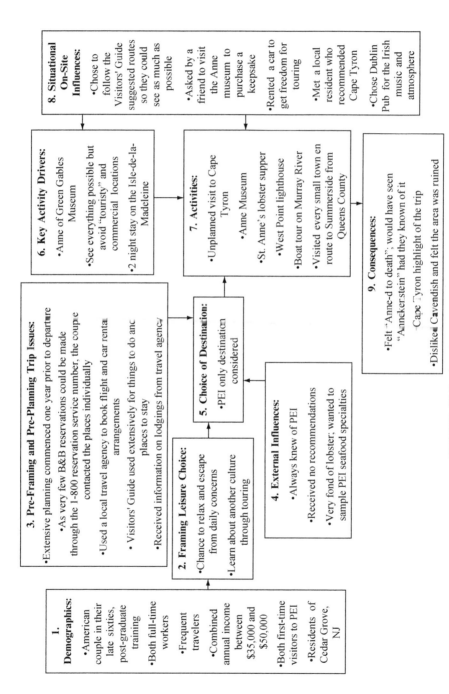

3. Pre-Framing and Pre-Planning Trip Issues:
•Extensive planning commenced one year prior to departure
•As very few B&B reservations could be made through the 1-800 reservation service number, the couple contacted the places individually
•Used a local travel agency to book flight and car rental arrangements
•Visitors' Guide used extensively for things to do and places to stay
•Received information on lodgings from travel agency

8. Situational On-Site Influences:
•Chose to follow the Visitors' Guide suggested routes so they could see as much as possible
•Asked by a friend to visit the Anne museum to purchase a keepsake
•Rented a car to get freedom for touring
•Met a local resident who recommended Cape Tyron
•Chose Dublin Pub for the Irish music and atmosphere

6. Key Activity Drivers:
•Anne of Green Gables Museum
•See everything possible but avoid "touristy" and commercial locations
•2 night stay on the Isle-de-la-Madeleine

7. Activities:
•Unplanned visit to Cape Tyron
•Anne Museum
•St. Anne's lobster supper
•West Point lighthouse
•Boat tour on Murray River
•Visited every small town en route to Summerside from Queens County

2. Framing Leisure Choice:
•Chance to relax and escape from daily concerns
•Learn about another culture through touring

5. Choice of Destination:
•PEI only destination considered

4. External Influences:
•Always knew of PEI
•Received no recommendations
•Very fond of lobster; wanted to sample PEI seafood specialties

9. Consequences:
•Felt "Anne-d to death"; would have seen "Annekerstein" had they known of it
•Cape Tyron highlight of the trip
•Disliked Cavendish and felt the area was ruined

1. Demographics:
•American couple in their late sixties, post-graduate training
•Both full-time workers
•Frequent travelers
•Combined annual income between $35,000 and $50,000
•Both first-time visitors to PEI
•Residents of Cedar Grove, NJ

FIGURE 10.9 American couple in late 60s.

230

Anne of Green Gables; however, this was not a conscious factor in their decision-making to come to PEI. MD already stated, "I felt *Anne*d to death."

When asked if they had seen "Annekenstein" (a parody production of the *Anne of Green Gables* musical; Annekenstein is held in Charlottetown), MD responded, "We would have loved to have seen it had we known about the play." MMI: although "*Anne*" is a traditional tourist attraction in PEI some individuals feel this theme has been overdone. Possibly more promotion of a satirical view of "Anne" could complement attendance at the regular musical.

PEI Recommended for this Trip?

MD reported no one recommended PEI as a vacation destination to them. They had never been to PEI before and felt it was an economical choice for a vacation destination. The main reason for the trip was to get away from daily concerns while learning of another culture while observing and experiencing nature.

Using the Visitors' Guide

MD reported extensive use of the Visitors' Guide prior to arriving on PEI. "The book is worn out," MD stated. The Visitors' Guide was used prior to arrival to plan their travel route and decide where to stay and what to do.

PEI Competitor Considered but Rejected

No other destination was considered as a principal destination.

Involvement in PEI Destination Choice

MD and her husband reported that they had equal shares in the decision of PEI as a destination choice. As well as being equally involved in the destination choice, MD and her husband were equally involved in the planning of their visit to PEI. They made use of a travel agent to plan getting to PEI and arrange their rental car. However, the travel agent in no way influenced their destination choice. Although they received the Visitors' Guide prior to arriving on PEI, it also in no way influenced their destination choice. The Visitors' Guide did, however, "clinch the deal" for the activities and attractions they would do and see once on PEI.

PEI Visit Questions

MD and husband spent 7 nights on PEI with two nights being spent on Iles-de-la-Madeleine. Being on PEI was the primary motivation leading to the add-on visit to Iles-de-la-Madeleine.

Main Motives for PEI Visit

MD reported three motives for their visit. MD assigned five votes to the chance to relax and escape from daily concerns. She assigned three votes to a chance to learn through touring about another "culture," its art, history, and cultural events, and two votes to a chance to observe and experience nature.

PEI Trip Route and Destinations

MD and husband had no principal destination for their PEI visit. They had planned on seeing as much of PEI as they could in their stay therefore choosing to follow the Visitors' Guide recommended routes. They began their visit in Queens County and explored this county extensively hitting Rocky Point, Canoe Cove, and every small town and shore en route to Summerside where they stayed their second night. Their third day was spent in the Evangeline area of Prince County, where they visited museums, other attractions, and the West Point Lighthouse, spending the night in O'Leary at the Thomas B&B. The fourth day they returned to Queens County where they visited "*Anne of Green Gables* Museum" (where they had been asked to visit and purchase a keepsake for a family member). An unplanned visit to Cape Tyron (recommended by a local) was the highlight of this day, "It was the most beautiful place we saw on PEI," MD reported. After dining on St. Ann's lobster dinners they spent the night in Darnley, once again at a B&B. The following (fifth day) was spent in Queens County and then their sixth day brought them into Kings County. MMI: the routes set out in the Visitors' Guide were used by this visiting party; PEI may want to continue to recommend the routes as used in the Visitors' Guide to parties who wish to see as much of PEI as possible in a limited time span, such as MD and husband.

Trip Mode and Route

MD chose to rent a car to allow them their freedom, although they would have taken a bus trip for the off-island excursion to Iles-de-la-Madeleine. They said that the ferry was "very expensive ($100.00 per car)" and upon return to PEI they needed a car to return them to the airport before departure. MMI: PEI tourism could consider a shuttle service to and from the airport for frequently visited PEI destinations. This particularly helps those who make off island excursions while visiting PEI as the Dougherty's did. MD reported only fleetingly considering alternative ways of getting to PEI, and a decision was made to fly based on the distance and time required to drive to PEI. MMI: market PEI as a "fly/drive" vacation destination for the American seniors market. The car rental agencies and airlines could work together to arrange a package best suited for this target, example: reduced rates on car rental when flying with local carriers. There was no choice offered to enter and exit the Iles-de-la-Madeleine, as there is no alternative ferry service.

PEI Activities and Attractions Visited

MD said, "We had planned to see the island and whatever we could do we'd do." They did such activities with aid of the Visitors' Guide. MD mentioned they also found things to do/visit on their own. MD reported going to many beaches; however, she could not remember the names, other than Cavendish, of the places that they did not enjoy. "They've ruined that area," MD reported.

They visited several museums, with educational/learning experience being the motive. "They were great," MD said. MD reported taking one boat tour on Murray River, a "Mussel Farm/Seal Watching Tour." MD said the tour was, "Enjoyable, but the only tour we knew of." MD reported trying to avoid "commercial, touristy places." MMI: PEI might improve marketing the provinces' outdoor activities and natural vistas for a target market such as the Doughertys. The Visitors' Guide could have a section dedicated to nature lovers.

Evening Restaurant Dining

MD reported having all their meals in restaurants; due to fondness for lobster, they had three lobster suppers. MD reported having chosen Dublin Pub to dine, for the Irish music. Otherwise they ate at local restaurants while en route to specific destinations. MMI: research the possibility of tours specifically designed for those who "love lobster," by means of traveling to differing lobster suppers, in conjunction with lobster fishing tours. In this manner two industries might complement each other and a greater awareness of each might be achieved.

Activities Not Engaged In

Available activities not engaged in by MD and her husband include deep sea fishing, golfing, farmers' markets, art galleries, and live theater. The two latter-mentioned activities MD reported not seeing advertisements for and therefore not being aware of. They tried to avoid all craft shops. MMI: this particular market would have participated in some of the aforementioned activities had they been more aware of these activities. Although this party was not at all interested in craft shops, there are other market segments that are more responsive target markets. PEI might consider ensuring that arts and crafts segments and arts and theater segments are separate entities within the Visitors' Guide.

The Accommodation Decision and Experiences

MD and husband made their accommodation choices in advance using B&B promotional brochures and the Visitors' Guide. They had no main accommodation and reported choosing their accommodations "just by chance," selecting them out of the book and coordinating their accommodations with their chosen route. MMI: the PEI Visitors' Guide should continue listing accommodations with routes, as this is an effective marketing tool for this particular target market.

Gifts and Other Purchases

DD reported leaving PEI with three purchases: *Anne of Green Gables* books and tape, valued at $43, earrings, valued at $15, and a collection of small gifts, valued at $90. DD reported having intended to return home with gifts; however, he had no specific gifts in mind other than *Anne of Green Gables* paraphernalia for a sister who is unable to travel and was raised on *Anne of Green Gables*. "Just like the Japanese," DD was quoted as saying. The other purchases were bought by chance while browsing; DD could not remember the names of the shops. DD particularly liked the earrings and wanted them for his wife. DD stated that "male supremacy" clinched the deal on the purchase of the earrings.

Expenditure Breakouts

DD reported their total expenditures as including the following amounts: $240.00 on accommodations; $80.00 recreation/entertainment; $250.00 meals in restaurants; $10.00 food and alcohol purchases in PEI stores; $150.00 gifts (golf shirt) anticipating another purchase; $240.00 rental car; and $85.00 gasoline purchase on PEI. Thus their total expenditures are estimated to equal $955 for their seven-night stay on PEI. This amount does not include their airfare to and from PEI or costs incurred involving their off-island excursion to Iles-de-le-Madeleine. MMI: if PEI implements specialized tour packages marketed in the U.S. geared towards specific interests of seniors, increased awareness of what PEI has to offer visitors may be necessary. The result of such awareness building may be placing PEI in these seniors' consideration sets, which would in turn lead to PEI as a preferred destination.

Observations About Customer Choice Processes

The decision to visit PEI by this party was made prior to receiving any promotional literature about PEI. Planning was done after receipt of the B&B brochure and Visitors' Guide. The Dougherty's eliminated the alternative of driving to PEI due to time and distance involved. They then allowed a travel agent to make route decisions regarding getting to PEI. The accommodations decisions were made by chance using promotional literature including the Visitors' Guide. The choices of restaurants were made due to their food preferences and choice of activities due to their interests. Their purchases were spontaneous other than the one gift purchase requested by a family member. In this case the location of shops is important in key areas to draw customers who have no specific purchases in mind prior to arrival.

Economic reasons and "never having been there" were key decisions in coming to PEI. The availability of bed and breakfasts on PEI is a key marketing item in this case, whereas higher priced accommodations would not attract this market.

Although their decision was made without aid of literature, the Visitors' Guide determined their routes once on PEI, and, therefore, sending the

Visitors' Guide to visitors in advance could encourage travel to rural areas on PEI and thus increase revenues in these areas.

This case study points to a market disinterested in Cavendish and *Anne*. This visiting party also could be influenced in purchasing package tours. Nature tours and lobster supper tours are an option in attracting this market, or a combination of the two themes. This visiting party had a large interest in understanding another culture and nature; therefore, information on regional agriculture/fishery festivals (e.g., Blueberry Festival, Oyster Festival, Potato Blossom Festival) may have increased their awareness and thus encouraged them to visit these areas.

PEI as a Primary Destination Choice with Off-Island Excursions

The fact that this PEI visit had included an off island excursion should be emphasized. The number of visiting seniors from the U.S. interested in touring the Maritime Provinces is likely to be substantial. Thus, marketing PEI as a primary destination with easily accessible off island excursions may be a successful strategy for reaching this target market. This strategy might also attract visitors residing in the Province of Quebec.

The Visitors' Guide and PEI Map as Marketing Tools

MD reported use of the Visitors' Guide extensively before arriving on PEI. It was not mentioned if it was used often once on PEI, although it was stated "the book is worn out". The Visitors' Guide did serve the function of drawing the visiting party to different rural areas. It created awareness of areas and attractions otherwise unknown to the visiting party. The description of the coastline on the visitor's map of PEI could be found as being partially responsible for DD's positive opinion of the coastline, expressed over telephone interview. Offering such descriptions may be beneficial, resulting in positive association with the coastline and thus PEI.

Grounded Theory Conclusions

This older American couple most likely visiting PEI for one-time only in their lifetimes is representative (and likely more typical than atypical) of a substantial market target segment for the province. The data on this case provides substantial support for all ten propositions, especially P2 concerning the influence of the Visitors' Guide on planning activities and place to stay. Such data indicates a likely double impact of the Visitors' Guide: (1) influencing the decision to visit PEI (though this couple did not verbally state such an influence) and (2) influencing what they did and where they spent their nights in PEI (the couple used the Visitors' Guide extensively for guiding their days in PEI). Using the Visitors' Guide appears to have been a necessary and sufficient attribution of several specific behaviors related to this couple's visit to PEI.

FIRST-TIME VISIT BY YOUNG EUROPEAN (AUSTRIAN) FRIENDS

This interview reports the responses of two Austrian tourists traveling around the world who spent three nights at PEI. Brigitte Binder (BB) and Gerti Lindmoser (GL) wanted to visit Halifax, but there was no flight to Halifax by their airline. They chose PEI because "it is the closest stop to Halifax," said BB. They used the Visitors' Guide to choose the places they wanted to see and they described the Visitors' Guide as "helpful." Though they had no expectations for PEI, they described the trip as follows: "It was okay. [We] enjoyed everything." The total expenditure of their three-night stay at PEI was $474. When asked about their intention to return to PEI in the near future, they reported that they are very unlikely to return: "[We] liked it very much but it is too far [from Austria]."

Description of the Travel Party and the Interview Site/Day

Demographics

The travel party included Brigitte Binder (BB) and her friend Gerti Lindmoser (GL). They are both in their twenties and they are both single. They both have some college level formal education. They are employed full time, and the annual income before taxes for each is between $35,001 and $50,000. They live in Austria.

Interview Site and Day

The interview was conducted at Charlottetown Airport when BB and GL were waiting for their plane to Boston. It was a Thursday and the interview started at 4:30 p.m.

Decision for the Total Trip

This trip for the two friends included a total of 30 days away from their Austrian home. They flew from Austria to Munich, Germany, and then flew to New York. In New York, they rented a car and drove to Ottawa and stayed there with their friends for three nights. From Ottawa, they drove to Montreal and stayed there for one day. They then drove back to Ottawa, stayed there one night, and drove to Toronto. From Toronto, they drove to the Niagara Falls and stayed there for one day. They then drove to Boston. From Boston, they flew to Charlottetown. They stayed there for one day and then rented a car and drove to New Brunswick. They stayed there for two days and visited Shediac and Moncton. From New Brunswick, they drove to PEI and stayed for three nights. After their two-day visit to PEI, they plan to fly back to Boston and fly to New Orleans for the weekend. From New Orleans, they will fly to Vancouver and stay there for one or two weeks with their relatives. They then plan to fly to New York. From New York, they will fly to Europe.

Planning Horizon

They reported engaging in some planning before they made the trip. BB said, "We live in different cities and didn't have time to meet. So we phoned each other to organize and create a rough plan." They wanted to visit Halifax, but the airline they took did not land in Halifax. So they chose PEI because it is the closest stop to Halifax. Halifax was their primary destination and they arrived at PEI by chance.

Assistance by Travel Professionals

BB reported visiting the OEKISTA travel agency in Salzburg, Austria, before their trip. "They arranged for our trans-Atlantic flights and car reservation for [our] first car rental," reported BB.

Requesting Information from Travel Offices Before Visiting

BB and GL did not contact any travel offices before they visited PEI. GL said, "Brigitte bought a book about Canada before we came here. We read it and picked out places we want to see."

PEI Planning Questions

First Learning About PEI

BB reported that they read articles in travelers' guides and wanted to go to Nova Scotia. "We learned about this place when we arrived here," she said.

PEI Recommended for this Trip? Why PEI Included?

BB and GL reported that no one recommended PEI for their trip. The only reason for them to choose PEI was, "It is closest to Halifax," said BB.

Using the Visitors' Guide

BB reported using the Visitors' Guide to some extent. "[The Visitors' Guide has a] map of the streets, accommodations, and sites. [It is] helpful," said BB. Note that Halifax was their primary destination and their PEI visit was because there was "no flight [to Halifax] with this airline," said BB.

Involvement in the PEI Destination Decision

BB and GL both reported that they were equally involved in making the decision.

PEI Visit

BB and GL stayed for three nights at PEI. They reported that their major destination was not PEI. BB said, "We plan to spend two weeks on the east coast and two weeks on the west coast." For the reason of this choice, she said, "It is most interesting. We have friends on east and west coasts."

Main Motives for the Trip

Out of ten votes, BB and GL assigned five votes to a chance to learn through touring about another culture. They assigned two votes to a chance to visit friends and relatives. They assigned one vote each to a chance to relax and escape from daily concerns and a chance to observe and experience nature.

PEI Trip Route and Destinations

On day one of their stay at PEI, BB and GL drove from Charlottetown to the National Park. They walked on the beach of North Rustico. They stayed at a bed-and-breakfast inn at Stanley Bridge. On day two, they drove to Summerside and exited PEI from Borden terminal to New Brunswick. On day three, they drove back from New Brunswick and entered PEI from the Borden terminal. They drove to Victoria. They visited the Chocolate Factory and the Borshaw Car Museum. They then drove to Charlottetown and stayed in a bed and breakfast inn in Meadowbank. On day four, they visited the Rock Point Indian Village and drove back to Charlottetown. They then stayed in the airport overnight to catch the 5:45 a.m. flight.

Trip Route and Mode

BB and GL chose a fly-and-drive mode for their trip. They reported to have not considered other alternatives because they said, "It is best to move around by car." They picked PEI as their destination because, "We thought this was closest to Halifax and we planned to go by 'bridge' to Halifax," said BB. Both BB and GL were involved in making this decision. As for ferry, they chose the closest terminal because there was a kilometer limit for the car (4 days = 800 kms). BB said, "We have no expectations for the ferry service, but it was okay."

PEI Activities and Attractions Visited

Prior to their trip, BB and GL did not plan on any particular activities. They visited the national park beach because BB reported, "The weather was fine and we wanted to exercise. The beach has fascinations. And we wanted to go to the National Park." They picked the car museum because, "It was raining and [the museum] looked interesting," said BB. They visited the Indian Village also because, "It looked interesting," as GL put it. They went to a craft studio called the House of Dolls near the Indian Village. They described their experience with these places visited as, "We had no expectations. But we really enjoyed everything," said GL.

Evening Restaurant Dining

BB and GL did not dine out in the evenings during their stay at PEI. They did spend about $60 on the meals in fast food restaurants.

Activities not Engaged in

BB and GL did not visit any art galleries and farmer markets. They did not engage in golfing, boat tours, and deep-sea fishing. They did not attend any theaters. They did not dine out in the evenings and did not have lobster supper. They did not visit any bars, either.

The Accommodation Decision and Experience

They stayed two nights in bed & breakfast inns at PEI and one night at the Charlottetown Airport. They stayed one night at the "Stallman's Inn" at Stanley Bridge and another night in the "Tighnabruaich Inn" at Meadowbank. They chose Stallman's because, "We saw another one in the guide but couldn't find it. And we saw this one on the road," said BB. Their experience with this inn was better than expected. "They were very friendly. It was clean and the food is good," reported BB. For another inn at Meadowbank, BB said, "The first impression wasn't terrific. There is no paved drive. But it was very nice." "They were there when we needed them and we didn't book any hotels [before we came here]," GL added. When asked about the things they would like to see changed at the inns, they said "nothing." Both BB and GL were involved in making the accommodation decision.

Gifts and Other Purchases

BB and GL did not plan to buy anything at PEI, and they bought nothing.

Expenditure Breakouts

BB and GL reported their total expenditures to include the following: $65 for accommodations; $30 for recreation/entertainment; $60 for meals in restaurants; $20 for food and alcohol purchases in PEI stores; $31 for ferry tickets; $45 for gasoline; $223 for car rental. The total expenditure of BB and GL during their three nights stay at PEI was approximately $474.

Grounded Theory Conclusions from the European Visit Case Study

At least two observations deserve emphasis. First, the impact of external situational influences is sometimes greater than the framing of leisure choices. These

European visitors represent "accidental tourists" in the truest sense of the concept—they had severely limited knowledge and no interest in visiting PEI during their trip to North America. The PEI visit was a glitch in their purchase consumption system that included a desire and plans to visit Nova Scotia.

Second, such accidental tourism can sometimes result in rather extensive overnight stays and trip activities. Thus, the seemingly unlikely theoretical conjunction of travelers not planning on visiting or staying overnight but who stay four nights or longer sometimes occurs. Studying such cases empirically enriches the development of a grounded theory as well as providing important clues for development of effective destination marketing strategies. For the latter, the data from other European visitors similar to what these two Austrian informants provide suggests that PEI may be unable to stand alone as a core destination for such markets. Planning joint marketing programs among the Canadian Maritime Provinces may benefit the smaller populated—and out of the way—provinces in particular. Designing visit packages and promoting joint visits to two or more Maritime Provinces during a single trip is likely to be appealing for such customer segments more than others.

LIMITATIONS AND SUGGESTIONS FOR FURTHER RESEARCH

The case studies presented provide investigative evidence on the value of systems thinking (Senge, 1990) in examining purchase consumption systems of leisure travel decision processes and behaviors. While such research provides data useful for building grounded theories of what is happening and why in the thinking and doing processes of customers, certainly large-scale surveys and field experiments of the impact of marketing and measured variables (e.g., demographic variables) are necessary to generalize the resulting theory to populations.

The case studies reported do go beyond the implicit models of destination marketing executives in indicating the immediate and "downstream" impacts of marketing tools, such as the impacts of *This Week in PEI* and the PEI Visitors' Guide. The findings suggest that the biggest impact of the Visitors' Guide is not in attracting visits but expanding the scope of visit behaviors. This conclusion is *not* meant to suggest that the marketing investment in the Visitors' Guide was unprofitable in causing visits to occur that would not otherwise have occurred; however, a substantial portion of the total Visitors' Guide impact likely due to its influence on increasing the range of behaviors—including length of stays—of visitors using the Visitors' Guide versus not using the Visitors' Guide.

CONTRIBUTIONS TO THEORY AND PRACTICE

Grounded theory serves to "put people back into marketing research" (Zaltman, 1997). Certainly collecting and mapping consumers' emic views of their planning and doing processes helps to revise and deepen the etic (i.e., researcher's) views of reality.

The main contribution to grounded theory from emic storytelling research in leisure travel may be the observation that no one dependent variable alone is both necessary and sufficient in influencing travelers' thoughts or actions. Even when a travel party reports experiences include bad accommodations, that alone is not sufficient to cause the entire trip to be judged a disaster; the conjunction of two bad accommodation experiences in a row and the lack of available alternative accommodations resulted in days of frustration and the final judgment that PEI is a bad place to visit.

Similarly, receiving the copy of *This Week in PEI* by itself was necessary but not enough to cause the leisure trip to PEI reported by the New Brunswick family. In reviewing Figure 10-3, several factors contribute for the family members reaching the unanimous decision to visit PEI—one or two of these factors appear neither necessary nor sufficient, such as the mother's remembering a visit to the *Anne* homestead years ago.

Figure 10-10 provides some summary information based in part on the findings in the case studies presented as well as large-scale survey research findings (details available in Woodside *et al.,* 1997). Figure 10-10 indicates the need to ensure design of effective PEI marketing strategies for three principal origin markets: residents in other Maritime Provinces, Ontario, and the U.S. (especially New England and the mid-Atlantic States). Focusing on such an exhibit raises interesting marketing strategy issues— such as, what would happen if PEI placed the Visitors' Guide in the hands of residents living in the other Maritime Provinces? Would the number of behaviors including their length of stays in PEI increase dramatically for these nearby consumers? Such an issue can be answered scientifically—with treatment and control groups, and such a study is suggested for future research.

Most likely three to five unique and valuable customer segments exist within each of the "Big 3" origin markets for PEI. Certainly not all PEI visitors from New Brunswick are young families and not all American visitors are seniors. The proposal here is that in-depth case studies employing the long interview method of about five travel parties (see McCracken, 1988) of each of three customer segments from each of the Big Three markets will provide both confirmatory evidence and additional nuances about visitors critical for achieving success in PEI's tourism export industry (i.e., about 45 in-depth case studies). Such a research approach is useful for building grounded theories of leisure travel for other destinations as well.

STORYTELLING THEORY AND STRATEGY APPLICATIONS

Given that a substantial share of unconscious thinking and learning occurs in stories (see Shank, 1999; Weick, 1995), in-depth reporting of real-life

Decision Area 2,0,S02	Destinations	Route/Mode to and in PEI	Accommodations During PEI stay	Activities in PEI	PEI Regions Visited	Attractions Visited, Including Restaurants	Gifts and Purchases Made
Consideration Set and Choices	Austria, Munich, New York, Ottawa, Montreal, Ottawa, Toronto, Niagara Falls, Boston, New Brunswick, PEI, New Orleans, Vancouver, New York, Europe	Fly to Charlottetown from Boston, drive to PEI, New Brunswick, Borden terminal to exit PEI	Smallman's B&B, Tighnabruaich, airport	National Park, Car Museum, Indian Village, Craft Studio	Charlottetown, Summerside, Stanley Bridge, North Rustico, New Brunswick, Victoria, Rocky Point	National Park, North Rustico Beach, Car Museum, Craft Studio, Indian Village, Rocky Point, Victoria, Chocolate Factory	Nothing
Motives	PEI was used as means to get to Halifax: "We have friends on the east and west coasts	It is best to move around by car	Found as needed, airport was very early flight	Beach fascinating; weather good; National Park: looked interesting car museum Indian village	Waited to drive to Halifax by bridge	Wanted to see National Park, weather good, looked interesting (car museum and Indian village)	No plan to buy anything

Information Search and Use	OEKISTA Travel Agency for PEI, book, "we learn about this place when we arrive here"	Visitors' Guide, for maps	Saw both inns on the route	Visitors' Guide	Visitors' Guide for maps	Visitors' Guide	N/A
Outcomes	No expectations but we like it very much	No expectations for ferry but it was OK.	Better than expected; Stallran's: friendly and clean, good food; Tiachmabruaich OK, though no paved drive.	No expectations, but enjoyed everything	No expectations, 'enjoyed everything'	No expectations, but enjoyed everything	N/A

FIGURE 10.10 Summary of a European duo's visit to Prince Edward Island (PEI) (Case 10). From Austria. Stayed three nights at various locations. Income range for each was between $35,000 and $50,000. Expenditures were $475. First-time visitors. Both are in their 20s and single. Work status: both full-time employed. Visitor segment: Far-distant, foreign, touring (world), young market. Both travelers are from Austria, though they live in different cities. They visited PEI on their way to Halifax. They spent three days of their 30-day trip on the island. Both were in their 20s, employed on a low-to-medium income. There was little or no preparation for PEI, though they used the Visitors' Guide to select the places to see on the island. They saw a range of places: national park, North Rustico beach, the chocolate factory, Rocky Point Indian Village, and the Borshaw Car Museum. They stayed in a B&B. The main aim of the trip was to see some of PEI as they were going to go near it to visit Halifax. They were unlikely to return in the near future as they felt it was a long way from Europe. Key words: foreign duo (not living together), low to medium income, three-day stay as part of a month-long trip, first-time visitors, unlikely to return, both from Austria, unplanned activities, short planning time frame, low involvement once on island.

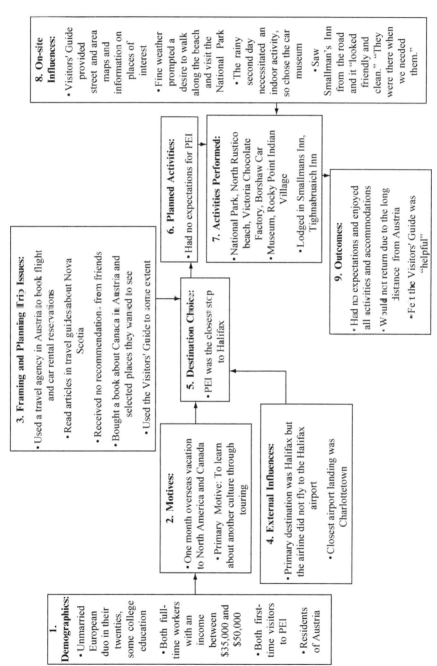

8. On-site Influences:
- Visitors' Guide provided street and area maps and information on places of interest
- Fine weather prompted a desire to walk along the beach and visit the National Park
- The rainy second day necessitated an indoor activity, so chose the car museum
- Saw Smallman's Inn from the road and it "looked friendly and clean." "They were there when we needed them."

6. Planned Activities:
- Had no expectations for PEI

7. Activities Performed:
- National Park, North Rustico beach, Victoria Chocolate Factory, Borshaw Car Museum, Rocky Point Indian Village
- Lodged in Smallmans Inn, Tighnabruaich Inn

3. Framing and Planning Trip Issues:
- Used a travel agency in Austria to book flight and car rental reservations
- Read articles in travel guides about Nova Scotia
- Received no recommendations from friends
- Bought a book about Canada in Austria and selected places they wanted to see
- Used the Visitors' Guide to some extent

5. Destination Choice:
- PEI was the closest stop to Halifax

9. Outcomes:
- Had no expectations and enjoyed all activities and accommodations
- Would not return due to the long distance from Austria
- Felt the Visitors' Guide was "helpful"

2. Motives:
- One month overseas vacation to North America and Canada
- Primary Motive: To learn about another culture through touring

4. External Influences:
- Primary destination was Halifax but the airline did not fly to the Halifax airport
- Closest airport landing was Charlottetown

1. Demographics:
- Unmarried European duo in their twenties, some college education
- Both full-time workers with an income between $35,000 and $50,000
- Both first-time visitors to PEI
- Residents of Austria

FIGURE 10.11 Young Austrian duo.

244

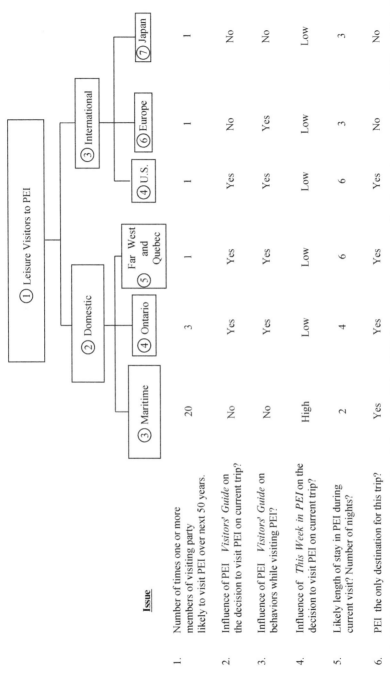

Issue	③ Maritime	④ Ontario	⑤ Far West and Quebec	④ U.S.	⑥ Europe	⑦ Japan
1. Number of times one or more members of visiting party likely to visit PEI over next 50 years.	20	3	1	1	1	1
2. Influence of PEI *Visitors' Guide* on the decision to visit PEI on current trip?	No	Yes	Yes	Yes	No	No
3. Influence of PEI *Visitors' Guide* on behaviors while visiting PEI?	No	Yes	Yes	Yes	Yes	No
4. Influence of *This Week in PEI* on the decision to visit PEI on current trip?	High	Low	Low	Low	Low	Low
5. Likely length of stay in PEI during current visit? Number of nights?	2	4	6	6	3	3
6. PEI the only destination for this trip?	Yes	Yes	Yes	Yes	No	No

FIGURE 10.12 Summary of findings. Numbers in boxes (see Tufte, 2003) for customer segments reflect the total export revenues for PEI contributed by tourism expenditures.

245

stories and advancing grounded theory of story-based thoughts and behavior is worthy of scholarly attention. Also, consider Shank's (1999, p. 96) conclusion: "When confronted with new problems, people almost inevitably search their memories for similar problems they have already solved (Johnson and Seifert, 1992; Gholson *et al.*, 1996). They are, in essence, recalling their own prior problem-solving stories." People make sense of their worlds and who they are from the stories of their experiences that they tell to themselves and others. Research on emic "sensemaking" is mostly research to collect introspective stories (Wallendorf and Brucks, 1993).

The application findings reported by Adaval and Wyer (1998) provide a very practical justification for thick descriptions of emic interpretations in whole stories. Whole-story based advertisements may have greater impact in building preference and action than simply listing benefits for visiting a destination. Thus, destination marketers may want to ground their advertising campaigns in real-life stories of successful visits—successful as illustrated by the emic stories learned from storytelling research. Can such ads be designed effectively without deep emic knowing? Likely not.

Consequently, advertising creative work and storytelling ads may be more effective if they build from emic knowledge (i.e., empirical, case-based, introspective, thick descriptions) rather than building using only the implicit etic views held by copywriters or from variable-based, empirical–positivistic, sample-based studies. How do seniors from America go about planning and doing their once-in-a-lifetime visits to PEI? How do repeat visitors to PEI from New Brunswick go about planning and doing their eighteenth visit? Thick descriptions of real-life stories told by participant/informants are likely to answer such questions well and provide information useful for effective storytelling ad copywriting and visualizations.

Emic storytelling research is likely to include reports of bad visits, such as the one described by the Ontario couple visiting PEI. The nuances reported in such bad visit stories suggest necessary design improvements in product and service offerings. Consequently, the practical value of emic storytelling research goes beyond creating advertisements effective in delivering visitors—such research helps identify specific product features that need to be redesigned, refurbished, quickly before customers' negative evaluations snowball into permanent customer loss and bad publicity.

PART V

LEARNING HOW INITIAL BEHAVIOR AFFECTS FUTURE BEHAVIOR

11

THE INFLUENCES OF BRAND IMPRINTING AND SHORT-TERM MARKETING ON SUBSEQUENT CUSTOMER CHOICES

Synopsis

When consumers are presented with traditional packaged goods (e.g., laundry detergent, bathroom tissue, sink cleaners) in a new purchasing environment, do they tend to keep buying the first brand that they try? If so, how widespread is this behavioral primacy effect? How do specific prices and other marketing variables work to reinforce or overcome the behavioral primacy effect? To answer these issues, a test market situation was created in which consumers were given the opportunity to purchase each week for 18 weeks from three product categories (bread, potato chips, and bathroom tissue) that included both real and simulated brands. During the study certain extraordinary influence strategies were implemented in order to observe their potential immediate and long-term influences on consumers' purchasing behavior. Findings: the behavioral primacy effect, purchasing a brand in the first week, has a significant impact on a brand's subsequent purchase share. Initial experience combined with the marketing influence strategies often greatly increases the probability of the purchase of a given brand.

INTRODUCTION: SHOULD ADVERTISERS PAY A PREMIUM FOR YOUNG AUDIENCES?

"My father introduced me to this beer when I was seven or so," said Mr. Schimmel, who has stuck to Iserlohner Pils [a German brand] all of his adult life. "Even before I ever drank it, it was part of a special ritual in my life," the younger Mr. Schimmel added (Fuhrmans, 2003, A5).

Researchers have been studying the purchasing behavior of consumers for decades in an attempt to understand what it is that drives such behavior and

---

This chapter was co-authored by Mark Uncles and Arch G. Woodside.

how consumer choices can be influenced. Much is known about purchasing behavior in established stationary (or approximately stationary) markets, especially concerning the limited brand repertoires that are so often maintained by consumers (Ehrenberg, 1988; Wright, Sharp, and Goodhardt, 2002; Ehrenberg, Uncles, and Goodhardt, 2004). But what is known about purchasing behavior in a new purchase environment? For example, when a consumer first starts buying a product (buying alcohol once over the permitted age), or after a move to a new location (coming to terms with a different mix of brands of bathroom tissues and potato chips after moving to a new city), or when marketers create new (sub-) categories or considerably alter existing (sub-) categories (the introduction of boutique ciders in the 1990s and branded vodka mixes in the 2000s, as well as the launch of specific new brands such as FCUK Spirit in Australia).

Does paying a premium price for advertising to reach younger versus older audiences make sense? For example, television commercial time on a nationwide David Letterman late night show may reach a smaller audience but be priced higher than on the competing Jay Leno show. The rationale for such a premium is that younger audiences are worth the higher price and that Letterman's audience is younger and more hip than Leno's. Such reasoning implies that a strategic window opens briefly for reaching customers who are relatively new to a choice context—a carryover effect occurs following first-time brand choice, and younger customers face new choice contexts more frequently than older customers.

For real and artificial brands in a highly controlled experimental design setting, this chapter confirms that an imprinting carryover effect on subsequent brand choices does occur. We present evidence supporting the view that advertising and marketing strategies for a given brand should be heavily weighted to achieve initial-trial purchases among consumers facing new choice contexts.

One finding from research on consumer brand choice behavior is that in a new purchase environment, initially consumers try several different brands that are available for them to buy—some consumers try all brands in the new environment if the number of brands is limited. After this initial exploration period, consumers tend to restrict their brand purchases to one or two brands (e.g., see Ehrenberg and Charlton, 1973; Ehrenberg, Hammond, and Goodhardt, 1994). However, heretofore the impact that the initial purchase of a brand has on consumers' purchasing behaviors in future purchase periods has not been examined in controlled (i.e., true experimental designed) conditions.

THEORY OF BEHAVIORAL PRIMACY EFFECT

The core "behavioral primacy effect" is that, given that the physical experience of buying and using a brand is satisfactory, consumers tend to repeat the purchase of the first brand that they purchased more frequently than other brands available in the same purchase environment (e.g., a supermarket or website with multiple brands available in adjacent spaces) that consumers also buy and use. We present evidence that confirms this proposition even for more mundane, less dramatic, first-time experiences than Mr. Schimmel's first beer.

Distinguishing behavioral primacy from cognitive primacy is useful from both theoretical and practical perspectives. Cognitive primacy refers to individuals remembering best what they learn first (see Arnould, Price, and Zinkhan, 2004, p. 370). Behavioral primacy is unique from cognitive primacy in focusing in the initial physical experience of touching, moving, transacting, and using experiences of one brand versus alternatively available brands experienced in later purchase periods; most communication studies estimate cognitive primacy effects using measures of recall or reported brand preference that first come to mind for the first brand seen or read about among several brands.

Operant conditioning theory and biological imprinting (Lorenz, 1952/1997) provide rationales for predicting subsequent behavioral preference (e.g., mating, refraining from cannibalizing, or initial purchase/use of a brand in a product category when in a new choice context). For example, among Wolf spiders, Hebets' Figure 1B (2003, p. 13392) shows 50 versus 12 percent rates of mating by adult females with adult males having black forelegs subsequent to the same adult females being exposed as "subadults" to adult males having black versus brown forelegs, respectively. The copulating rates by adult females with adult males having brown forelegs subsequent to the same adult females being exposed when subadults to adult males having brown versus black forelegs was 38 versus 14 percent, respectively. Such imprinting experiences served to eliminate cannibalism of males by the female spiders; Hebets' (2003, Figure 1B) shows zero cannibalism when female subadults were exposed to adult male spiders with brown versus black forelegs followed by mating or meal opportunities when the females became adults and then were exposed to adult males with brown versus black forelegs, respectively. However, the rates of cannibalism of males by females was 28 percent for black-foreleg-male subadult exposure followed by the brown adult male treatment and 16 percent for brown-foreleg-male subadult exposure followed by the black adult male treatment.

In a human context, brand imprinting (i.e., incumbency, see Muthukrisnan, 1995) is predicted to result subsequently in more repeat purchases for the imprinted brand compared to competing brands available in the same purchase environment. If using the brand initially purchased in a new choice context results in positive reinforcement, the experience serves as the exemplar for comparing subsequent use experiences when buying competing brands. Moreover, given that consumers have difficulty differentiating brands for many packaged goods (Foxall, 1999; Steinberg, 2003), consumers tend to stick with the brand (or brands) that satisfied them first. This is behavioral brand imprinting. Such a behavioral process need not be based on conscious thinking (see Bargh, 2002). Indeed, many consumers tend toward conserving cognitive effort possibly for searching, evaluating, and making tradeoffs for more critical issues in life than evaluating alternative packaged goods brands.

Mental processing theory and the empirical findings of Muthukrishnan and Kardes (2001) help to explain further the brand imprinting phenomenon: consumers become familiar with the brands that they purchased initially and they remember their experiences—even if such remembering occurs unconsciously (i.e., the remembering is not retrievable in a conscious process, see Kagan, 2002; Zaltman, 2003). If the experience was favorable, they likely attribute this positive conclusion to the brand and are much more likely to buy the brand again. After such experiences the tendency is to persist with the focal attributes in subsequent choices and the tendency to associate certain key benefits of the product primarily with the target attributes even for neutral evidence (see Muthukrishnan, 1995; Muthukrishnan and Kardes, 2001). Consumers look for anything associating with the product to reinforce their experience with the brand and they use what they find from this search to develop their preferences for the brand that they are familiar with.

Consistent findings from studies of marketing influences on brand choice through multiple time periods for packaged goods are that the effects of manipulating marketing variables (e.g., price changes, special store displays, advertising) are such that effects are substantial but short lived—after the treatment period ends (e.g., special price offer), the share of sales for the treated brand reverts back to the share held before the treatment period (see Eskin and Baron, 1977; Ehrenberg, Hammond, and Goodhardt, 1994; Jedidi, Mela, and Gupta, 1999; Motes and Woodside, 1984). For instance, an analysis of 150 price promotions in Britain, Germany, Japan, and the U.S. showed that before-to-after repeat-buying was unaffected (i.e., there was no learning), there was no before-to-after sales increase, and there were no/few new buyers (Ehrenberg, Hammond, and Goodhardt, 1994). Thus, marketing influences on a brand's market share tend to be transitory.

This suggests that once established, the behavioral primacy effect is enduring. But, there may be more to it than this. For the first brand (or brands) chosen, it is possible that the marketing influences interact to reinforce the behavioral primacy effect.

In order to examine the uncertainties previously mentioned, this chapter continues the research of consumer purchasing behavior with the further analysis of data from Motes and Woodside (2001) of a multi-week in-home shopping experiment. Motes and Woodside (2001) report the impacts of immediate and long-term impacts of extra-ordinary and regular influence strategies on consumer brand choice. This chapter probes the primacy effect of purchasing a brand in the initial buying period (i.e., week one) and how it influences further purchasing behavior and brand preference. In addition, we consider here the interaction effects of brand imprinting and implementing certain influence strategies for short periods of time.

Propositions

Two propositions are examined:

P_1: Due to brand imprinting, purchasing a brand in the initial time period (week one) increases the likelihood of a consumer's purchasing the same brand in future shopping trips.

P_2: A brand imprinting and unique marketing interaction effect exists; that is, the brand priming impact is prevalent especially when combined with the implementation of short-term marketing influence strategies for the brand first experienced.

Figure 11-1 illustrates the two propositions. Without brand imprinting Brand X's long-term share of purchases will be low, whereas with imprinting the long-term share of purchases will be at a medium level (P_1). A strong positive interaction effect for brand imprinting by special, short-term marketing programs results in Brand X having a high long-term share of purchase (P_2). The rationale for P_2 is that consumers are consciously as well as unconsciously vigilant to special, short-term inducement offers to the first brand that they experience—all first-brand experiences may be thought to include some rite of passage no matter how mundane the product category and no matter if consumers can consciously retrieve the name of the brand. By contrast, without brand imprinting Brand X's long-term share of purchases remains low—despite exposure to short-term marketing programs.

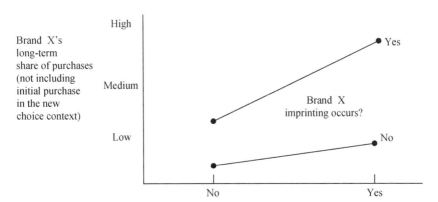

FIGURE 11.1 Theoretical predictions for brand imprinting and special, short-term marketing program influences on a brand's long-term share of purchases.

Method

To test the propositions, the present study further analyzes the data from the 18-week market test reported by Motes and Woodside (2001). The market test was performed by providing competing brands in three product categories in an in-home shopping experiment. A total of 114 subjects participated in all 18 weeks of the study. The Ss were adult females and males aged 24 to 57 living in a southeastern U.S. metropolitan area. Each subject was given the opportunity to purchase one brand each week of each of three product categories: bread, bathroom tissue, and potato chips. Before the start of the study, Ss selected had to be buyers of at least two of the three product categories in addition to roughly representing medium to heavy buying households. They were not required to purchase each week nor were they restricted from buying similar products from outside sources to allow for more realism in the study.

The subjects were assigned randomly to one of five separate treatment groups, one of which was a control group (i.e., no special, short-term, marketing programs occurred for selected subjects (Ss) in the control group over the 18 weeks), for implementation of the different influence strategies. The design of the study and selection of subjects builds on the Ehrenberg and Charlton (1973) study, with several extensions. The more recent study was performed over an 18 week period as opposed to 15 weeks and offered both real brands (for potato chips) as well as artificial brands (for bread and toilet paper). The formal use of a control group to compare treatment group results against was also new in the author study compared to Ehrenberg and Charlton's study. (Burke *et al.* (1992) describe the relative merits of making real-world observations and using simulated environments.)

Product Categories and Manipulations

Bread

Four different brands of bread were offered and distinguished solely by the letter C, J, M, or V on the otherwise blank packaging. Each brand of bread was identical in all aspects (which fact the subjects were not made aware of) and sold at a price of 45¢. Over the duration of the study, different influence strategies were implemented in 3-week intervals for each treatment group. For treatment groups 1 and 2 a 10¢ price reduction for Brand J was offered in weeks 7–9 and 13–15, respectively for each group. An advertising message was attached to Brand J bread for treatment group 3 in weeks 7–9 and for treatment group 4 in weeks 13–15. Also during weeks 7–9 Brand M bread was temporarily out of stock for treatment group 4. This situation was not of major concern for the present chapter but a brief examination showed that there was not a significant effect on the consumers' purchase behavior following the stock out. Brand M's purchase share returned to its normal level in the following weeks, an outcome consistent with the long-held view that very temporary out-of-stocks need not lead to a longer-term loss of sales (Charlton *et al.*, 1972).

Bathroom Tissue

Three different brands of bathroom tissue were offered and were separable by their prices of 10¢, 15¢, and 20¢. There were no other brand distinctions. Treatment groups 1 and 2 were exposed to an advertising message for both the 10¢ and 20¢ brands. The advertising message was used during weeks 10–12 in treatment group 1 and weeks 16–18 for treatment group 2.

A coupon was attached to the 15¢ brand during weeks 10–12 for treatment group 3 and during weeks 16–18 for treatment group 4. The coupon offer was, "Buy one at the regular price, get one extra for 10¢." A new two-ply brand of tissue was introduced in treatment group 2 during weeks 7–9, and then removed in week 10. The new brand was offered at a premium price of 25¢. Like the stock out situation of Brand M bread, the introduction of a new brand is also not of direct concern in this report. The procedure here is similar to that used by Ehrenberg, Scriven, and Barnard (1997).

Potato Chips

The final product category offered to the subjects was potato chips. This category was comprised of three real brands: Charles, Lay's, and Wise. They were sold as they would appear in grocery stores, but with a price of 70¢. The well-established Lay's brand was used for the implementation of price manipulations in each treatment group. During weeks 4–6 the price of Lay's was increased by 20¢ for treatment group 1 and by 10¢ for treatment group 2 in the same time period. Treatment group 3 was exposed to a 10¢ price decrease in weeks 4–6 while treatment group 4 was given a reduction of 20¢. The different price levels were used to represent moderate and drastic changes in price to examine if each had significantly different impacts. Also the impact of a price reduction of a real brand is compared with that of a simulated brand of bread.

RESULTS

P_1: Behavioral Primacy Effect and Brand Imprinting

The findings support P_1: buying in the first week of the study has a significant impact on the subjects' future purchasing behavior. The Ss purchased a brand more often if they had purchased that brand in the first week. Treatment groups 1 and 2 and the control group were used to test this theory on the impact of buying a brand of bathroom tissue in the first week. The probability of purchasing a certain brand of bathroom tissue increases given that the subject purchased the same brand in week 1 (see Figure 11-2; group level analysis results: adjusted R^2 = .87, df = 2, 3; p < .02).

The later purchase share of each brand (10¢, 15¢, and 20¢) was greater if the brand was purchased in week 1 than if the brand had not been purchased initially. Similar graphs illustrate the imprinting effect for the purchase of Brand J bread; see Figures 11-3 and 11-4. (Multiple regression results [individual-level analysis]: Buy Brand J = 1.366 – 2.725 Price$_j$ + .709 Buy J$_{wk1}$ – 1.298 Price$_j$ × Buy J$_{wk1}$; adjusted R^2 = .07, df = 3, 1202; F = 32.82; p < .0001; the coefficients have a similar profile [i.e., all significant statistically] using binary logistic regression.)

These findings indicate a behavioral primacy effect and are consistent with the theoretical rationale provided earlier (e.g., Foxall, 1999; Bargh, 2002; Muthukrishnan, 1995; Muthukrishnan and Kardes, 2001).

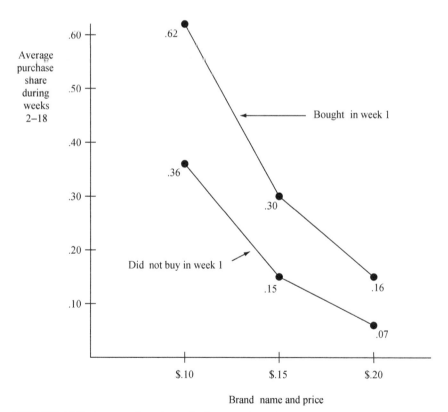

FIGURE 11.2   Impact of purchase of toilet paper in week 1 on average brand purchase share for all groups.

P₂: Brand Imprinting and Special Marketing Program Interaction Effects

The findings partially support P_2. A brand imprinting and unique marketing interaction effect occurs for Brand J bread and the short-term price reduction; that is, the brand priming impact is prevalent especially when combined with the implementation of short-term marketing influence strategies for the brand first experienced; see Figure 11-3. However, no significant interaction effect occurs for Brand J bread and the short-term advertising for Brand J; see Figure 11-4.

The findings for Lay's potato chips confirm a strong interaction effect between imprinting and price levels for the brand's lower and raising price (i.e., Lay's; group level analysis: adjusted $R^2 = .89$; $F = 24.7$, $df = 3, 6$, $p < .001$; standardized model: Z_Share$_{t>1}$ = $- .58$ Z_Price + 1.60 Z_Imprinting – 1.12 Z_Price-by-Imprinting). Figure 11-5 shows the three effects.

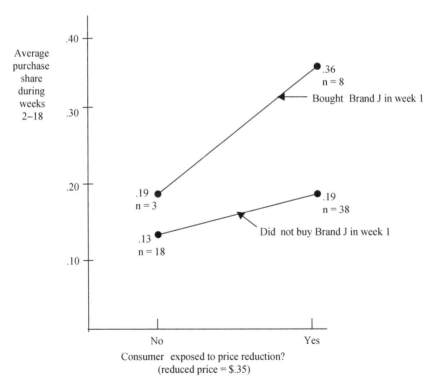

FIGURE 11.3 Impacts of Brand J bread purchase in week 1 and short-term price reduction on average Brand J purchase share. Multiple regression results: Buy Brand J = 1.366 – 2.725 Price$_j$ + .709 Buy Jwk1 – 1.298 Price$_j$ x Buy Jwk1; adjusted $R^2 = .073$, $df = 3, 1202$; $F = 32.82$; $p < .0001$.

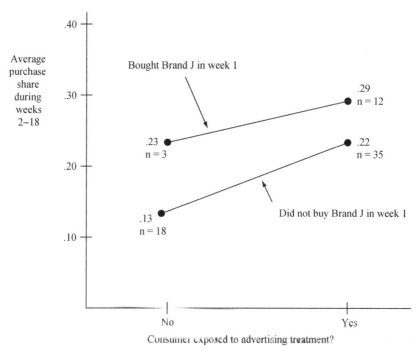

FIGURE 11.4   Impacts of Brand J bread purchase in week 1 and short-term advertising on subsequent average Brand J purchase share.

No interaction effect is found for the price of Lay's and imprinting for the two brands competing with Lay's. However, both a brand imprinting effect and a competitor's price main effect are found for each of these two competing brands (Wise and Charles). Figures 11-6 and 11-7 summarize both the predictions from the respective group level models and the actual findings for these two brands for the Lay's price and incumbency conditions.

Venn Diagram Illustrations of Brand Imprinting and Special, Short-Term Marketing Influences

Figure 11-8 presents further details of brand imprinting and exposure to special, short-term marketing influences on Brand J bread's purchase shares. For example, among Ss who did buy Brand J bread in the first week and were exposed to the price reduction for Brand J, Brand J's long-term purchase share was .36 (i.e., p (Bj | (Bj t=1 ∪ Exposed Price J=.35) = .36, n = 8). But the purchase share drops to .19 for Ss exposed to the price reduction for Brand J bread and who did not buy J in the first week (i.e., p (Bj | ((Exposed Price J=.35) ∩ Bj t=1) = .19, n = 38).

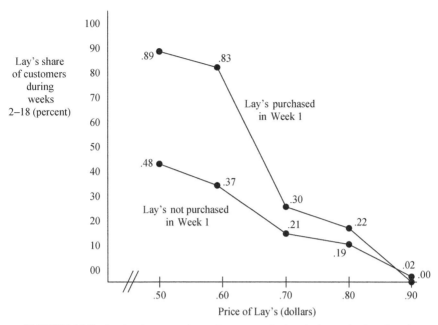

FIGURE 11.5   Lay's subsequent share of customers by imprinting and price of Lay's.

Summary and Meta-Analysis of the Findings

The results for the brands in the other two product categories support the same finding: brand imprinting serves to achieve a positive impact on long-term purchase share for brands that fail to result from special, short-term, marketing manipulations.

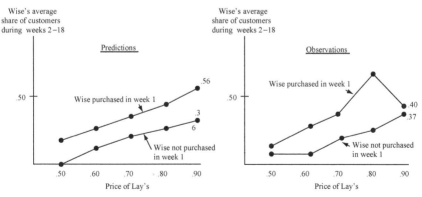

FIGURE 11.6   Predicted and observed customer share for brand incumbency for Wise and price of Lay's.

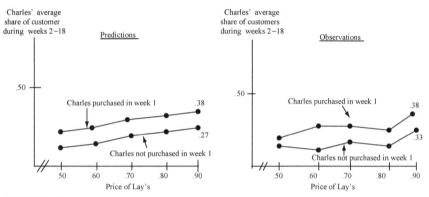

FIGURE 11.7 Predicted and observed customer share for brand incumbency for Charles, and price of Lay's.

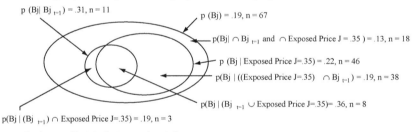

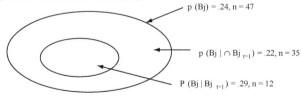

FIGURE 11.8 Venn diagram and Bayesian analysis of price treatment results for Brand J: Brand J choice shares across the 18 weeks of the study. Quasi–control group (T3 and T4) subjects were not exposed to Brand J price = .35 (price-reduced treatment periods) but were exposed to advertising treatments for Brand J, and T4 subjects were exposed to Brand M's being out of stock during weeks 7–9.

Table 11-1 summarizes the imprinting results for all ten brands across the three product categories. The summary includes statistically significant brand imprinting influences in the direction predicted by the H_1. In the table, the meta analysis using a paired sample t-test supports the conclusion that brand imprinting has a moderate effect size on subsequent brand choice behavior.

GENERAL DISCUSSION

In a new environment, initially consumers try (i.e., "trial purchase") several different brands—some consumers will try all brands in the new environment if the number of brands is limited (e.g., less than five). After this initial exploration period, consumer brand purchases for some consumers are restricted to a few (one or two) brands, and other brands available in the environment are rarely purchased. This is evident in the limited repertoire purchasing of established brands in stationary (or approximately stationary) markets (Ehrenberg, 1988; Ehrenberg et al., 2004).

A favorable impact on the probability of repurchasing a brand occurs if the brand is purchased initially. The following process might be at work: customers build preferences based on how well a product meets their needs and expectations and even the most insignificant attributes can serve as an influence on these preferences (Carpenter et al., 1994; Muthukrishnan and Kardes, 2001)—even if the attribute may be in the nature of first-brand experience.

These findings support the view by some marketers that it is very important for a customer to try the marketer's brand as early as possible—i.e., immediately after launch, or as soon as a consumer moves to a new location, or at the time she experiences a new (sub-) category. The message for management from these brand-imprinting results is "get them early": (a) Overly weight marketing efforts to attract first-time product users; (b) Identify consumers who are likely to be experiencing a product for the first time or in a new way (e.g., those moving to a new city); (c) Ensure those making initial trial purchases have a satisfactory experience (e.g., when launching brands into a new product [sub-] category or into a considerably altered existing [sub-] category).

Of course, to be effective, early trial and brand imprinting also must be supported by such marketing basics as making the brand available to target customers and minimizing systemic out-of-stock conditions (factors not manipulated in the multi-week in-home shopping experiment).

A question not addressed here is how quickly the consumer moves from trial purchase to steady state purchasing. One view is that the process is slow; however isolated examples show that some brands can establish market share very quickly (with all the associated patterns of repeat buying expected for

TABLE 11-1 Summary and Meta-Analysis of Brand Imprinting Influence for Brands in Three Product Categories

Product	Brand	Imprinting? (Share in Weeks 2–18)		Difference (%)	$F\ (df = 1, 1936)$	One-tail $p <$	Eta^2
		Yes (%)	No (%)				
Bread	J	26	20	+ 6	6.84	.006	.004
	C	17	13	+ 4	2.98	.042	.002
	M	15	17	− 2	2.10	n.s.	.000
	V	16	15	+ 1	0.06	n.s.	.000
Potato chips	Lay's	31	22	+ 9	17.60	.000	.009
	Charles	29	19	+ 10	28.34	.000	.014
	Wise	37	18	+ 19	75.26	.000	.037
Bathroom tissue	10 Cents	61	37	+ 24	119.69	.000	.058
	15 Cents	24	16	+ 8	12.35	.000	.006
	20 Cents	12	8	+ 4	5.49	.008	.003
Unweighted average (meta-analysis results)		27	19	+ 8	$t = 3.31, df = 10$ (paired)	.1205	.125

that level of share) (Wellan and Ehrenberg, 1988). Analysis of a further 22 cases shows that the previously isolated examples may be more common than previously supposed (Ehrenberg and Goodhardt, 2000). These findings point to quite fast transitions from trial purchase to steady state purchasing.

More in-depth studies and cases of the impact of influence strategies and the brand primacy effect are needed, and these may result in revised estimates of the likely range of impacts for both effects. They might also reveal how quickly the brand primacy effect takes hold. But this study provides a basic idea of how such variables affect consumers, their brand choices, and their long-term choice behaviors.

First-time brand experiences may occur at any age and they are likely to occur for consumers in the second half of their lives for some product categories (e.g., incontinent care and drugs for erectile dysfunction). Thus, the association between age and first-time brand experience is likely to be moderate rather than large. However, additional research (e.g., see Woodside and Wilson, 1995) confirms Mr. Schimmel's brand imprinting from early family-ritual experiences with Iserlohner Pils: for some product categories, first-time brand imprinting occurs via modeling and vicarious exploration (see Price and Ridgway, 1982).

This view that a greater share of subsequent purchases accrues for a brand due to modeling or choice imprinting experiences is not necessarily grounded in information that consumers can retrieve from their long-term memories. Given the scientific evidence that most thinking occurs automatically/unconsciously (see Bargh, 2002; Kagan, 2002; Zaltman, 2003), direct questioning may be ineffective in learning the subsequent effects of consumers' actual brand imprinting experiences. The great promise for accurately measuring short-term marketing effects by designing long-term experiments that Ehrenberg and Charlton (1973) advocated and reported in the *Journal of Advertising Research* more than 30 years ago extends to learning about long-term brand imprinting influence and how such brand imprinting experience interacts with marketing tools on subsequent choice behavior.

12

CUSTOMER VARIETY-SEEKING INFLUENCE ON SUBSEQUENT BRAND CHOICE BEHAVIOR

Synopsis

For fast-moving consumer goods (FMCGs), such as bread, potato chips, and toilet paper, do consumers who exhibit variety-seeking behavior in new buying contexts (i.e., buy different brands at least once over initial buying episodes) also exhibit unique longer-term brand and product purchase behaviors than do non–variety seeking consumers? Are high variety seekers more influenced than low variety seekers to buy a brand during short-term special marketing offers (e.g., price specials)? Evidence from field experiments for three FMCGs partially supports two propositions. Firstly, a greater share of high variety seekers more frequently buys each brand available in future purchase time periods; however, two types of low variety seekers exist, and they differ in their responses to a brand's short-term marketing tactics. Secondly, short-term marketing tactics (e.g., price specials) have greater impact on increasing a brand's share of customers among high versus low variety seekers. Thus, a brand benefits two ways from high versus low variety-seeking behavior: higher penetration (i.e., share of households buying the brand) and greater response to short-term marketing tactics.

INTRODUCTION: HOW INITIAL VARIETY-SEEKING AFFECTS LONG-TERM BRAND CHOICE

Consumers frequently find themselves in moderately unfamiliar choice contexts, such as shopping at a given supermarket for the first time or when one or two new brands are made available at a familiar store or internet display for a given product category. Consumers frequently switch their purchases among different brands in such choice contexts. While the literature on consumer variety seeking focuses on predicting and explaining such switching behavior (e.g., Howard and Sheth, 1969; Menon and Kahn, 1995; McAlister and Pessemier, 1982; Raju, 1980; Venkatesan, 1973), Chapter 12 probes the views that (1) consumers can be segmented by variety-seeking behavior for fast moving consumer goods such as competing brands of bread, potato chips, and toilet paper—not all consumers exhibit a desire to try all unfamiliar brands in unfamiliar choice contexts while others do engage in such choice behavior; and (2) a strong interaction effect occurs between prior variety-seeking behavior and short-term marketing tactics on current brand choice behavior—a greater share of consumers quickly trying all brands in a new choice context respond to later short-term marketing tactics compared to consumers exhibiting less variety-seeking behavior.

The findings support these views and contribute to building a nuance-filled theory of variety-seeking behavior that includes the following propositions: (1) Consumers can be segmented by their variety-seeking brand-choice behaviors. (2) Consumers not purchasing a variety of brands in new purchase contexts include two subcategories: consumers with buying loyalties to one or two brands and consumers who frequently do not buy any brands in the product category during buying episodes. (3) Consumers exhibiting fast variety purchase behavior in new buying contexts are more sensitive to short-term marketing strategies compared to slow variety seekers, brand loyal buyers, and consumers frequently not buying any brands. If these propositions are confirmed by additional research, the information is useful for FMCGs brand managers trying to understand why short-term marketing strategies work well in some markets and poorly in others and for planning which customers to target for individual-level short-term marketing strategies.

VARIETY-SEEKING BEHAVIOR

Theoretically, variety-seeking behavior is defined in the consumer research literature as an individual's change in alternatives (e.g., brands) selected in different choice opportunities (e.g., back-to-back shopping trips) due to a desire to try something different—a person may engage in exploration of the environment (e.g., variety-seeking or novelty-seeking behaviors) in order to achieve a satisfactory or optimum level of stimulation (see Berlyne, 1960; Driver and Streufert, 1965; Fiske and Maddi, 1991; Hunt, 1963; Joachimsthaler and Lastovicka, 1984). "For instance, a consumer may choose a 7-Up following a choice of Coke not because of his or her preference for Coke has changed but just because he or she wants something different. Thus, variety-seeking behavior can occur when preferences for the items remain constant (as is frequently true in mature product classes) but a need for increased variety or stimulation exists" (Menon and Kahn, 1995, p. 286).

Operationally, variety-seeking behavior is defined in the consumer research literature in terms of observed alternative-choice switching behavior (e.g., see Faison, 1977; Pessemier, 1985; Menon and Kahn, 1995) without examining the psychological or social antecedents of such behavior. However, the observed variety-seeking behavior may be due to reasons unrelated to the concept of an optimal level of stimulation and trying something different (e.g., a competing explanation for choosing a 7-Up in the next purchase episode after selecting a Coke that is due to a decision to limit caffeine choices to every once-in-awhile or some other heuristic). The points being made here are that (1) behavioral science theory and empirical evidence are lacking in the development and testing of competing rationales for observed variety-seeking behavior, and (2) the theoretical and operational definitions of variety-seeking behavior need to match one another.

Thus, this chapter defines variety-seeking behavior as an individual's change in alternatives (e.g., brands) selected in different choice opportunities (e.g., back-to-back shopping trips). Further, consumer research would benefit from distinguishing variety-seeking behavior from novelty-seeking behavior in that novelty-seeking behavior includes trying different, and previously unknown to the person, alternatives (e.g., unknown brands in a new choice context) whereby each alternative represents a new experience to the person. Variety-seeking behavior includes both novelty-seeking behavior as well as choice-switching behavior among previously known and/or experienced alternatives.

PROPOSITIONS

The focus here is on some of the consequences to initial variety-seeking versus non-variety-seeking behavior. Thus, the propositions and the following empirical study examine variety-seeking behavior as an independent measured (i.e., chronic) variable.

H_1: Consumers can be segmented by their degree of initial variety-seeking behavior—some consumers quickly engage in variety-seeking behavior as indicated by trying all brands available in a new choice context; other consumers engage more slowly in similar variety-seeking behavior; other consumers fail to try all brands and quickly display repeat loyalty to a limited number of brands; and other consumers fail to try all brands as well as select a brand infrequently (50% or less during choice opportunities). Rationale: while shopping for FMCGs and comparing brands of such products may be consciously as well as unconsciously exciting for many consumers (e.g., for an early examination of this view, see Cox, 1967), other consumers are likely to be rather bored by the prospect, as Kassarjian (1997, xiii) tellingly observes:

> Yet, because to us [consumer researchers] a brand of toilet paper may be important, we have projected that belief onto the consumer. A one percent share of market can mean thousands of dollars of net profit to a company. That one brand has greater shearing strength or is more quickly biodegradable or has more sheets per roll may be quite important to the consumerist, to the environmentalist, or to the readers of *Consumer Reports*. That panel

data on the purchase of toilet paper over a seventeen-year period exists may be titillatingly exciting to the academic researcher, but the average consumer who blithely purchases, consumes, and discards the product, most likely could care less. Unconcernedly he or she makes the purchase, switches brands, ignores commercials, and worries about the important decisions in his life and not the purchase of toilet paper.

P_2: Future brand and product category choice shares vary systematically among consumers segmented by their initial variety-seeking behavior. For example, consumers quickly seeking variety among alternative brands and consumers initially buying less often (50% or less in initial buying episodes) exhibit similar (highest and lowest) purchase shares in future buying time periods. Rationale: the belief that product and brand involvement varies as a chronic psychological variable among consumers serves as the rationale for P_2. Thus, quickly choosing different available brands of toilet paper by some consumers is indicative of greater inherent interest in such shopping behavior compared to taking longer to choose all the available brands and especially compared to not bothering to try all the brands available. This inherent interest manifests in more/less frequent purchases of different brands and the product category in later purchases.

P_3: consumers' sensitivity to short-term marketing tactics varies directly with their speed exhibited in initial variety-seeking behavior—fast variety seekers are the most sensitive and non–variety seekers who often do not buy the product category in initial periods in the choice context are the least sensitive. Rationale: initial variety-seeking behavior indicates vigilance and excitement about what's happening in the marketplace. The fast variety seekers are attentive—ready—to respond to more favorable market conditions in a given context, more so than the other three segments of customers; and the non–variety seekers who often do not buy in initial periods are the least attentive, for example, the benefit of responding to a lower price for a given brand is more likely to go unnoticed by this segment, and if noticed, is less appealing than null choice of not buying the product category at all.

METHOD

This chapter provides the details of the method used to collect data to test the propositions. This section offers only a brief description of the method. Please refer to the method section in Chapter 11 for additional details.

A market test was performed by providing competing brands in three product categories in an in-home shopping experiment. A total of 114 subjects participated in all 18 weeks of the study. Each subject was given the opportunity to purchase one brand each week of each of three product categories: bread, toilet paper, and potato chips. Before the start of the study, subjects selected had to be buyers of two of the three product categories in addition to roughly representing medium to heavy buying households. They were not required to purchase each week nor were they restricted from buying similar products from outside sources to allow for more realism in the study. The subjects were assigned randomly to one of five separate treatment groups, one of which was a control group (i.e., no special, short-term, marketing programs occurred for Ss in the control group over the 18 weeks), for implementation of the different influence strategies.

Product Categories and Manipulations

Bread

Four different brands of bread were offered and distinguished solely by either the letter C, J, M, or V on the otherwise blank packaging. Each brand of bread was identical in all aspects (which the subjects were not made aware of) and sold at a price of 45¢. Over the duration of the study different influence strategies were implemented in three-week intervals for each treatment group. For treatment groups 1 and 2 a 10¢ price reduction for Brand J was offered in weeks 7–9 and 13–15, respectively, for each group. An advertising message was attached to Brand J bread for treatment group 3 in weeks 7–9 and for treatment group 4 in weeks 13–15. Also during weeks 7–9 Brand M bread was temporarily out of stock for treatment group 4. This situation was not of major concern for the present chapter but a brief examination showed that there was not a significant effect on the consumers' purchase behavior following the stock out. Brand M's purchase share returned to its normal level in the following weeks.

Toilet Paper

Three different brands of toilet paper were offered and were distinguished by their prices of 10¢, 15¢, and 20¢. There were no other brand distinctions. Treatment groups 1 and 2 were exposed to an advertising treatment for both the 10¢ and the 20¢ brands. The advertising message was used during weeks 10–12 in treatment group 1 and weeks 16–18 for treatment group 2.

A coupon was attached to the 15¢ brand during weeks 10–12 for treatment group 3 and during weeks 16–18 for treatment group 4. The coupon offer was, "Buy one at the regular price, get one extra for 10¢." A new two-ply brand of tissue was introduced in treatment group 2 during the weeks 7–9, and then removed in week 10. The new brand was offered at a premium price of 25¢. Like the stock out situation of Brand M bread, the introduction of a new brand is also not of direct concern in this report.

Potato Chips

The final product category offered to the subjects was potato chips. This category was comprised of three real brands: Charles, Lay's, and Wise. They were sold as they would appear in grocery stores, but with a price of 70¢. The well-established Lays brand was used for the implementation of price manip-ulations in each treatment group. During weeks 4–6 the price of Lay's was increased by 20¢ for treatment group 1 and by 10¢ for treatment group 2 in the same time period. Treatment group 3 was exposed to a 10¢ price decrease in weeks 4–6 while treatment group 4 was given a reduction of 20¢. The dif-ferent price levels were used to represent moderate and drastic changes in price to examine if each had significantly different impacts. Also the impact of a price reduction of a real brand is compared with that of a simulated brand of bread.

OPERATIONAL DEFINITIONS OF NOVELTY-SEEKING AND VARIETY-SEEKING BEHAVIORS

The study applies high-hurdle operational definitions to identify novelty-seeking and variety-seeking behaviors. For bread, fast novelty-seeking behavior (FNSB) is trying all four previously unknown brands within the first four weeks of the experiment; slow novelty-seeking behavior (SNSB) is taking eight weeks to try all four previously unknown brands. For toilet paper, FNSB is trying all three previously unknown brands within the first three weeks of the experiment; SNSB is taking six weeks to try all three brands.

For the three well-known brands of potato chips, fast variety-seeking behavior (FVSB) is trying all three brands within the first three weeks of the experiment; slow variety-seeking behavior (SVSB) is taking six weeks to try all three brands.

Findings

The findings provide strong support for most parts of all three proposi-tions—however, only the fourth segment (non–variety seekers who do not buy in most initial time periods) differs in the shares of later brand purchases compared to initially fast and slow variety seekers and brand loyal con-sumers. Also, the mean differences in product category purchases supports are highly significant only for comparisons of the first three segments versus the last segment (non–variety seekers who do not buy in most initial time periods). Thus, H_2 receives limited support.

Bread

For bread, four time periods were required to enable choice of all four brands; 16 Ss completed such purchase behavior and are classified as fast variety seekers for bread. A total of 51 Ss completed purchases of all four brands in more than four but less than eight weeks; these Ss are classified as slow variety seekers for bread. A total of 20 Ss did not buy all four brands within the first eight weeks but did buy in most of the first eight-week time periods; these Ss are classified as initial brand loyals. A total of 27 Ss did not buy all four brands within the first eight weeks and did not buy in most of these initial time periods; these Ss are classified as the less frequent buying non–variety seekers. Finding such distinct choice patterns for the brands of bread supports H_1.

Figure 12-1 illustrates the influence of initial variety-seeking behavior on the patterns of later brand and product category choices. P_2 receives limited support in that segment D (non–variety seekers who do not buy in most initial time periods) does have significantly lower bread choices in weeks 10–18 compared to the other three segments (F = 88, d.f. = 3, 1022, p < .000; Tukey HSD test, p < .05; ξ^2 = .21). Note in Figure 12-1 that the fast initial variety seekers (A) have the highest level of choice activity—a pattern that repeats for the other two product categories.

Figure 12-2 illustrates strong but not perfect support for H_3. For the low price treatment condition the increase in Brand J's share of customers is dramatic for the fast initial variety seekers (A) and paltry in comparison for

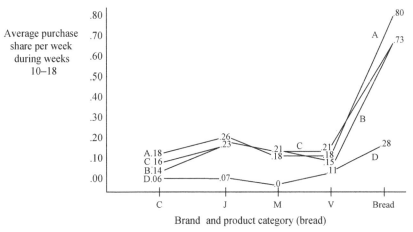

FIGURE 12.1   Average brand and product category purchase per week for bread brands during weeks 10–18 among consumers (A) trying all four brands in the first four weeks (fast variety seekers); (B) consumers taking eight weeks to try all four brands (slow variety seekers); (C) consumers loyal to one or two brands and not trying all brands in the first eight weeks (early brand-loyal buyers); (D) consumers low in variety and buying product category four weeks or less during the first eight weeks. The penetrations of the product category during weeks 10–18 were similar for buyers segmented in groups A, B, and C and significantly higher (p <.01 by ANOVA and a Tukey test) compared to buyers in segment D. Thus, buyers not exhibiting variety in trying all brands and buying 50 percent or less during the first eight weeks remain non–variety and low penetration buyers in future time periods.

segment D. Note the magnitude of the increases in J's share of customers for the four segments in comparison to the increases possible (e.g., for A this increase equals $((.67 - .21) / (1 - .21) = 58\%)$:

A, fast initial variety seekers. 58%
B, slow initial variety seekers 22
C, initial brand loyal 33
D, non-variety and not buying for most initial periods 17

Potato Chips

For chips, three weeks were necessary to enable selection of all three available brands. A total of 25 Ss did so, and these Ss are classified as fast initial variety seekers. A total of 25 Ss took more than three and less than seven weeks to select all three brands; these Ss are classified as slow initial variety seekers.

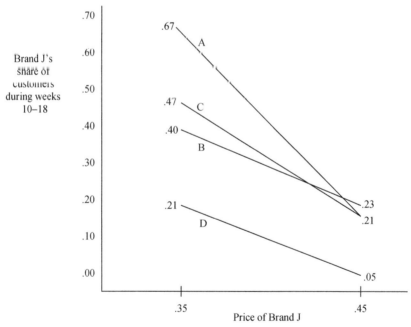

FIGURE 12.2   How initial variety seeking boosts the influence of a bread brand's short-term marketing tactic (during weeks 10–12) on share of customers among (A) trying all four brands in first four weeks (fast variety seekers); (B) consumers taking eight weeks to try all four brands (slow variety seekers); (C) consumers loyal to one or two brands and not trying all brands in first eight weeks (early brand loyal buyers); (D) consumers low in variety and buying product category four weeks or less during the first eight weeks. Price special (short-term reductions) increases Brand J's share of customers for each group of buyers segmented by variety seeking behavior and J's share boost due to price special is greater for the fast variety seekers compared to the other three segments.

A total of 43 Ss bought chips in most periods in the first six weeks but did not buy all three brands over the six weeks; these Ss are classified as initial brand loyals. A total of 21 Ss did not try all three brands in the first six weeks and did not buy in most weeks during the first six weeks. The finding of these four patterns supports P_1.

Figure 12-3 illustrates a significantly lower product category share for the D segment compared to the variety and loyal segments (A-C) for chip purchases during weeks 4–18. Similar to the findings for bread, the fast initial variety seekers for chips have the highest share of product category purchases during weeks 4–18 even though the average share differences between segments A-C are not significant statistically. Thus, H_2 receives limited support for chips.

The findings for chips in Figure 12-4 provide strong support for H_3. A strong interaction effect occurs for short-term price reductions and initial variety-seeking behavior for chips. The increases in observed versus possible shares of customers for Lay's potato chips during weeks 4–18 for the 50¢ versus 70¢ price vary in a pattern exactly to what H_4 predicts:

A, fast initial variety seekers 69%
B, slow initial variety seekers 53
C, initial brand loyal 26
D, non-variety and not buying for most initial periods 11

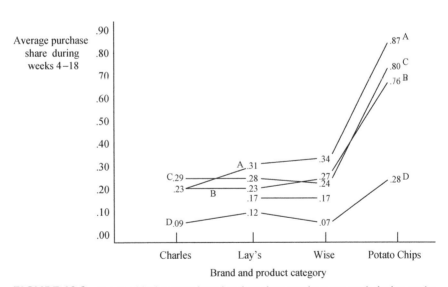

FIGURE 12.3 Potato chips' average brand and product purchase per week during weeks 4–18 for (A) customers trying all three brands in the first three weeks (fast variety seekers); (B) customers taking six weeks to try all three brands (slow variety seekers); (C) customers loyal to one or two brands and not trying all brands in the first six weeks; (D) consumers low in variety seeking and buying the product category three weeks or less in the first six weeks.

Toilet Paper

For toilet paper a total of 22 Ss tried all three brands in the first 3 weeks; these Ss are classified as the fast initial variety seekers. A total of 13 Ss took longer than three weeks but less than seven weeks to try all three brands; these Ss are classified as the slow initial variety seekers. A total of 57 Ss displayed loyalty to one or two brands and did not try all three brands in the first six weeks; these Ss are classified as initial brand loyals. A total of 22 Ss displayed incomplete variety-seeking behavior in the first six weeks and did not buy in most purchase occasions in the first six weeks; these Ss are classified as the non–variety seekers buying 50 percent or less of the time during the first six weeks. Being able to identify these four segments supports H_1.

Figure 12-5 shows that P_2 receives some support. Brand purchases and the product category purchases do vary systematically during weeks 10–18 among consumers segmented by their initial variety-seeking behavior. However, the fast initial variety seekers are now shown to purchase more of the product category compared to the slow initial variety seekers and the loyals. The loyals' choice of the 10¢ brand during weeks 10–18 is significantly greater than the other three segments.

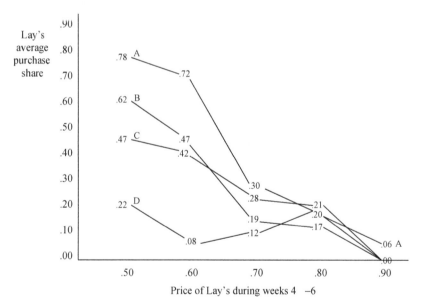

FIGURE 12.4   Influence of five price points on Lay's (during weeks 4–6) on average purchases per week for weeks 4–18 for (A) customers trying all three brands in the first three weeks (fast variety seekers); (B) customers taking six weeks to try all three brands (slow variety seekers); (C) customers loyal to one or two brands and not trying all brands in the first six weeks; (D) consumers low in variety seeking and buying the product category three weeks or less in the first six weeks. The price of Lay's during weeks 1–3 and 7–18 was $.70.

Figure 12-6 provides some support for H_3. All Ss in the two variety-seeking segments exposed to the special offer responded consistently by choosing the special offer, while many of the loyals stuck with buying the 10¢ brand, and the non-variety-seeking light buyers (the D segment Ss) did not increase their choice of the 15¢ brand in response to the coupon offer. Generally, the pattern of findings in Figure 12-6 supports the view that variety seekers are more responsive to short-term marketing strategies compared to non–variety seekers.

The pattern of observed response to special marketing stimulation versus response possible is consistent for toilet paper compared to the other two product categories:

A, fast initial variety seekers 100%
B, slow initial variety seekers 100
C, initial brand loyal 43
D, non-variety and not buying for most initial periods 0

Limitations and General Discussion

The findings and support described for the three propositions are limited to a laboratory experiment that includes in-home experiments of marketing manipulations for 114 households over 18 weeks. The experimental design provides for greater control than non-obtrusive field experiments, and Ehrenberg (1988) provides a lively defense of the value of in-home, extended

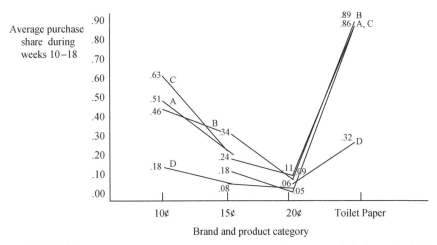

FIGURE 12.5 Toilet paper average brand and product purchase per week during weeks 4–18 for (A) customers trying all three brands in the first three weeks (fast variety seekers); (B) customers taking six weeks to try all three brands (slow variety seekers); (C) customers loyal to one or two brands and not trying all brands in the first six weeks; (D) consumers low in variety seeking and buying the product category three weeks or less in the first six weeks.

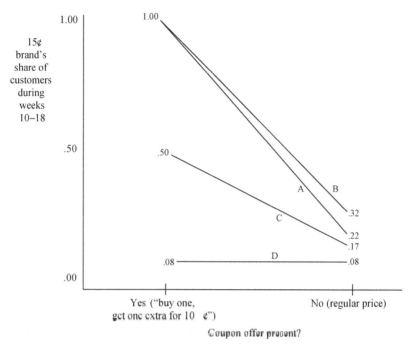

FIGURE 12.6 How initial variety-seeking in toilet-paper brands boosts the influence of a brand's short-term marketing tactic on share of customers among (A) those trying all four brands in first four weeks (fast variety seekers); (B) consumers taking eight weeks to try all four brands (slow variety seekers); (C) consumers loyal to one or two brands and not trying all brands in first eight weeks (early brand loyal buyers); (D) consumers low in variety and buying product category four weeks or less during the first eight weeks.

time-period experiments—including the vision that using well-controlled experimental designs in marketing provides benchmark, effect-size information as to the extent that marketing stimuli affects household brand and product penetrations and buying frequencies. Such information is crucial for conducting meta-analyses of marketing influences, as well as the influence of consumer-measured variables (such as variety-seeking behavior).

This report serves to confirm and extend Hoyer and MacInnis's (1997, p. 262) speculation that "certain consumers are higher in the need for stimulation and are less tolerant of boredom than others. These *sensation seekers* are more likely to engage in variety seeking than others and are more likely to be the first to try new and trendy products" [bold in the original]. Within a controlled experimentally designed context, Chapter 12 confirms the view that initial variety-seeking behavior occurs in selecting among competing brands in three product categories among some segments of consumers—but not all consumers.

This chapter serves to more explicitly develop and empirically examine the existence of both brand sensation seekers and avoiders. It presents evidence that both segments respond differently to short-term brand strategies—with a greater share of sensation seekers (defined as consumers trying all available brands quickly or somewhat slowly in initial choice opportunities) being more sensitive to short-term marketing inducements presented by one of the competing brands compared to sensation avoiders (defined as consumers not trying all three or four brands as soon as possible or in double the choice opportunities necessary to try all the brands).

The findings presented serve to refine Kassarjian's (1997) observation about the average consumer of toilet paper "who blithely purchases, consumes, and discards the product, most likely could care less." Just as some consumers may watch *The Home Shopping Network* on television for hours while others never do, some consumers do exhibit variety-seeking behavior while others do not when buying toilet paper and other FMCGs. Here the focus on the average consumer needs to be redirected to spotlight consumers who do exhibit care versus those who do not.

With respect to initial brand choice non-variety-seeking behavior divides naturally into two subcategories: repeat brand buyers who do not try all available brands and buyers not trying all brands combined with frequently not selecting any brands in the product category. It is only the consumers in the very last subcategory (non–variety seekers who frequently do not select any brand) that could care less—if not caring is defined as little to no response to subsequent short-term marketing inducements.

Given that the study confirms the propositions for three different product categories—two using artificial brands and one using real brands—strengthens basic tenants for a theory of brand variety-seeking behavior. These tenants include the propositions that consumers can be segmented into at least four groups according to their initial variety-seeking behavior; consumers segmented by their initial variety-seeking behavior exhibit different patterns in their later brand and product category choice behaviors; and, initial variety seekers are more sensitive to short-term marketing tactics compared to initial variety avoiders—especially variety avoiders not buying during most initial buying opportunities.

This report takes a small step in rectifying Kassarjian's lament, expressed in the following first sentence, and to refine his view in the third sentence expressed during the close of his Association for Consumer Research 1977 Presidential Address:

> It is too bad that so few of us have chosen to study learning theory in consumer behavior in recent years, and so few of us have turned to the study of low involvement behavior. Whether we like it or not, low involvement, low risk, the unimportant, is what much of consumer behavior is all about. Whether or not we anthropomorphize our own values onto the consumer, and whether or not we chose to be unparsimonious in our thinking, the facts

do not change that under most conditions, for most types of goods and decisions, the behavior of the consumer is just not important from his point of view. (Kassarjian, 1977, p. xiv)

FUTURE RESEARCH

While the consumer research literature offers several speculations as to the antecedents to variety-seeking behavior (e.g., satiation and boredom, see Venkatesan, 1973; Hoyer and Ridgway, 1984), empirical evidence is lacking to confirm these views. Also, such views do not address the causes of initial variety-seeking and avoidance behaviors—behaviors in new contexts in which consumers have yet to make repetitive choices even though they have likely made similar choices for FMCGs in prior contexts. Similarly, empirical evidence is lacking that supports the view that "repetitive purchasing causes the internal level of stimulation to fall below the OSL [i.e., "optimal stimulation level," an internal ideal level of stimulation], "and buying something different is a way of restoring it" (Hoyer and MacInnis, 1997, p. 262). Research to support this view would seem to require researchers to identify consumers' OSL and engage them in repetitive purchasing enough to cause falls below their OSL to observe if they switch their buying behaviors.

Future research that examines the demographics, values, and personalities of sub-segments of variety seekers and avoiders, as well as research examining how choice contexts affect variety-seeking behavior (e.g., Menon and Kahn, 1995), may be more beneficial than confirming OSL-related propositions. Who are the consumers who do and do not exhibit initial sensitivities to different brand choice opportunities and changes in marketing stimuli for such low-involvement choices as toilet paper and potato chips? How might marketers or others (public policy implementers) design contexts encouraging or preventing desired variety-seeking behaviors?

Given that additional research confirms the view that fast, initial variety seeking relates positively to subsequent frequent product use and high sensitivity to short-term marketing inducements, the benefits for marketers and social policy makers of designing contexts effective in stimulating initial variety-seeking behavior becomes clear. For example, such research may establish that designing initial contexts that effectively promote variety-seeking behavior leads to frequent hygienic behaviors (teeth brushing) and responsiveness to special offers to buy clinically proven, more effective brands of toothpaste—another mundane FMCG. Thus, the further study of the antecedents and consequences of initial variety-seeking behavior for FMCGs is worth the attention of marketers, policymakers, and consumers.

REFERENCES

Adaval, R., and R. S. Wyer (1998), "The Role of Narratives in Consumer Information Processing," *Journal of Consumer Research*, 7 (3), 207–245.

Allport, G. W. (1985). The historical background of social psychology. In G. Lindzey and E. Aronson (Eds.), *Handbook of social psychology*, Volume 1, (pp. 1–46). New York: Random House.

Alpert, M. I. (1971), "Identification of Determinant Attributes," *Journal of Marketing Research*, 8, 2, 184–191.

Andreasen, A. R. (1985). Backward market research. *Harvard Business Review*, 63 (May-June), 176.

"Are You Purchasing MRO Supplies?" (1986). N.A.P.M. Insight, The Newsletter of the National Association of Purchasing Management, Inc., 4 (7), 4.

Arnould, E. J., and M. Wallendorf (1994), "Market-Oriented Ethnography: Interpretation Building and Marketing Strategy Formulation," *Journal of Marketing Research*, 31 (November), 484–503.

Arnould, E. J., Price, L. L., and Zinkhan, G. M. (2004), *Consumers*, Boston: McGraw-Hill Irwin.

Arnould, E. J., & Price, L. L. (1993). River magic: Extraordinary experience and the extended service encounter. Journal of Consumer Research, 20, 24–45.

Axelrod, J. N. (1968). Attitude measures that predict purchase. Journal of Advertising Research, 8, 3–17.

Axelrod, J. N. (1986). Minnie, minnie tickled the parson. Journal of Advertising Research, 26, 89–93.

Bagozzi, R. P., & Dabholkar, P. A. (2000), Discursive psychology: An alternative conceptual foundation to means-end chain theory, Psychology & Marketing, 17 (7), 535–586.

Bandura, A. (1977), *Social Learning Theory*, Upper Saddle River, NJ: Prentice-Hall.

Bargh, J. A. (1989). Conditional automaticity: Varieties of automatic influence in social perception and cognition. In J. S. Uleman & J. A. Bargh (Eds.), Unintended thought (pp. 3–51). New York: Guilford Press.

Bargh, J. (2002), "Losing Consciousness: Automatic Influences on Consumer Judgment, Behavior, and Motivation," *Journal of Consumer Research*, 29 (September), 280–285.

Bargh, J. A., Chen, M., & Burrows, L. (1996), Automaticity of social behavior: Direct effects of trait construct and stereotype activation on action. Journal of Personality and Social Psychology, 71 (2), 230–244.

Bargh, J. A. (1994), The four horsemen of automaticity. In R. S. Wyer & T. K. Srull (Eds.), *Handbook of Social Cognition* (pp. 1–40). Hillsdale, NJ: Erlbaum.

Barrett, J. (1986), "Why Major Account Selling Works," *Industrial Marketing Management*, Vol. 15, February, pp. 63–73.

Bearden, W. O., & Woodside, A. (1978). Consumption occasion influence on consumer brand choice. Decision Sciences, 9 (April), 274–281.

Becker, H. S. (1998). Tricks of the trade: How to think about your research while you're doing It. Chicago: University of Chicago Press.

Belk, R. (1974). An exploratory assessment of situational effects in buyer behavior. Journal of Marketing Research, 11 (May), 156–163.

Belk, R., Güliz Ger, and S. Askegaard (2003), The Fire of Desire: A Multisited Inquiry into Consumer Passion, *Journal of Consumer Research*, 30 (December), 326–351.

Belk, R. W., and J. A. Costa (1998), "The Mountain Man Myth: A Contemporary Consuming Fantasy," *Journal of Consumer Research*, 25 (December), 218–240.

Berkowitz M. (1986), "New Product Adoption by the Buying Organization: Who are the Real Influencers?" *Industrial Marketing Management*, 15 (1), 33–44.

Bettman, J. R. (1974), "Toward a Statistics for Consumer Decision Nets Models," *Journal of Consumer Research*, 1 (June), 71–80.

Bettman, J. K (1979), *An Information Processing Theory of Consumer Choice*, Addison-Wesley, Reading, Massachusetts.

Bettman, J. R. (1970), "Information Processing Models of Consumer Behavior," *Journal of Marketing Research*, 7 (3), 370–376.

Bettman, J. R., and C. W. Park (1980), "Effects of Prior Knowledge, Experience, and Phase of the Choice Process on Consumer Decision Processes: A Protocol Analysis," *Journal of Consumer Research*, 7, 234–248.

Biemans, W. G. (1989), *Developing Innovations within Networks*, Groningen, the Netherlands, University of Groningen.

Bougon, M. G., and J. Komocar (1990), "Directing Strategic Change: A Dynamic Wholistic Approach," in *Mapping Strategic Thought*, ed. by Anne Sigismund Huff, Chichester, UK: Wiley.

Braun, K. A., & Zaltman, G. (1998). Backward framing through memory reconstruction. Working paper, report no. 98–109 (42 pages). Boston: Marketing Science Institute.

Brisoux, J. E. (1980), *The Evoked Set Phenomenon: Its Dimensions and Contents*. Unpublished Ph.D. dissertation, Quebec City. University of Laval.

Brisoux, J. E. and Michel Laroche (1980), "A Proposed Consumer Strategy of Simplification for Categorizing Brands," in *Evolving Marketing Thought for the 1980's*, John D. Summey and Robert D. Taylor (Ed.). Atlanta: Southern Marketing Association, 112–114.

Brisoux, J. E., and Michel Laroche (1981), "Evoked Set Formation and Composition: An Empirical Investigation Under a Routinized Response Behavior Situation." In *Advances in Consumer Research*, 8, Kent B. Monroe (Ed.), Ann Arbor: Association for Consumer Research, 357–361.

Brown, S. (1998), The Wind in the Wallows: Literary Theory, Autobiographical Criticism and Subjective Personal Introspection, *Advances in Consumer Research*, 25, 25–30.

Bruner, J. S. (1986). Actual minds, possible worlds. Cambridge, MA: Harvard University Press.

Bruner, J. S. (1990). Culture and human development: a new look. Human Development, 33, 344–355.

Bruner, J. S., J. J. Goodnow and G. A. Austin (1959), *A Study of Thinking*, New York: Wiley.

Burke, R. R., Harlam, Bari A., Kahn, Barbara E, Lodish, Leonard M. (1992), "Comparing Dynamic Consumer Choice in Real and Computer-Simulated Environments," *Journal of Consumer Research*, 19 (1), 71–83.

Calder, B. J. (1977), "Structural Role Analysis of Organizational Buying: A Preliminary Investigation," in *Consumer and Industrial Buying Behavior*, ed. by A.G. Woodside, J. N. Sheth, and P. D. Bennett, Elsevier, New York.

Campbell, D. T. (1975), "Degrees of Freedom in the Case Study," *Comparative Political Studies*, 8 (July), 178–193.

Campbell, D. T. (1969), "Reforms as Experiments," *American Psychologist*, 24, 409–429.

Campbell, P. M. (1969). *The Existence of Evoked Set and Determinants of its Magnitude in Brand Choice Behavior*, Unpublished Ph.D. dissertation. New York: Columbia University.

Campbell, D. T., and Julian C. Stanley (1966), *Experimental and Quasi-Experimental Designs for Research*, Chicago: Rand McNally.

Carlsmith, J. M., P. C. Ellsworth, and E. Aronson (1976), *Methods of Research in Social Psychology*, Reading, MA: Addison-Wesley.

Carpenter, G. S., R. Glazer, and K. Nakamoto (1994), "Meaningful Brands from Meaningless Differentiation: The Dependence on Irrelevant Attributes," *Journal of Marketing Research*, 31 (3), 339–350.

Charlton, P., Ehrenberg, A. S. C. and Pymont, B. (1972), "Buyer Behavior Under Mini-Test Conditions," *Journal of the Market Research Society*, 14, 171–183.

Chilsen, J. (1999). Volkswagen sued for Holocaust acts. Baton Rouge, LA: The Advocate (May 6, p. 23A).

Choffray, J. M., and Lilien, G. L., (1980), *Market Planning for New Industrial Product*, Wiley, New York.

Christensen, C. M. (1997), *The Innovator's Dilemma*, Cambridge, MA: Harvard Business School Press.

Christensen, G. L., and J. C. Olson (2002), "Mapping Consumers' Mental Models with ZMET," *Psychology & Marketing*, 19 (6), 477–502.

Cialdini, R (1983), *Influence*, Morrow, New York.

Cohen, L. (1966), "The Level of Consciousness: A Dynamic approach to the Recall Technique," *Journal of Marketing Research*, 3 (2), 142–148.

Collins, J., & Loftus, E. F. (1975). A spreading activation theory of semantic processing. Psychological Review, 87, 407–428.

Cook, T. D., and D. T. Campbell (1979), *Quasi-Experimentation*, Boston: Holt Mifflin.

Corey, E. R. (1978), *Procurement Management: Strategy. Organization, and Decision-Making*, Boston: CBI.

Corey, E. R., F. V. Cespedes, and V. K. Rangan (1989), *Going to Market: Distribution Systems for Industrial Markets*, Cambridge: Harvard Business School Press.

Corstjens, M., and P. Doyle (1989), "Evaluating Alternative Retail Repositioning Strategies," *Marketing Science*, 8, 2, 170–180.

Cox, D. F. (1967), "Risk Handling in Consumer Behavior—an Intensive Study of Two Cases, in D. F. Cox (ed.), *Risk Taking and Information Handling in Consumer Behavior*, Graduate School of Business Administration, Harvard University, Boston, 18–81.

Cyert, R. M., Simon, H. A., and Trow, D. B. (1956), "Observation of a Business Decision," *Journal of Business*, 29 (October), 237–238.

Dauten, D. (1996), "Studying Obits for Businesses," *Sunday Advocate*, Baton Rouge, Louisiana, April 14, p. 20.

Dean, J. W. (1986), "Decision Processes in the Adoption of Advanced Technology," working paper, College of Business Administration, Pennsylvania State University, University Park, PA.

Denzin, N. K (1983), "Interpretive Interactionisms," in Morgan, G. (ed.) *Beyond Method*, Sage, Beverly Hills, California.

Dichter, E. (1985). *Dichter on consumer motivation*. New York: Elsevier North-Holland.

Doyle, J. R., and Sims, D. (2002). Enabling strategic metaphor in conversation. In A. S. Huff & M. Jenkins, *Mapping Strategic Knowledge* (pp. 63–85). London: Sage.

Dyer, W. G., Jr., and Wilkins, A. L. (1991), "Better Stories, Not Better Constructs, to Generate Better Stories,": A Rejoinder to Eisenhardt," *Academy of Management Review*, 16 (3), 613–619.

Ehrenberg, A. S. C. (1988), *Repeat buying: theory and applications, 2nd edition*. New York: North-Holland.

Ehrenberg, A. S. C., and Charlton, P. (1973), "An Analysis of Simulated Brand Choice," *Journal of Advertising Research*, 13 (1), 21–33.

Ehrenberg, A. S. C., and Goodhardt, G. J. (2000), "New Brands: Near-Instant Loyalty," *Journal of Marketing Management*, 16 (6), 607–617.

Ehrenberg, A. S. C., Uncles, M. D., and Goodhardt, G. J. (2004), "Understanding Brand Performance Measures: Using Dirichlet Benchmarks," *Journal of Business Research* (in press).

Ehrenberg, A. S. C., Scriven, J., and Barnard, N. (1997), "Advertising and Price," *Journal of Advertising Research*, 37 (3), (May-June), 27–35.

Ehrenberg, A. S. C. (1988), *Repeat Buying: Theory and Applications*, 2nd Edition, New York: Elsevier.

Eisenhardt, K. (1989), "Building Theories from Case Study Research," *Academy of Management Review*, 14 (4), 532–550.

Ellis, C. (1991). Sociological introspection and emotional institution. *Symbolic Interaction*, 14 (1), 23–50.

Ellis, P., and A. Pecotich (2001), "Social Factors Influencing Export Initiation in Small and Medium-Sized Enterprises," *Journal of Marketing Research*, 38 (February), 119–130.

Epstein, S. (1994). Integration of the cognitive and the psychodynamic unconscious. American Psychologist, 49 (8), 709–724.

Ericsson, K. A., and H. A. Simon (1993), *Protocol Analysis: Verbal Reports as Data*, Cambridge, MA: MIT Press.

Eskin, G. J. (1975), "A Case for Test Market Experiments," *Journal of Advertising Research*, 15 (2), 30–36.

Faison, E. W. J. (1977), "The Neglected Variety Drive," *Journal of Consumer Research*, 4 (December), 172–75.

Farley, J. U., and J. A. Howard (1975), *Control of 'Error' in Market Research Data*, Lexington, MA: Lexington Books.

Farquhar, P. H., Herr, P. M., & Fazio, R. H. (1990). A relational model of category extensions of brands. In M.E. Goldberg, G. Gorn, & R. W. Pollay (Eds.), Advances in Consumer Research (pp. 97–105). Provo, UT: Association for Consumer Research.

Fauconnier, G. (1997), *Mapping in Thought and Language*, Cambridge, UK: Cambridge University Press.

Fazio, R. H., M. C. Powell, and P. M. Herr (1983), "Toward a Process Model of the Attitude-Behavior Relation: Accessing One's Attitude Upon Mere Observation of the Attitude Object," *Journal of Personality and Social Psychology*, 44, 6, 723–735.

Fazio, R. H. (1986), "How do Attitudes Guide Behavior?" in R. M. Sorentino and E. T. Higgins (eds.), *Handbook of Motivation and Cognition: Foundation of Social Behavior*, New York: Guilford, 204–243.

Fazio, R. H., M. C. Powell, and C. J. Williams (1989), "The Role of Attitude Accessibility in the Attitude-to-Behavior Process," *Journal of Consumer Research*, 16, 4, 280–288.

Fazio, R. H. (1990). Multiple processes by which attitudes guide behavior: The mode model as an integrative framework. Advances in Experimental Social Psychology, 23, 75–109.

Feldman, J. M., & Lynch, Jr. J. G. (1988). Self-generated validity and other effects of measurement on belief, attitude, intention, and behavior. Journal of Applied Psychology, 73 (3), 421–435.

Fischer, E. (1999). Tales of Food and eating. In E. J. Arnould & L. M. Scott (Eds.), Advances in consumer research, 26. Montreal: Association for Consumer Research, 483.

Fisher, R. (1993). Social desirability bias and the validity of indirect questioning. *Journal of Consumer Research*, 20 (September), 303–315.

Fiske, D. W., and S. R. Maddi (1961), *Functions of Varied Experience, Homewood*, IL: Dorsey.

Fodness, D., and B. Murray. (1999). "A Model of Tourist Information Search Behavior," *Journal of Travel Research*, 37 (3), 220–230.

Fournier, S. (1998), "Consumers and Their Brands: Developing Relationship Theory in Consumer Research," *Journal of Consumer Research*, 24 (4), 343–374.

Foxall, G. R. (1999), "The Substitutability of Brands," *Managerial and Decision Economics*, 20, 241–257.

Frazer, K. (1991), *Bad Trips*. New York: Doubleday.

Freud, S. ([1908] 1965). *The interpretation of dreams*, (J. Strachey, Trans.). New York: Avon.

Fuhrmans, V. (2003), "In One German Town, Residents Measure Civic Pride by the Beer," *Wall Street Journal*, June 20, A1, A5.

Fulgoni, G. M., and G. J. Eskin (1983), "The BehaviorScan Research Facility for studying Retail Sopping Patterns," in W. R. Darden and R. F. Lusch, *Patronage Behavior and Retail Management*, New York: North-Holland, 263–274.

Geertz, C. (1973), *The Interpretation of Cultures*, New York: Basic Books.

Geertz, C. (1973), "Thick Description: Toward an Interpretive Theory of Culture," in Gilovich, T. (1991), *How We Know What Isn't So*, New York: Free Press.

Gladwin, C. H. (1989), *Ethnographic Decision Tree Modeling*, Thousand Oaks, CA: Sage.

Gladwell, M. (2000), *The Tipping Point: How Little Things Can Make a Big Difference*, Boston: Little, Brown.

Glaser, B. G., and A. L. Strauss (1967), *The Discovery of Grounded Theory*, Chicago: Aldine.

Gholson, B. D., A. Smither, A. Buhrman, M. K. Duncan, and K. A. Pierce (1996), "The Sources of Children's Reasoning Errors during Analogical Problem Solving, *Applied Cognitive Psychology*, 10 (5), S85–S97.

Gilovich, T. (1991), *How We Know What Isn't So*, New York: Free Press.

Goldstein, D. G., R. G. Gigerenzer, R. H. Hogarth, A. Kacelnik, Y. Kareev, G. Klein, L. Martignon, J. W. Payne, and K. H. Schlag (2002), "Group Report: Why and When Do Simple Heuristics Work," in *Bounded Rationality: the Adaptive Toolbox*, ed. by Gerd Gigerenzer and Reinhard Selten, Cambridge, MA: The MIT Press, 172–190.

Gorman, R. H. (1971), "Role Conception and Purchasing Behavior," *Journal of Purchasing*, 7 (1), 56–61.

Gould, S. J. (1991). The self-manipulation of my pervasive, perceived vital energy through product use: an introspective-praxis perspective. *Journal of Consumer Research*, 18 (2), 194–207.

Gould, S. J. (1995). Researcher introspection as a method in consumer research: applications, issues, and implications. *Journal of Consumer Research*, 21 (4), 719–722.

Grice, H. P. (1975). Logic and conversation. In P. Cole and J. L. Morgan (Eds.), *Syntax and semantics: volume 3, speech acts* (pp. 41–58). New York: Academic Press.

Grunert, K. (1988), "Research in Consumer Behavior: Beyond Attitudes and Decision-making." *European Research: The Journal of the European Society for Opinion and Marketing Research*, 16, 5, 172–183.

Grunert, K. G. (1990), *Kognitive Strukturen in der Konsumforschung*, Heidelberg, Physica-Verlag.

Gutman, J. (1997). Means-end chains as goal hierarchies. Psychology & Marketing, 14 (6), 545–560.

Gutman, J., & Reynolds, T. J. (1978). An investigation of the levels of cognitive abstraction utilized by consumers in product differentiation. In J. Eighmey (ed.), Attitude Research under the Sun. Chicago: American Marketing Association, 57–64.

Haines, G. H., Jr. (1974), "Process Models of Consumer Decision-Making" in *Buyer/Consumer Information Processing*, G. David Hughes and Michael L. Ray (Eds.). Chapel Hill: University of North Carolina Press, 89–107.

Hakansson, H., Ed. (1982), *International Marketing and Purchasing of Industrial Goods*, New York: Wiley.

Haley, R. I., & Case, P.B. (1979). Testing thirteen attitude scales for agreement and brand discrimination. Journal of Marketing, 43, 20–32.

Hall, R. I. (1984), "The Natural Logic of Management Policy Making: Its Implications for the Survival of an Organization, *Management Science*, 30, 905–927.

Hall, R. I. (1991), "The Policy Maps of Managers," Working Paper, Winnipeg, Drake Centre for Management Studies, University of Manitoba.

Hall, R. I. (1976), "A System Pathology on an Organization: The Rise and Fall of the Old Saturday Evening Post," *Administrative Science Quarterly*, 21 (2), 185–211.

Hall, R. I., and W. B. Menzies (1983), "A Corporate System Model of a Sports Club: Using Simulation as an Aid to policymaking in a Crisis," *Management Science*, 29 (1), 52–64.

Hakansson, H. (1982), *International Marketing and Purchasing of Industrial Goods*, Wiley, Chichester.

Hakansson, H., and Wootz, B. (1975), "Supplier Selection in an Industrial Environment – An Experimental Study," *Journal of Marketing Research*, Vol. 12, February, pp. 48–51.

Haves, W. L. (1972), *Statistics for Psychologists*. New York: Holt, Rinehart and Winston.

Hebets, E. (2003), "Subadult Experience Influences Adult Male Choice in an Arthropod: Exposed Female Wolf Spiders Prefer Males of a Familiar Phenotype," *Proceedings of the National Academy of Science*, 100, 23 (November 11), 13390–5.

Heider, F. (1958), *The Psychology of Interpersonal Relations*, John Wiley and Sons.

Heisley, D. D., and Levy, S. J. (1991), "Autodriving: A Photoelicitation Technique, *Journal of Consumer Research*, 18 (December), 257–272.

Hersen, M., and D. H. Barlow (1976), *Single-case Experimental Designs: Strategies for Studying Behavior Change*, New York: Pergamon.

Hill, R. W, and Hiller, T. J. (1979), *Organizational Buying Behaviour*, Macmillan, London.

Hilton, D. J. (1995). The social context of reasoning: conversational inference and rational judgment. *Psychological Bulletin*, 118 (2), 248–271.

Hirschman, E. (1986) "Humanistic Inquiry in Marketing Research: Philosophy, Methods, and Criteria," *Journal of Marketing Research*, Vol. 13, August, pp. 237–49.

Hirschman, E. C. (1992). The consciousness of addiction: toward a general theory of compulsive consumption. *Journal of Consumer Research*, 19 (September), 155–179.

Hirschman, E. C. (1985), "Scientific Style and the Conduct of Consumer Research," *Journal of Consumer Research*, 12 (September), 225–239.

Hlavacek. J. D., and T. J. McCuistion, "Industrial Distributors—When, Who, and How?" *Harvard Business Review,* 61, 96–101.

Hogarth, R. (1987), *Judgement and Choice, 2nd Edition*, Chichester: Wiley.

Holbrook, M. B. (1995), *Consumer Research: Introspective Essays on the Study of Consumption*, Thousand Oaks, CA: Sage.

Holbrook, M. B. (1986). I'm hip: an autobiographical account of some consumption experiences. In R. J. Lutz (Ed.) *Advances in Consumer Research, 13* (pp. 614–618). Provo: UT: Association for Consumer Research.

Holbrook, M. B. (1999). *Consumer value: a framework for analysis and research*. London: Routledge.

Holbrook, M. B. (1984), "Theory Development is a Jazz Solo: Bird Lives," in *AMA Winter Educators' Conference Proceedings*, eds. Paul F. Anderson and Michael J. Ryan, Chicago: American Marketing Association, 48–52.

Holbrook M. B. (2003). Time travels in retrospace: unpacking my grandfather's trunk—some introspective recollections of life on Brule River. In S. Brown & J. Sherry (Eds.), *Retroscapes*. Thousand Oaks, CA: Sage.

Holbrook, M. B. (2004). Customer value and autoethnography: subjective personal introspection and the meanings of a photograph collection. *Journal of Business Research*, forthcoming.

Holbrook M. B., & Kuwahara, T. (1998). Collective stereographic photo essays: an integrated approach to probing consumption experiences in depth. *International Journal of Research in Marketing*, 15 (2), 201–221.

Holden, S. J. S., and R. J. Lutz (1992), "Ask Not What the Brand Can Evoke; Ask What Can Evoke the Brand?" in: J. F. Sherry, Jr. and B. Sternthal (eds.) *Advances in Consumer Behavior*, 19, Provo, Utah: Association for Consumer Research, 101–107.

Holden, S. J. S. (1993), "Understanding Brand Awareness: Let Me Give You a C(l)ue," in L. McAlister and M. L. Rothschild (eds.), *Advances in Consumer Research*, 20, Provo, Utah: Association for Consumer Research, 383–388.

Homans, G. C. (1974), Social Behavior: Its Elementary Forms, New York: Harcourt, Brace, and Jovanovich.

Howard, J. A., and W. M. Morgenroth (1968), "Information Processing Model of Executive Decision," *Management Science*, 14 (3), 416–428.

Howard, J. A., J. Hulbert, and J. U. Farley (1975), "Organizational Analysis and Information-Systems Design: A Decision-Process Perspective," *Journal of Business Research*, 3 (April), 133–148.

Howard, J. A. (1963), *Marketing Management, Analysis and Planning,* Homewood. Illinois: Irwin.

Howard, J. A. (1977). *Consumer Behavior: Application of Theory,* New York: McGraw Hill.

Howard, J. A., and J. N. Sheth (1969), *The Theory of Buyer Behavior,* New York: Wiley.

Howard, J. A. and J. N. Sheth (1969), *The Theory of Buyer Behavior,* New York: Wiley.

Hoyer, W. D., and D. J. MacInnis (1997), *Consumer Behavior,* Boston: Houghton Mifflin.

Hoyer, W. D., and N. M. Ridgway (1984), "Variety Seeking as an Explanation for Exploratory Purchase Behavior: A Theoretical Model, in ed. Thomas C. Kinnear, *Advances in Consumer Research, 11,* Ann Arbor, MA: Association for Consumer Research, 114–9.

Huff, A. S. (1990), *Mapping Strategic Thought,* Chichester, UK: Wiley.

Hulbert, J. M., Farley, J. U., and Howard, J. A. (1972), "Information Processing and Decision Making in Marketing Organizations," *Journal of Marketing Research* 9 (1) (February) 75–77.

Hulbert, J. M. (1981), "Description Models of Marketing Decisions," in Schultz, R.I., and Zolters, A. A (Eds.) *Marketing Decision Models,* North-Holland, New York, pp. 19–53.

Hunter, J. E., F. L. Schmidt, and G. B. Jackson (1982), *Meta-Analysis: Cumulating Research Findings Across Studies,* Thousand Oaks, CA: Sage.

Irwin, F. W., & Gebhard, M. E. (1946). Studies in object-preferences: the effect of ownership and other social influences. American Journal of Psychology, 59, 633–651.

Jarvis, L. P., and J. B. Wilcox (1973), "Evoked Set Size—Some Theoretical Foundations and Empirical Evidence." In *Combined Proceedings,* Thomas V. Greer (Ed.), Chicago: American Marketing Association, 236–240.

Joachimsthaler, E. A., and J. L. Lastovicka (1984), "Optimal Stimulation Level—Exploratory Behavior Models, *Journal of Consumer Research,* 11 (December), 830–35.

Johnson, H. M., and C. Seifert (1992), "The Role of Predictive Features in Retrieving Analogical Cases, "Journal *of Memory and Language,* 31 (4), 648–667.

Kagan, J. (2002), *Surprise, Uncertainty and Knowledge* Structures (Cambridge, MA: Harvard University Press).

Kaplan, A. (1984), "Philosophy of science in Anthropology," *Annual Review of Anthropology,* Vol. 13, pp. 25–39.

Kassarjian, H. H. (1978), "Presidential Address, 1977: Anthropomorphisms and Parsimony," *Advances in Consumer Research, Volume 5,* 1978, xiii–xiv.

Keysuk, K. (2002), "Output Sector Munificence and Supplier Control in Industrial Channels of Distribution: a Contingency Approach," *Journal of Business Research,* 55, Issue 6, June 2002, 427–440.

Koerner, J. (1998). Personal interview with the CEO of Barq's. New Orleans, February 20.

Koll, O. (2000). Personal communication via email from *oliver.koll@uibk.ac.at.*

Kotler, P. (2000), *Marketing Management,* 10th edition, Englewood Cliffs, NJ: Prentice-Hall.

Krugman, H. (1965). The impact of television advertising: Learning without involvement. Public Opinion Quarterly, 29, 349–356.

LaDoux, J. E. (1996). The emotional brain: The mysterious underpinnings of emotional life. New York: Simon and Schuster.

Langley, A, Mintzberg, H., Pitcher, P., Posada, E., & Saint-Macary, J. (1995). Opening up decision-making: the view from the black stool. *Organization Science,* 6 (3), 260–279.

Langley, A. (1999), "Strategies for Theorizing from Process Data," *Academy of Management Review,* 24 (4), 691–710.

Lapersonne, E., G. Laurent, and Jean-Jacques Le Goff (1995), "Consideration Sets of Size One," An Empirical Investigation of Automobile Purchases, *International Journal of Research in Marketing,* 12 (1), May 1995, 55–66.

Laroche, M., J. Rosenblatt, J. E. Brisoux, and R. Shimotakahara (1983), "Brand Categorization Strategies in RRB Situations: Some Empirical Results," in *Advances in Consumer Research,* Vol. 10. San Francisco: Association for Consumer Research.

Leszczyc, Peter T. L. Popkowski, & Timmermans, H. (2001). Experimental choice analysis of shopping strategies. *Journal of Retailing,* 77, 493–509.

Levy, S. J. (1981), "Interpreting Consumer Methodology: A Structural Approach to Consumer Behavior," *Journal of Marketing*, 45 (Summer), 49–61.

Lilien, G. I., and Wong, M. A. (1984), "An Exploratory Investigation of the structure of the Buying Center in the Metalworking Industry", *Journal of Marketing Research*, Vol. 21, pp. 1–11.

Lindquist, J. D. (1975), "Meaning of Image," *Journal of Retailing*, 50, 4, 29–38.

Loewenstein, G. (2001), "The Creative Destruction of Decision Research," *Journal of Consumer Research*, 28 (December), 499–505.

Lorenz, K. (1952/1997), *King's Solomon's Ring*, New York: Penguin Books.

March, J. G., and R. I. Sutton (1997), "Organizational Performance as a Dependent Variable, *Organizational Science*, 8 (6), 698–706.

May, E. G. (1975), "Practical Applications of Recent Retail Image studies," *Journal of Retailing*, 50,4, 5–20.

McAlister, L., and E. Pessemier (1982), "Variety-Seeking Behavior: An interdisplinary Review," *Journal of Consumer Research*, 9 (December) 311–22.

McCracken, G. (1988), *The Long Interview*, Thousand Oaks, CA: Sage Publications.

Menard, S. (1995), *Applied Logistic Regression Analysis*, Thousand Oaks, CA: Sage.

Menon, S., and B. E. Kahn (1995), "The Impact of Context on Variety Seeking in Product Choices, *Journal of Consumer Research*, 22 (December), 285–95.

Merton, R. K. (1957), *Social Theory and Social Structure*, (2nd Ed.) Free Press, Glencoe, Illinois.

Meyers, J. H. (1979), `Methodological Issues in Evoked Set Formation and Composition." in *Advances in Consumer Research, 6*, William L. Wilkie (Ed.). Urbana, Illinois: Association for Consumer Research, 236–237.

Miles, M. B., and A. M. Huberman (1994), *Qualitative Data Analysis: An Expanded Sourcebook*, 2nd ed. Thousand Oaks, CA. Sage Publications.

Miller, D. (1975), Evolution and Revolution: a Quantum View of Structural Change in Organizations, *Journal of Management Studies*, 19, 131–151.

Miller, G. A. (1956), "The Magic Number Seven. Plus or Minus Two: Some Limits on Our Capacity for Processing Information," *The Psychological Review*, 63. 8 1–97.

Mintzberg, H. (1979), "An Emerging Strategy of `Direct' Research," *Administrative Science Quarterly*, 24 (December), 582–589.

Mintzberg, H. (1973), *The Nature of Managerial Work*, New York: Harper and Row.

Mitroff, I. I., & Kilmann, R. H. (1976). On organization stories: an approach to the design and analysis of organizations through myths and stories. In R. H. Kilman, L. R. Pondy, & D. P. Slevin (Eds.), The Management of Organization Design (Vol. 1, pp. 189–207). New York: North-Holland.

Mitroff, I., and R. H. Kilmann (1978), *Methodological Approaches to Social Science*, San Francisco, CA: Jossey-Bass.

Möller, K. (1983), *Research Paradigms in Analysing Organizational Buying Process*, Helsinki: Helsinki School of Economics and Business Administration.

Montgomery, D. F. (1975), "New Product Distribution: An Analysis of Supermarket Buyer Decisions," *Journal of Marketing Research*, 12 (August), 255–264.

Moore, C. G. (1969). "A Descriptive Model of the Industrial Purchasing Process: The Supplier Selection Routine." in *Management Action: Models of Administrative Decisions,* C. F. Weber and G. Peters (Eds.), Scranton, Pennsylvania: International Textbook, 76–114.

Morgenroth, W. M. (1964), "A Method for Understanding Price Determinants," *Journal of Marketing Research*, 1 (3), 17–26.

Motes, W. H., and A. G. Woodside (1984), "Field Test of Package Advertising Effects on Brand Choice Behavior," *Journal of Advertising Research*, 24 (1), 39–47.

Motes, W. H., and A. G. Woodside (2001), "Purchase Experiments of Extra-Ordinary and Regular Influence Strategies Using Artificial and Real Brands, *Journal of Business Research*, 53 (1), 15–35.

Mudambi, S., and R. Aggarwal (2003), "Industrial Distributors: Can They Survive in the New Economy?" *Industrial Marketing Management*, 32 (4), 317–325.

Muthukrishnan, A. V. (1995), "Decision Ambiguity and Incumbent Band Advantage," *Journal of Consumer Research*, 22 (June), 98–109.

Muthukrishnan, A. V., and Kardes, F., "Persistent Preferences for Product Attributes: The Effects of the Initial Choice Context and Uninformative Experience," *Journal of Consumer Research*, Vol. 28, June 2001, pp.89–104.

Naravana, C. L., and R. Markin, Jr. (1975), "Consumer Behavior and Product Performance: An Alternative Conceptualization." *Journal of Marketing,* 39, 1–6.

Narus, J. A., and J. C. Anderson (1986), "Industrial Distributor Selling: The Roles of Outside and Inside Sales," *Industrial Marketing Management*. 15 (1), 55–62.

Nicosia, F. M., and Wind, Y. (1977), "Behaviour Models of Organizational Buying Processes," in Nicosia, F.M and Wind, Y. (Eds.) Behavioural Models for Market Analysis: *Foundations for Marketing Action*, Dryden, Hinsdale, Illinois, pp. 96–120.

Nielsen, R. L. (1986), Personal interview, Lincoln. Nebraska: SRI Research Center.

Nittoli, S. (2003), A Confirmatory Personal Introspection of My University Choice," Working paper, Department of Marketing, Boston College, 28 pp.

Nutt, P. C. (1993), "The Formulation Processes and Tactics Used in Organizational Decision Making," *Organization Science*, 4 (2), 226–251.

Orr, J. E. (1990). Sharing knowledge, celebrating identity: community memory in a service culture. In D. Middleton & D. Edwards (Eds.), Collective remembering (pp. 169–189). London: Sage.

Park, C. W., Hughes, R. W., Thurkal, V., & Friedman, R. (1981). Consumers' decision plans and subsequent choice behavior. *Journal of Marketing*, 45 (Spring), 33–47.

Payne, J. W., J. Bettman, & Johnston, (1993), *The Adaptive Decision Maker*, New York: Cambridge Press.

Payne, S. L. (1951). *The art of asking questions*. Princeton: NJ: Princeton University Press.

Pieters, R., Baumgartner, H., & Allen, D. (1995). A means-end chain approach to consumer goal structures. International Journal of Research in Marketing, 12 (3), 227–244.

Pessemier, E. A. (1985), "Varied Individual Behavior: Some Theories, Measurement Methods, and Models," *Multivariate Behavioral Research*, 20 (January), 69–94.

Peter, J. P (1983), "Construct validity: A Review of Basic Issues and Marketing Practices," *Journal of Marketing Research*, Vol 18, May, pp. 133–45.

Pettigrew, A. M. (1995), "Longitudinal Field Research on Change: Theory and Practice," in *Longitudinal Field Research Methods*, ed. by George P. Huber and Andrew H. Van De Ven, Thousand Oaks, CA: Sage, 91–125.

Pettigrew, A. M. (1973), *The Politics of Organizational Decision Making*. London: Tavistock.

Pettigrew, A. M. (1975), "The Industrial Purchasing Decision as a Political Process," *European Journal of Marketing*, 9 (March), 4–19.

Pettigrew, A. M. (1979), "On Studying Organizational Cultures," *Administrative Science Quarterly*, 24 (December), 570–581.

Pettigrew, A. M. (1992), "The Character and Significance of Strategy Process Research," *Strategic Management Journal*, 13 (Winter Special Issue), 5–16.

Petty, R. E., & Cacioppo, J. T. (1986). Communication and persuasion: Central and peripheral routes to attitude change. New York: Springer Verlag.

Petty, R. E., Unnava, R., & Strathman, A. J. (1991). Theories of attitude change. In T. S. Robertson & H. H. Kassarjian (Eds.), Handbook of consumer behavior (pp. 241–280). Englewood Cliffs, NJ: Prentice-Hall.

Posner, G. (1998). VW Day, Sometimes buying a car means burying the past. New York Times Magazine, Sunday, October 4, 128.

Price, L. L., and N. M. Ridgway (1982), "Use Innovativeness, Vicarious Exploration and Purchase Exploration: Three Facets of Consumer Varied Behavior, in ed. Bruce Walker, *American Marketing Association Educators' Conference Proceedings* (Chicago: American Marketing Association), pp. 56–60.

Ragin, C. C. (1987). *The Comparative Method: Moving Beyond Qualitative and Quantitative Strategies*. Berkeley: University of California Press.

Raju, P. S. (1980), "Optimum Stimulation Level: Its Relationship to Personality Demographics and Exploratory Behavior," *Journal of Consumer Research* 7 (December), 272–82.

Ram, S. (1987), "A Model of Innovation Resistance, *Advances in Consumer Research, Volume 14*, M. Wallendorf and P. Anderson, eds., Provo, UT: Association for Consumer Research, 193–197.

Richmond, B. (1987), "The Strategic Forum: from Vision to Strategy to Operating Policies and Back Again," available from High Performance Systems, Inc., Box B 1167, Hanover, NH 03755.

Russo, J. E., Johnson, E. J., & Stephens, D. L. (1989). The validity of verbal protocols. Memory and Cognition, 17, 759–769.

Sanday, P. R. (1979), "The Ethnographic Paradigm(s)," *Administrative Science Quarterly*, 24 (December), 539–550.

Sawyer, A., and P. Peter (1983). "The Significance of Statistical Significance Tests in Marketing Research," *Journal of Marketing Research*. 20 (2), 122–133.

Schank, R. C. (1999), *Dynamic Memory Revisited*, Cambridge, UK: Cambridge University Press.

Schank, R. C. (1990). Tell me a story: A new look at real and artificial memory. New York: Charles Scribner's Sons.

Schank, R. C., & Abelson, R. P. (1977). Scripts, plans, goals, and understanding: An inquiry into human knowledge. Hillsdale, NJ: Erlbaum.

Schwarz, N. (1999). Self-reports: how the questions shape the answers. *American Psychologist*, 54 (2), 93–105.

Senge, P. M. (1990), *The Fifth Discipline*, New York: Doubleday.

Siegel, S. (1956), *Nonparametric Statistics for the Behavioral Sciences*, New York: McGraw-Hill.

Shank, R. C. (1999), *Dynamic Memory Revisited*, Cambridge, UK: Cambridge University Press.

Sherif, C. W., M. Sherif, and R. E. Nebergall (1965), *Attitude and Attitude Change: The Social Judgment-Involvement Approach*. Philadelphia: Saunders.

Sherry, J. F., M. A. McGrath, and S. J. Levy (1995), "Monadic Giving: Anatomy of Gifts Given to the Self," in *Contemporary Marketing and Consumer Behavior*, ed. by John F. Sherry, Jr., Thousand Oaks, CA: Sage Publications.

Simon, H. A. (1957), *Administrative Behavior*, New York: Macmillan.

Simon, H. A. (1990), "Invariants of Human Behavior," *Annual Review of Psychology*, *41*, 1–19.

Simon, H.A. (1974), "How Big is a Chunk," *Science*, 183 (4124), 482–488.

Sims, D. B. P., & Doyle, J. R. (1995). Cognitive sculpting as a means of working with managers' metaphors. *OMEGA*, 23 (2), 117–124.

Sirsi, A. K., J. C. Ward, and P. H. Reingen (1996), "Microcultural Analysis of Variation in Sharing of Causal Reasoning about Behavior," Journal of Consumer Research, 22 (4), 345–372.

Skinner, B. F. (1996), "Operant Behavior," in W. K. Honig (ed.), *Operant Behavior: Areas for Research and Application*, New York: Appleton-Century-Crofts, pp. 12–32.

Smith, R. A., & Lux, D. S. (1993). Historical method in consumer research: developing causal explanations of change. *Journal of Consumer Research*, 19 (March), 595–610.

Spekman, R. E, and Stern, L.W. (1979), "Environmental Uncertainty and Buying Group Structure: An Empirical Investigation," *Journal of Marketing*, Vol. 43, Spring, pp 54–64.Stubbart, Charles, and Arkalgud Ramaprasad (1988), "Probing Two Chief Executives' Schematic Knowledge on the U.S. Steel Industry by Using Cognitive Maps," *Advances in Strategic Management*, 5, 139–164.

Spiggle, S., and M. A. Sewall (1987), "A Choice Sets Model of Retail Selection," *Journal of Marketing*, 51 (2), 86–96.

Steinberg, B. (2003), "Brawny Man Gets a Sexy Makeover," *Wall Street Journal*, June 13, B7.

Thelen, E. M., and A. G. Woodside (1997), "What Evokes the Brand or Store?" *International Journal of Research in Marketing*, 14 (November), 125–143.

Thompson, J. R., and R. D. Cooper (1979), "Additional Evidence on the Limited Size of Evoked and Inept Sets of Travel Destinations," *Journal of Travel Research*, 18, 23–25.

Tigert, D. J., (1983), "Pushing the Hot Buttons for a Successful Retailing Strategy," in W. R. Darden and R. F. Lusch, eds., *Patronage Behavior and Retail Management*, New York: North-Holland, 89–114.

Thompson, C. J., Locander, W. B., & Pollio, H. R. (1989). Putting consumer experience back into consumer research: the philosophy and method of existential-phenomenology. *Journal of Consumer Research*, 16 (September), 133–147.

Tufte, E. (2003), *The Visual Display of Quantitative Information*, Cheshire, CT: Graphic Press.

Van Maanan, J. (1979), "The Fact of Fiction in Organizational Ethnography, *Administrative Science Quarterly*, 24 (December), 34–41, 539–550.

Van Someren, M. W., Barnard, Y. F., and Sandberg, J. A. C. (1994), *The Think Aloud Method*, Academic Press, London.

Venkatesan, M. (1973), "Cognitive Consistency and Novelty Seeking," in *Consumer Behavior: Theoretical Sources*, ed., Scott Ward and Thomas S. Robertson, Englewood Cliffs, NJ: Prentice-Hall, 355–84.

Vyas, N., and Woodside, AG. (1984) "An Inductive Model of Industrial Supplier Choice Processes," *Journal of Marketing*, Vol. 48, Winter, pp. 30–45.

Wallendorf, M., and M. Brucks (1993), "Introspection in Consumer Research: Implementation and Implications, *Journal of Consumer Research*, 20 (3), 339–359.

Wallendorf, M., and E. J. Arnould (1991), "'We Gather Together': Consumption Rituals of Thanksgiving Day," *Journal of Consumer Research*, 18 (June), 13–31.

Warwick, D. P. (1975), *A Theory of Public Bureaucracy: Politics, Personality, and Organization in the State Department*, Cambridge, MA: Harvard University Press.

Webb, E. J., D. T. Campbell, R. D. Schwartz, and L. Sechrest (1966), *Unobtrusive Measures*, Chicago: Rand McNally.

Webb, E., and K. E. Weick (1979), "Unobtrusive Measures in Organizational Theory," *Administrative Science Quarterly*, 24 (December), 650–659.

Webster, F. Jr., and Wind, Y. (1972), *Organizational Buying Behavior*, Prentice-Hall, Englewood Cliffs, New Jersey.

Wegner, D. M. (2002), *The Illusion of Conscious Will*, Cambridge, MA: Bradford Books, MIT Press.

Weick, K. (1995), *Sensemaking in Organizations*, Thousand Oaks, CA: Sage.

Weick, K. (1993). *Sensemaking in organizations*. Thousand Oaks, CA: Sage.

Weick, K. E. (1969), *The Social Psychology of Organizing*, Reading, MA: Addison Wesley.

Weick, K. E. (1979), *The Social Psychology of Organizing*, 2nd edition, Reading, MA: Addison Wesley.

Weitz, B. A., Sujan, H., and Sujan, M. (1986), "Knowledge, Motivation, and Adaptive Behavior," *Journal of Marketing*, 50 (4), 174–191.

Wellan, D. M., and A. S. C. Ehrenberg (1988), "A Successful New Brand: Shield," *Journal of the Market Research Society,* 30 (1) (January), 35–44.

Wells, W. D. (1993). Discovery-oriented consumer research. *Journal of Consumer Research*, 19 (March), 489–504.

Wells, W. D. (1995), "Afterword: Learning to See II," in *Contemporary Marketing and Consumer Behavior*, ed. by John F. Sherry, Jr., Thousand Oaks, CA: Sage.

Westrum, R. (1982), "Social Intelligence about Hidden Events," *Knowledge*, 3 (3), 381–400.

Whyte, W. F. (1990), *Participatory Action Research*, Newbury Park, CA: Sage.

Whyte, W. F. (1991), *Social Theory for Action*, Newbury Park,CA: Sage.

Whyte, W. F. and E. L. Hamilton (1965), *Action Research for Management*, Homewood, IL: Irwin-Dorsey.

Williams, J. D. (1992). Reflections on a black middle-class consumer: caught between two worlds or getting the best of both? In J. F. Sherry, Jr. and B. Sternthal (Eds.) *Advances in Consumer Research, 19* (pp. 850–856). Provo, UT: Association for Consumer Research, 850–856.

Wilson, C. E. (1981), "A Procedure for the Analysis of Consumer Decision Making," *Journal of Advertising Research*, 21 (2), 31–38.

Wilson, E. J., G. L. Lilien, and D. T. Wilson (1991), "Developing and Testing a Contingency Paradigm of Group Choice in Organizational Buying," *Journal of Marketing Research*, 28 (November), 452–466.

Wilson, E. J., R. C. McMurrian, and A. G. Woodside (2000), "How Business-to-Business Buyers Frame Problems and the Influence of Value-Added Customer Services (VACS) on Supplier Choice," in *Designing Winning Products*, Arch G. Woodside (ed.), Amsterdam: Elsevier Science, 245–254.

Wilson, E. J., and D. T. Wilson (1988), "'Degrees of Freedom' in Case Study Research of Behavioral Theories of Group Buying," *Advances in Consumer Research*, 15, 587–594.

Wilson, E. J., and A. G. Woodside (1999), "Degrees-of-Freedom Analysis' of Case Study Data in Business Marketing Research," *Industrial Marketing Management*, 28 (3), 215–231.

Wilson, T. D. (2002), *Strangers to Ourselves: Discovering the Adaptive Unconscious*, Cambridge, MA: Belknap Press of Harvard University Press.

Witte, E. (1972), "Field Research on Complex Decision-Making Processes—The Phase Theorem," *International Studies of Management and Organization*, 2 (October), 156–182.

Wolf, M. (1990), "Chinanotes: Engendering Anthropology," in *Fieldnotes*, ed. by Roger Sanjek, Ithaca, NY: Cornell University Press, 343–355.

Woodside, A. G., and E. J. Wilson (1995), "Applying the Long Interview in Direct Marketing Research," *Journal of Direct Marketing*, 9 (1), 37–55.

Woodside, A. G., Floyd-Finch, N., & Wilson, E. J. (1986). Pscyhodrama and beverage consumption. In *Proceedings 13th International research seminar in marketing*, ed. by Michel Laroche & Alain Strazzieri, Aix-en-Provence, France: Institute d'Administration des enterprises, University of Marseille, 478–511.

Woodside, A. G., & Chebat, J.-C. (2001). Updating Heider's balance theory in consumer behavior. Psychology & Marketing, 18 (5), 475–496.

Woodside, A. G., and R. C. McMurrian (2000), "Automatic Cognitive Processing and Choice of Suppliers by Business-to-Business Customers," in *Designing Winning Products*, Arch G. Woodside (ed.), Amsterdam: Elsevier Science, 245–254.

Woodside, A. G., ed. (1996), Case Studies for Industrial and Business Marketing, Stamford, CT: JAI Press.

Woodside, A. G., and E. J. Wilson (2000), "Constructing Thick Descriptions of Marketers' and Buyers' Decision Processes in Business-to-business Relationships," *Journal of Business & Industrial Marketing*, 15 (5), 354–369.

Woodside, A. G. (1987), "Customer Awareness and Choice of Industrial Distributors," *Industrial Marketing & Purchasing*, 2 (2), 47–68.

Woodside, A. G., ed. (2000a), *Getting Better at Sensemaking*, Stamford, CT: JAI Press.

Woodside, A. G., and M. Sakai (2001), *Meta-Evaluation*, Champaign, IL: Sagamore Publishing.

Woodside, A. G., (ed.) (1992), *Mapping How Industry Buys, Advances in Business Marketing, Volume 5*, JAI Press, Greenwich, CT.

Woodside, A. G., and D. C. Sherrell (1980), "New Replacement Part Buying," *Industrial Marketing Management*, 9, 123–132.

Woodside, A.G., and Sammuel, D.M. (1981), "Observation of Centralized Corporate Procurement," *Industrial Marketing Management*, Vol. 10, August, pp. 191–205.

Woodside, A. G., and R. A. Fleck, Jr. (1979), "The Case Approach to Understanding Brand Choice," *Journal of Advertising Research*, 19 (2), 23–30.

Woodside, A. G. (2000b), "When Superior New Technologies are Rejected," in *Designing Winning Products*, Arch G. Woodside, ed., Amsterdam: Elsevier

Woodside, A.G., and Vyas, B. (1983), "Buying Behavior for an Industrial Commodity: A Descriptive model of One's Firm's Decision Process," in Murphy, P.E and Lacziniak, G. R. (Eds.), *1983 AMA Educators' Proceedings*, American Marketing Association, Chicago, pp. 51–7.

Woodside, A. G., and Wilson, E. J. (2002), "Respondent Inaccuracy," *Journal of Advertising Research*, 42 (6), 1–13.

Woodside, A. G. (1994). Modeling linkage advertising: Going beyond better media comparisons. Journal of Advertising Research, 34, 22–31.

Woodside, A. G., and R. J. Trappey, III, (1992a), "Finding Out Why Customers Shop Your Store and Buy Your Brand: Automatic Cognitive Processing Models of Primary Choice," *Journal of Advertising Research*, 32 (November), 59–78.

Woodside, A. G., and R. J. Trappey, III (1992b), "Incorporating Competition in Attidude Accessibility Models of Customers' Primary Store Choice," in William R. Darden and Robert F. Lusch, eds., *The Cutting Edge, Proceedings of the 1991 Symposium on Patronage Behavior and Retail Strategy*, Baton Rouge, LA: Louisiana State University, 295–310.

Woodside, A. G., and D. L. Sherrell (1980), "New Replacement Part Buying," *Industrial Marketing Management*, 9 (2), 191–205.

Woodside, A. G., and D. M. Samuel (1981), "Observation of Centralized Corporate Procurement," *Industrial Marketing Management*, 10 (3), 191–205.

Woodside, A. G., and E. J. Wilson (1985), "Effects of Consumer Awareness of Brand Advertising on Preference," *Journal of Advertising Research*, 35 (4), 41–48.

Woodside, A. G., and K. Möller (1992), "Middle Range Theories of Industrial Purchasing Strategies, *Advances in Business Marketing and Purchasing, Volume 5*, JAI Press, 21–59.

Woodside, A. G., and D. L. Sherrell (1977), "Traveler Evoked, Inept, and Inert Sets of Vacation Destinations," *Journal of Travel Research*, 16 (1), 14–18.

Woodside, A. G., and E. M. Moore (1983), "Direct Response Marketing: Understanding Patronage Behavior and Testing Competing Strategies," in *Patronage Behavior and Retail Management*, ed. by William R. Darden and Robert F. Lusch, New York: North-Holland, 179–205.

Woodside, A. G. (1990), "Measuring Advertising Effectiveness in Destination Marketing Strategies," *Journal of Travel Research*, 29 (Fall), 3–8.

Woodside, A. G., and C. Dubelaar (2002), "A General Theory of Tourism Consumption Systems: A Conceptual Framework and an Empirical Exploration," *Journal of Travel Research*, 41 (November), 120–132.

Woodside, A. G., and R. King (2001), "Tourism Consumption Systems: Theory and Empirical Research, *Journal of Travel & Tourism Research*, 10 (1), 3–27.

Woodside, A. G., and E. J. Wilson (1995), "Applying the Long Interview in Direct Marketing Research," *Journal of Direct Marketing*, 9 (1), 37–55

Woodside, A. G., R. MacDonald, and R. J. Trappey III (1997), "Measuring Linkage-Advertising Effects on Customer Behavior and Net Revenue," *Canadian Journal of Administrative Sciences*, 14 (2), 214–228.

Wright, M., B. Sharp, and G. J. Goodhardt (2002), "Purchase Loyalty is Polarised into either Repertoire or Subscription Patterns," *Australasian Marketing Journal*, 10 (3), 7–20.

Yin, R. K. (1994), *Case Study Research*, Thousand Oaks, CA: Sage.

Zaltman, G. (2003), *How Customers Think*, Boston: Harvard Business School Press.

Zajonc, R. B., & Markus, H. (1982). Affective and cognitive factors in preferences, Journal of Consumer Research, 9, 123–131.

Zaltman, G. (2003). How Consumers Think. Cambridge, MA: Harvard Business School Press.

Zaltman, G. (1997). Rethinking market research: Putting people back in. Journal of Marketing Research, 34, 55–67, 424–437.

Zaltman, G., & Coulter, R. H. (1995). Seeing the voice of the customer: Metaphor-based advertising research. Journal of Advertising Research, 35, 35–51.

Zaltman, G. (2003), *How Customers Think*, Boston: Harvard Business School Press.

Zuikier, H. (1986). The paradigmatic and narrative modes in goal-guided inference. In R. M. Sorrentino & E. T. Higgins (Eds.), Handbook of Motivation and Cognition (pp. 465–502). New York: Guillford.

—— (1975), "The Industrial Purchasing Decision as a Political Process," *European Journal of Marketing*, Vol. 9, pp 4–19.

INDEX

Routinized response behavior (RRB)
in automatic thinking, vendor choices,
141–142
RRB. *See* Routinized response behavior

Senior management participation
in large purchase order streams, mapping
contingent thinking, 49f, 56–57
Sensation seekers
in variety-seeking, brand choice behavior,
276
Sensemaking, 3–4, 8f, 9, 16
advancing from SPI to CPI and, 111, 124
automatic thinking, vendor choices of
industrial distributors and, 141
in balanced, unbalanced/unconscious-
conscious thinking, 73–75
in CSR, thinking, deciding, acting, 22
in holistic case-based modeling, 198, 246
Service guarantees
Rosemont case study, applying long
interview methods and, 173, 185
Short-term marketing. *See* Brand imprinting,
short-term marketing influences
Similarities
executive/customer thinking, deciding,
acting and, 3, 4–5, 7, 8f, 9, 11–12, 14,
15–16
Slow novelty-seeking behavior (SNSB)
in variety-seeking, brand choice behavior,
270
Slow-variety-seeking behavior (SVSB)
in variety-seeking, brand choice behavior,
270
Small purchase order streams, mapping
contingent thinking
delivery requirements in, 59
design recommendations in, 51f, 58–59
situational considerations in, 59–60
SNSB. *See* Slow novelty-seeking behavior
Special marketing programs
brand imprinting, short-term marketing
and, 257–258, 257f, 258f, 259f, 260f
SPI. *See* Subjective personal introspection
Stay-the-Course theories
long interview methods and, 174–175,
177t, 181, 182, 186, 188–189
Steelcase, case study
mapping contingent thinking and, 52–54
Stimulation. *See also* Optimal stimulation
level
in variety-seeking, brand choice behavior,
266–267, 268, 278

Storytelling
balanced, unbalanced/unconscious-
conscious thinking and, 66,
73–75, 74f
emic-based, 191, 193, 241, 246
SPI to CPI and, 117, 118f–119f
Strategic cognitive processing
in customer automatic thinking, store
choice, 130
Subjective personal introspection (SPI)
guided introspection and, 107
interactive introspection and, 107
reflexivity/ethnographic studies and, 107
researcher introspection and, 104
syncretic combinations and, 107
Subjective personal introspection (SPI), CPI
advanced from
buying choice and, 117, 118f–119f, 120
cohort auditors and, 112–113, 114f
confirmatory personal introspection and,
107–109
CPs in buying process and, 110–111, 125
creative destructing and, 103–104
emic representations in, 124
etic representations in, 124
experimental issues for, 106t
FMET and, 113, 115f–116f, 117
formal survey protocols and, 111
humanistic inquiry paradigm and, 111
inside auditors and, 112
introspection, case studies, theories and,
108–110
introspective conscious thought-retrieval
and, 104, 105f
iterative feedback process and, 109
learning while talking in, 112
metaphor elicitation and, 103–104
multi-methods approach and, 103,
108–109, 120, 122f, 124–125
research introspectors and, 112–113
RID and, 112–113, 120, 121f, 122f
RPD and, 112–113, 120, 121f, 122f
sensemaking and, 111, 124
storytelling and, 117, 118f–119f
subjective personal introspection and,
104–107
TD and, 112–113, 120, 121f, 122f
theory construction and, 123–124
thick descriptions in, 103
unconscious motives and, 109
unconscious thought-retrieval and, 104,
105f
SVSB. *See* Slow-variety-seeking behavior

*For Product Safety Concerns and Information please contact
our EU representative GPSR@taylorandfrancis.com Taylor & Francis
Verlag GmbH, Kaufingerstraße 24, 80331 München, Germany*

T - #0020 - 230425 - C0 - 229/152/18 [20] - CB - 9780750679015 - Gloss Lamination